THE BASICS OF AMERICAN POLITICS

THE BASICS OF AMERICAN POLITICS
SECOND EDITION

by **Gary Wasserman**

with **Edmund Beard**

Marsha Hurst

Little, Brown and Company
Boston   Toronto

Copyright © 1979 by Gary Wasserman
Copyright © 1976 by Little, Brown and Company (Inc.)

All rights reserved. No part of this book may be reproduced in any form or by any electronic or mechanical means including information storage and retrieval systems without permission in writing from the publisher, except by a reviewer who may quote brief passages in a review.

Library of Congress Catalog Card No. 78-24683

ISBN 0-316-924210

10 9 8 7 6 5 4

HAL

*Published simultaneously in Canada
by Little, Brown & Company (Canada) Limited*

Printed in the United States of America

Drawings by David Omar White

To My Students

Preface

The first edition of this text was written after I had taught an introductory American government course at an inner city college for several years. My students and I needed a text that was basic, cheap, easy to read, and short. I couldn't find such a book, so I wrote one.

Since then I have taught American government at an Ivy League college. Perhaps it was only a surprise to their teacher, but the needs of the two very different groups of students were basically the same. Both groups generally lacked a solid foundation in the structure and practices of American politics; both wished to acquire these basics quickly and painlessly in order to spend time on issues they found more interesting. The first edition allowed them to do that.

In *The Basics of American Politics*, politics is sometimes compared to a game in that it involves competing players more or less following certain rules and trying to win. But politics is no lighthearted sport; it is complex, important and deadly serious. This book is intended to provide a start for both understanding and playing the political game.

The second edition has been extensively revised and, somewhat regretfully, expanded. New sections have been added on voters and elections, presidential power, civil liberties and the media. The book has been updated to cover a new president and congress and their changes in practice. Recent events such as the Bakke decision, bureaucratic reforms, energy legislation, the continuing decline of seniority in congress and the rise of media influence, find a place in this edition.

A number of people helped on the text. Although I am responsible for writing this edition, the basis of Chapter 4 remains what Ed Beard had written previously. Similarly, sections of Chapters 6 and 7, benefit from Marsha Hurst's writing in the first edition. Ed Wasserman wrote the draft on which the media section is based. Dennis Quinn of Columbia University provided invaluable research. I am grateful to all of them. I also wish to thank the following people for their expert help in fashioning the finished product: Peggy Freund, Thomas A. Horne, James L. Hutter, Herbert Jacob, Alan Platt, Richard Pious, Wilbur C. Rich, Bruce L. R. Smith and Elise T. Snyder. Greg Franklin and Barbara Garrey of Little, Brown and Company improved the book with their judgment. Any errors that remain are undoubtedly my own. But if this book helps someone learn about American politics, it is probably because of what my students taught me. That is why the book is dedicated to them.

G. W.

Contents

1 What Is Politics?   3
An Overheard Conversation   3
Politics and Power   4
The Need for Government   7
The Study of Politics   11
What Is This Book About?   16
Thought Questions   17
Suggested Readings   18

2 The Constitution: Rules of the Game   21
Background to the Constitution   21
The Framers   25
Ratification and the Bill of Rights   28
Four Major Constitutional Principles   30
How Is the Constitution Changed?   37
Why Has the Constitution Survived?   40
Case Study: The Evolution of a Constitutional Right, Freedom of Speech   43
Wrap-up   47
Thought Questions   49
Suggested Readings   50

3 The Executive Branch: The President and the Bureaucracy   53
The President and the Constitution   53
History of the Presidency   55
Types of Presidents   59
Presidential Roles   62
The President and the Public   69
The Federal Bureaucracy   69
The Problems of Bureaucracy   75
The President and the Bureaucracy   78
Case Study: Three Examples of Presidential Power   79
Wrap-up   85
Thought Questions   87
Suggested Readings   87

4 The Legislative Branch: Congress   91

Makeup of the Senate and House   92
How Does Congress Operate?   104
The Committee System   109
The Other Powers of Congress   119
Case Study: Congress and the Campaign
    Finance Reform Bill   121
Wrap-up   125
Thought Questions   128
Suggested Readings   128

5 The Judicial Branch: The Supreme Court and the Federal Court System   131

The Federal Court System   131
The United States Supreme Court   135
Case Study: Separate But Equal?   146
Strengths and Weaknesses of the Supreme Court   152
Wrap-up   157
Thought Questions   159
Suggested Readings   159

6 Voters and Political Parties   161

Voters   161
Political Parties   169
Party Functions   174
View from the Inside: Party Organizations   175
View from the Outside: The Two-Party System   180
Wrap-up   182
Thought Questions   183
Suggested Readings   184

7 Interest Groups and the Media   187

Interest Groups   187
Media   196
Case Study: Electing a Senator   208
Wrap-up   213
Thought Questions   214
Suggested Readings   215

8 Who Wins, Who Loses: Pluralism versus Elitism — 219

Pluralism 219
Power Elite 224
The Debate 227
Wrap-up 229
Thought Questions 230
Suggested Readings 230

Appendixes — 231

The Declaration of Independence 231
The Constitution of the United States 235

Index — 257

THE BASICS OF AMERICAN POLITICS

What Is Politics? 1

AN OVERHEARD CONVERSATION

"There are some very strange dudes teaching here this year. The first day of my American government class the prof comes in and asks us to sit in alphabetical order. Is this believable, I ask myself. Of course all the freshman sheep do it forthwith. But since I am sitting next to a most attractive lady I am very put out by this. So I ask him whether he might not want us to wear Mickey Mouse ears to his next class. A bit too cute perhaps, because he asks me if I think politics goes on in the classroom. I reply no, we are alleged to study politics, but very few of us actually indulge. Incorrect, the dude responds, and would I mind removing myself from his class. Yes I would very much mind, I say, considering the costs of my first seven years at college. Will you pleeeze leave, he says. Seeing no gain from further dialogue, I start to exit. He then stops me and asks why I am departing. I remind the gentleman that while he may have missed it, he has just requested my absence. But he insists, inquiring why I'm doing what he asked. I am beginning to think I have missed something and I retort that he is numero uno here, the teach, while I am but a lowly student. In other words, he says, my power or authority as the teacher of this class influenced you to do something you didn't want to do. In fact it influenced everyone's behavior by getting the class to sit in alphabetical order. So we just saw a process of influence in this classroom that affected a group of people. That's politics. Now you may sit down, and I'm sorry I put you through all that. Not at all, I graciously respond, it was a pleasure to assist in instructing my fellow students."

What the above dialogue reveals is that there is a process of influence between the teacher and the students. This relationship is not only an educational one, but a political one as well. It's political in the sense of political scientist Harold Lasswell's definition of politics as *the process of who gets what, when, and how.* The teacher (who) gets the student to leave the class (what) immediately (when) by using his authority to persuade and threaten him (how). This indeed is politics.

Our definition of politics centers on interactions among a number of people involving influence. How do people get others to do what they wish? How does our society or any society (like that classroom) distribute its valued things, such as wealth, prestige, and security? Who gets these valued things, which political scientists call *values,* and how? The dialogue hints at an answer to these questions. That answer lies in the concepts of *power* and *authority.*

POLITICS AND POWER

Notice in the dialogue that the teacher influenced the student to do something the student didn't want to do (leave the class). The teacher demonstrated that he or she had power over the student. Power is simply *the ability to influence another's behavior.* Power is getting someone to do something he or she wouldn't otherwise do. Power may involve force (often called *coercion*), or persuasion, or rewards. But its essence is the ability to change another's actions in some way. The more power one has over another, the greater the change, or the easier the change is to accomplish. Having more power could also mean influencing more people to change.

Power always involves a relationship between people and groups. When someone says that a person has a lot of power, one should ask: Power to influence whom to do what? What is the power relationship being discussed? For example, take the statement, "The United States is the most powerful nation in the world today." If this means that because of its huge wealth, large army, and educated population, the United States can influence any other country however it wishes, the statement is wrong. These resources (wealth, army, and population) can only give a *capacity* for power. Whether this capacity is converted into actual influence will depend on the relationship in which it is applied. Certainly the United States had greater wealth, population, and troops than North Vietnam. Yet in attempting to halt a national movement with foreign troops in the Vietnam War the United States had very limited power to change that small Asian country's behavior.

People generally do not seek power only for its own sake. They usually want it for the other values it can get them — for the fame or wealth or even affection they think it will bring. Power, like money, is a means to other ends. Most people seek money for what it can buy, whether possessions, prestige, or security. Just as some people go after money more intently than others, so some people seek power more than others. Of course power, just like money, does not come to everyone who seeks it.

Elites

Those who do gain power are often called the *elite*. The elite are those who get most of the values society has available (such as wealth and respect). We could answer the "who" part of the question "who gets what, when, and how" by saying the elite are those who get the most.

There may be different elites depending on what value is being considered. In a small town, for example, the owner of the largest business may be getting most of the wealth in the community, while the poor but honest mayor has most of the respect. In most cases, however, the values overlap. The wealthy businessman will get plenty of respect and the mayor will use people's respect for him or her to make income-producing contacts and investments.

To see the difference between the elite and the rest of us we can look at one value (wealth) in one society (America). Clearly wealth is not distributed equally among the population — some (an elite) get more than others. About 1.6

percent of the population owns 80 percent of all stocks, 100 percent of all state and city bonds, and 88.5 percent of all corporate bonds. The richest 20 percent of Americans receives almost 45 percent of our national income. On the other side, the bottom 20 percent of American families gets less than 6 percent of the national income. Almost 80 million Americans live on incomes estimated to be below the adequate minimum by the Department of Labor. Forty million, the majority of them white, are classified as very poor. Twelve million Americans, a 1973 report by a Senate committee found, do not get enough to eat. These differences show the division between the elite and the bulk of the population in the way our society's value of wealth is distributed.

Authority: Legitimate Power

Often members of an elite reinforce their position by gaining authority. Authority is *legitimate power*. By *legitimate* we mean even more than "legal": The word implies a *rightness* or *correctness*. This rightness or legitimacy is connected in people's minds to both the position and the wishes of the authority. People generally recognize certain others as having the right to influence their behavior in certain ways. Most people feel a secretary of state *should* follow the wishes of the president; students *should* listen to their teacher; children *should* obey their parents. In all these cases there is a personal moral quality to the influence. Other reasons why people obey authorities include habit, the authority figure's personal appeal, desire to be accepted by the group, and self-interest. But although they may not always follow it, people widely recognize authority as deserving obedience, and that is what gives it legitimacy.

Authority, then, is an efficient form of power. If people feel that they *should* follow the wishes of an authority, then there is no need to force or even to persuade them to do so. The cost of influence is lowered for the authority. It takes little effort for a policeman to get a group of teenagers to stay on the sidewalk — as long as they respect his authority. But in Watts, the black ghetto of Los Angeles, on August 11, 1965, getting those teenagers to obey required hundreds of police and started a riot dangerous to all involved. Because the police had lost their legitimacy in the eyes of the teenagers, the cost to the police of influencing the teenagers' behavior went up. The police still could *force* agreement (and an element of force lies behind most authority); but anybody can clear a street with a gun. Only a recognized authority can do it with just a word.

Power and authority, then, are central to politics. They are also central to many other aspects of life — certainly almost all human interactions show people trying to influence others. We could in a political science course study the politics of a school or a hospital or a family — who influences, who is influenced, and the process of influence. But most of us are interested in a bigger question: How does the whole society decide who gets what, when, and how? To find out, we need to study the most important organization that decides who is to get the valued things of our society — government.

THE NEED FOR GOVERNMENT

Government is one of humanity's oldest and most universal institutions. History records very few societies that have existed with no government. *Anarchy* (a society without government) may be an interesting theory, but it seldom has been applied for long. Instead, people have lived under forms of government varying from the chief of an American Indian village to the complex government of the Soviet Union. Why is government so common?

One answer is that government is as common in society as is political conflict — disputes over the distribution of a society's valued things. These values (such as wealth) are fairly limited, but peoples' demands for them are pretty unlimited. This means conflict. Whenever people have lived together they have needed a way to regulate the conflicts among them. The question is not *whether* there will be conflict but *how* the conflict will be handled. Who will decide on the rules that determine who wins and loses? And how does one get the loser to accept the decision? The usual way to channel political conflict and thus preserve society is to have some form of government.

Most governments in the world today claim to be democratic. A *democracy* is a form of government in which all people effectively participate. Because it is generally impractical for all the people to take part in their government directly, their participation is usually through representatives whom they choose in free elections. Hence the people rule themselves indirectly, through their representatives, and the government is often called a *representative democracy*.

Yet establishing governments, even democratic ones, to settle conflicts creates new problems. Government allows some people to have their way by coercing others even more effectively than they could if government didn't exist. And to control government is to have great power over many others. As the mass murders of Jews in Nazi Germany illustrated, having control of government may even mean having the power to kill millions of people.

In the next chapter we will see that the men who wrote the United States Constitution recognized this problem. They set up a number of checks and divisions of power to limit the future leaders of the United States government. Of course, these may not always work. For example, someone commented that the Cuban missile crisis of October, 1962, showed how the actions of an elderly ex-blacksmith (Soviet Premier Khrushchev) and the son of a millionaire (United States President Kennedy) could determine whether millions of people would live or die.

What Is Government?

Government is a political association which does two things:

1. It makes rules determining who will get the valued things of a society.
2. It alone regulates the use of legitimate force in society.

The first part of the definition deals with how society distributes the valued things it has available — wealth, respect, safety, and so on. The second part deals with how these decisions are enforced. Government, then, has the final word over who gets what, and the ultimate say over how it will be done.

This does not mean that the goverment always *directly* determines who will get the valued things in a society. In theory, the United States government only protects and legitimizes the private distribution of most of society's val-

ues. That is, our government is set up to allow people to get what they can without government interference. But this noninterference also can be viewed as a decision supporting the status quo or existing distribution of values in American society. The government not only refuses to interfere but also prevents others from interfering in the status quo. For example, it enforces laws such as those supporting repayment of debt and punishment of robbery. In practice these and other government functions, such as providing a sound currency, protecting from domestic unrest, and safeguarding private property, do mean government intervention. Most groups favor government intervention, if it is in their favor.

At the same time, the government sets limits on the private distribution of values. While allowing people to accumulate wealth, the government puts higher taxes on those with higher incomes (though tax loopholes used by the wealthy tend to undercut this). It also supports welfare programs to help the people who are getting the least of society's wealth. Both taxes and welfare illustrate the government's use of its legitimate power (authority) to place limits on the private distribution of this value.

Making and Supporting Decisions

The government may also intervene more directly in disputes among its citizens. For example, citizens of a town near a river may not be able to swim there because a paper mill dumps sewage into it. The citizens of the town or the owners of the mill may ask the government to settle the dispute. The appropriate part of the government may respond by passing a law or making a court ruling that decides whether the town or the paper mill will get the use of the river (the "valued thing").

How the government supports its decision brings us to the second aspect of government — its exclusive regulation of legitimate force. In enforcing its decisions, the government may employ, allow, or prevent the use of force. Either the paper mill or the town's swimmers may be ordered not to use the river. If they try they may be fined or arrested. The government alone is allowed to regulate what kind of force is used, and how.

This is not to say that the government is the only group in society that can legitimately use force. Parents may spank their children to keep them from swimming, or the paper mill may employ guards to keep people off their property. But only the government can set limits on this force. Most governments, while permitting parents to spank their kids, forbid cruel punishment of children. The paper mill's guards may be forbidden to use guns to keep swimmers out. Government does not *monopolize* the use of legitimate force, but it alone sets limits to its use.

THE STUDY OF POLITICS

Political scientists, as we have seen, are interested in finding out how society decides who gets what, when, and how. But what do political scientists *do?* What is the study of politics? One thing you will notice about political science is that it's a lot like other disciplines such as history, economics, sociology, anthropology, and psychology. Each studies aspects of the interactions among people. In any large group of people many social relations are going on. Each of these disciplines may look at the same group and ask different questions about the relationships going on there. This division of labor is partly traditional and partly a way of separating complicated human relations into more easily understood parts. Political science fits in by studying one type of interaction between people — that involving power and authority. An example may make the approaches of the other disciplines clearer and distinguish them from political science.

Political Science and General Motors

What questions would an economist, a psychologist, and a historian ask about the operations of a "society" like the giant automobile maker, General Motors? An *economist* might ask questions about the production and distribution of the Chevys, Pontiacs, Cadillacs, and trucks that GM makes. How are the raw materials converted into a finished product? At what cost? How efficiently does the assembly line operate? How are the cars marketed? A *psychologist* would center on the motives and interactions of people at GM. How do the workers or executives view their jobs and the company? Why? What is the psychological makeup of successful executives? of dissatisfied workers? A *historian* might look at the origins and development of General Motors. What factors within the company and in the country generally have accounted for GM's expansion? Why did it become the world's second largest corporation (with assets of over $25 billion) while competitors fell by the wayside?

Of course none of these fields are watertight compartments. They overlap. Members of one discipline are often interested in the findings of another. The economist may find answers to his or her questions about the efficiency of the assembly line in the works of the psychologist. The historian might ask the economist about GM's marketing activities to determine the reasons why the corporation has expanded. Certainly the economist and psychologist would want to know about the history of the giant industry before studying their particular parts of it.

A political scientist, although interested in the other disciplines' findings, would most likely focus on our central question: *who is getting what, when, and how?* Who runs General Motors? How do they run it? How do the heads of GM reach decisions? How do unions or the government influence the decisions of GM? (Strikes? Taxes?) How do GM's leaders get their decisions carried out? How did these people get to the top and how do they stay there? Political science focuses on the study of power and authority; on the powerful, the ways they exercise their authority, and the effects they produce.

As Lasswell wrote, "The study of politics is the study of

influence and the influential."[1] That is the core of what a political scientist would want to find out about General Motors.

Why Give a Damn about Politics?

After looking at what politics is and what government and political scientists do, you could still be asking one basic question: Who cares? Why give a damn about politics? Often students say: "Politics is just ego-tripping. I don't want to get involved in it." But you *are* involved. Apathy is as much a political position as is activism. Either position will influence who gets what in our society. Safe streets, good schools, clean food are political decisions influenced by who participates in them, who is prevented from participating, and who chooses not to participate.

Our lives are webs of politics. From the moment we wake up in the morning we are affected by someone's political choices. Think of what you've done today and how politics has influenced you. What you had (or didn't have) for breakfast was probably influenced by the price and availability of the food. The quality of the food you ate was regulated by a government agency that made sure those Grade A eggs were Grade A and that the milk was indeed pasteurized. The cost of that milk or those eggs was affected by the decisions of government to aid farmers, as well as the ability of farmers' groups to influence the government (through campaign contributions, for instance). The news you heard on the radio of what the government was doing for the economy was conditioned by what officials felt they should tell the public, and what media editors felt was newsworthy. The lack of good public transportation to take you to school may have been a result of government decisions to put money into highways rather than buses or trains. The college you attend, the tuition you pay, the GI benefits or other aid you

---

[1] Harold Lasswell, *Politics: Who Gets What, When, How* (New York: World, 1936, 1958), p. 13.

may or may not receive, are all the results of someone's choices in the political game.

Let's take a personal example to make the point clearer. Students of American government generally have agreed that federal regulatory commissions often do not effectively regulate the businesses they oversee. Detached from the rest of the government's bureaucracy, these commissions have tended to be closely tied to the powerful economic interests they supervise. The lesson was brought home several years ago.

In July, 1972, the cargo door blew off of an American Airlines DC-10 flying over Windsor, Canada, causing violent decompression. The pilot managed to land the empty jumbo jet safely. The independent National Transportation

Safety Board investigated the near-disaster. Their recommendations went to the Federal Aviation Administration (FAA), the government regulatory commission in charge of airline safety. The Safety Board recommended that the FAA order that all cargo doors have modified locking devices and that McDonnell Douglas, the plane's builders, be required to strengthen the cabin floor.

The FAA, headed by a political appointee, was operating under a policy of "gentleman's agreements" with the industries it was regulating. After discussions with the plane's manufacturers (who were large campaign contributors to President Nixon's re-election), they allowed McDonnell Douglas to modify the door on its own instead of under FAA supervision and to simply issue advisory service bulletins for the 130 or so DC-10s already in operation. McDonnell Douglas was allowed to reject as "impractical" the idea of strengthening the floor.

Somehow the changes on the door of a DC-10 flown by Turkish Airlines had not been made. The plane, flying from Paris to London in March, 1974, crashed, killing all 346 people aboard. It was at the time the world's worst air disaster. The cargo door had blown off. This produced an explosive decompression, collapse of the cabin floor, and loss of control. Passengers still strapped in their seats were sucked from the plane. A subcommittee of the House of Representatives, in a report on the crash, attacked the FAA for its "indifference to public safety" and for attempting to "balance dollars against lives."[2]

A teacher and friend of the authors of this book, Professor Wayne Wilcox of Columbia University, was on the plane. With him were his wife and two children.

We have no choice over *whether* to be involved in the political game. But we can choose *how* to be involved. We can choose whether to be a *subject in* the political game or an *object of* that game. The question is not whether politics affects us. It does, and will. The question is whether we will

[2] *The Times* (London), December 29, 1974.

affect politics. The first step in this decision is the choice of how aware we wish to be of the game. This book may, with luck, be a start of your awareness, and your willingness to be a *player* rather than merely *played upon.*

WHAT IS THIS BOOK ABOUT?

This book is, in a way, a scorecard covering the major players in the game of national politics. This first chapter introduces some of the terms and substance of politics — the means (power and authority) and goals (valued things) of the game. The next chapter discusses the formal constitutional rules under which the competition proceeds. The following three chapters deal with the governmental players — the president and bureaucracy, Congress, and the federal courts — their history and structure, their strengths and weaknesses. Chapters 6 and 7 are about several important nongovernmental players — voters, political parties, interest groups, and media. That they are not formal parts of the government does not mean they do not have great influence over the outcome of political conflicts. Finally, the last chapter goes into different theories of who wins and loses, who plays and doesn't play the game.

Let's be clear about this "game"; it is not Monday night football. It is vital, complex, ever changing, never ending, and played in deadly seriousness. There are actually many games going on at the same time with overlapping players and objectives. They are games in which the participants seldom agree, even on the goals. For the goals (unlike the touchdown in football) vary with the objectives of the players. A business group may seek higher profits from its involvement in a political issue; a consumer organization may want a better-quality product; and a labor union may demand higher wages for its workers. They may all compete for their differing objectives over the same issue. They all seek to use power to obtain the values they consider important. We can analyze fairly objectively how they play the game, but which side we root for depends on our own interests and ideals.

Another problem is that the players we've grouped together may not see themselves as being on the same team. Each participant, whether the bureaucracy, Congress, or media, is hardly a single player seeking a single goal. They are not only players but *arenas* in which competition goes on. We may read of Congress opposing the president on an issue. But a closer look will find the president's congressional supporters and opponents fighting it out in the committees of Congress. Some of the media may oppose a certain political movement, while allowing or limiting the use of TV and radio as an arena for publicizing the movement's views.

Finally, in this brief introductory text all the political players are not discussed. State and local governments are certainly important in national politics. Ethnic groups and even foreign governments may have a role in the outcome of the competition. An even more central omission, as one student remarked, are the people. What ever happened to the people in this game? Are they players or spectators?

For the most part, politics today is a spectator sport. The people are in the audience. To be sure, people do influence the players. The president and Congress are selected by election, labor unions depend on membership dues for support, and political parties need popular backing for their activities. But though it is played for the crowd and paid for by them, the game doesn't generally include them directly. Whether it will depends on the players, the rules and nature of the competition, and the people watching.

THOUGHT QUESTIONS

1. In the opening dialogue of this chapter, we discovered politics in what may seem an unlikely place — a classroom. Describe some other common situations where politics goes on.
2. How do authorities gain legitimacy? How do they lose it? Can you think of recent examples of both?

3. Why do you think many people are apathetic about national politics? Is apathy encouraged? If so, how? By whom?
4. In what ways has your life been affected by governmental action? Did you have anything to say about those actions? If you didn't, do you know who did?

SUGGESTED READINGS

1. Golding, William G. *Lord of the Flies.* New York: Capricorn Books, 1959. Pb.
   A somewhat pessimistic novel of what happens to a group of British children on a deserted island without adults or government, but with lots of politics.
2. Korda, Michael. *Power.* New York: Ballantine Books, 1975. Pb.
   A witty best-selling manual about the role of power in our daily lives with tips on how to "make it" in the power game.
3. Lasswell, Harold D. *Politics: Who Gets What, When, How.* New York: World, 1958.
   A brief, well-known introduction to politics.
4. Orwell, George. *Animal Farm.* New York: Harcourt, Brace, Jovanovich, 1946. Pb.
   The famous barnyard tale where the animals overthrow the farmer and set up a government in which pigs are more equal than others.
5. Schattschneider, E. E. *The Semisovereign People.* New York: Holt, Rinehart, and Winston, 1961. Pb.
   This landmark work presents a basic explanation of how and why some people get into the political game and some stay out.

The Constitution: Rules of the Game   2

So far we have discussed what the political game is about, what winning means, and why one plays. This chapter deals with the principles and procedures of the competition. The Constitution contains the official rules of the American political game; and it also establishes three major players and their powers — the president, Congress, and the Supreme Court. Further, it places limits on how the game can be played, and provides protection for the losers, through its safeguards on individual rights. And by establishing a central government sharing power with state governments, the Constitution marks out the arenas of play. What led to the adoption of these rules, what they mean, how they have changed, and how much influence they have today, are the central questions of this chapter.

BACKGROUND TO THE CONSTITUTION

In July, 1776, the Declaration of Independence proclaimed the American colonies "Free and Independent States." This symbolized the beginning not only of a bitter fight for independence from Great Britain, but also of a struggle to unify the separate and often conflicting interests, regions, and states of America. Only after a decade of trial and error was the Constitution written and accepted as the legal foundation for the new United States of America.

The men who gathered in Philadelphia in May, 1787, to write the Constitution were not starting from scratch. They were able to draw on (1) an English legal heritage, (2) American models of colonial and state governments, and (3) their experience with the Articles of Confederation.

The English political heritage the framers were part of included the Magna Charta, which in 1215 had declared that the power of the king was not absolute. It also included the idea of natural rights, expressed by English philosophers, most notably John Locke, who wrote that people were "born free" and formed society to protect their rights. Many colonists felt that they were fighting a revolution to secure their traditional rights as Englishmen, which had been denied them by an abusive colonial government.

During their 150 years as colonies, the states had learned much about self-government that now went into the Constitution. Even the earliest settlers had been determined to live under written rules of law resting on the consent of the community: the *Mayflower Compact* was signed by the Pilgrims shortly before they landed at Plymouth in 1620. Similar documents existed in most of the colonies. Other aspects of colonial governments, such as two-house legislatures, also were later to appear in the Constitution. After the Revolution, in reaction to the authority of the royal governor, the colonists established the legislature as the most important branch in their state governments. Most of the colonies had a governor, a legislature, and a judiciary, a pattern that would evolve into the constitutional separation of powers. Most had regular elections, though generally only white, propertied males could vote. There was even an uneasy basis for the federal system of local and national governments in the sharing of powers between the American colonies and a central government in England. Perhaps most important was the idea of limited government and individual rights written into the state constitutions after the Revolution.

But unity among the colonies was evolving only slowly. Attempts to tighten their ties during the Revolution were a limited success. The First Continental Congress in September, 1774, had established regular lines of communication among the colonies and given a focus to anti-British sentiment. The Second Continental Congress, beginning in Philadelphia in May, 1775, created the Declaration of Independence. At the same time a plan for confederation — a loose union among the states — was proposed. The Articles of Confederation were ratified by the states by March, 1781, and went into effect even before the formal end of the American Revolution in February, 1783.

The Articles of Confederation (1781–89)

Pointing out the shortcomings of the Articles of Confederation is not difficult. There was really no national government set up in the articles. Rather they established a "league of friendship" among the states, which didn't have much more authority than the United Nations does today. The center of the federation was a *unicameral* (one-house) congress. Each state had one vote regardless of its size. Most serious actions required approval by nine states, and amendments to the articles needed the approval of all thirteen.

The confederation had no executive branch and no national system of courts. But perhaps most important, the congress had no ability to impose taxes, only to *request* funds from the states. Each state retained its "sovereignty, freedom, and independence." Nor did the congress have any authority over citizens, who were subject only to the government of their states. In short, the congress had no ability to enforce its will on either states or citizens.

The confederation did have many strengths, however. Unlike the United Nations, it had the power to declare war, conduct foreign policy, coin money, manage a postal system, and oversee an army made up of the state militias. The articles were also startlingly democratic in requiring compulsory rotation in office. That is, no member of the congress could serve more than three years in any six. Finally, there were real accomplishments under the articles, such as the start of a national bureaucracy and the passing of the Northwest Ordinance, which established the procedure for admitting new states into the union.

But by 1787 the inadequacies of the articles were more apparent than the strengths. Too little power had been granted to the central authority. The confederation was in deep financial difficulty: not enough funds were coming from the states, the currency was being devalued, and the states were locked in trade wars, putting up tariff barriers against each other. Shays' Rebellion in late 1786, an angry protest by Massachusetts farmers unable to pay their mortgages and taxes, reinforced the fears of many of the propertied elite that strong government was needed to avoid "mob rule" and economic disruption.

The Constitutional Convention

Against this background the convention met in Philadelphia from May 25 to September 17, 1787. The weather was hot and muggy, making tempers short. All the meetings were held in strict secrecy. One reason for this was that the congress had reluctantly called the convention together "for the sole purpose of revising the Articles of Confederation." Yet within five days of its organization the convention had adopted a Virginia delegate's resolution "that a national government ought to be established consisting of a *supreme* legislative, executive, and judiciary." In other words, the convention violated the authority under which it had been established, and proceeded to write a completely new United States Constitution in a single summer.

The Constitution was a product of a series of compromises. The most important compromise, because it was the most divisive issue, was the question of how the states would be represented in the national legislature. The large states proposed a legislature with representation based either on the taxes paid by each state to the national government, or on the number of people in each state. The small states wanted one vote for each state no matter what its size. After a long deadlock an agreement called *The Great Compromise*, established the present structure of Congress: representation based on population in the lower house

(House of Representatives) and equal representation for all states in the upper one (Senate).

Other compromises came a bit more easily. Southern delegates feared the national government would impose an export tax on their agricultural goods, and interfere with slavery. A compromise was reached which gave Congress the power to regulate commerce but not to put a tax on exports. In addition, the slave trade could not be banned before 1808. The slave issue was also central in what was perhaps the weirdest agreement — the "Three-Fifths" Compromise. Here the debate was over whether slaves should be counted as people for purposes of representation and taxation. It was finally agreed that slaves should be counted as three-fifths of a person for both. (This was later changed by the Thirteenth Amendment.) Another central issue, that of the right of a state to withdraw or *secede* from the union, was simply avoided. The questions of secession and slavery had to wait for a later generation to answer in a bloody civil war.

THE FRAMERS

Given the importance of the Constitution, it is a little surprising how quickly and painlessly it was drafted. No doubt this was due partly to the wisdom of the men at Philadelphia. The universally respected General Washington chaired the meetings; the political brilliance of Alexander Hamilton and James Madison illuminated the debates; and Benjamin Franklin at eighty-two added the moderation of age. The delegates themselves possessed a blend of experience and learning. Of the fifty-five delegates, forty-two had served in the Continental Congress. More than half were college-educated and had studied political philosophy. They were a relatively young group, the average age being forty. In this they may have reflected a generation gap of their own time. Having politically matured during the Revolutionary period, they were less tied to state loyalties than were older men whose outlook was formed before the war. They were nationalists building a nation, not merely defending the interests of their states.

But there was more to the consensus than this. The framers were not exactly a representative sample of the population of America at the time. They were wealthy planters, merchants, and lawyers. Fifteen of them were slaveholders, fourteen were land speculators. The small farmers and workers of the country, many of whom were suffering from an economic downturn, were not represented at Philadelphia. Nor did leading liberals in the elite who might speak for this poorer majority, such as Thomas Jefferson (who was in Paris as ambassador) or Patrick Henry (who stayed away because he "smelt a rat"), attend the convention. Only six of the fifty-six men who signed the Declaration of Independence were at the convention. The delegates were a conservative, propertied elite, worried that continuing the weak confederation would only encourage more and larger Shays' Rebellions. Thus the debates at the convention were not between the haves and the have-nots, but between the haves and the haves over their regional interests.

Motives behind the Constitution

Much scholarly debate has gone on over the motives of the framers since Charles Beard published his book, *An Economic Interpretation of the Constitution of the United States* in 1913. Beard argued that the convention was a counterrevolution engineered by the delegates to protect and improve their own property holdings by transferring power from the states to an unrepresentative central government. Certainly the forty delegates who held nearly worthless confederation securities stood to profit from a new government committed to honoring these debts. Certainly as creditors and property holders their interests would be better protected by a strong central government. Nor did the delegates particularly favor democracy. Most thought that liberty had to be protected *from* democracy (which they thought of as "mob rule") and agreed with Madison's statement in *The Federalist Papers* (No. 10) that "Those who hold and those who are without property have ever formed distinct interests in society."

Critics of Beard's theory argue that the framers' motives were more varied. They reason that the delegates sought to build a new nation, to reduce the country's numerous political disputes, and to promote economic development that would benefit all. They point out that having a central government able to raise an army to protect the states from foreign attack appeared to be the most important reason why George Washington, among others, backed the Constitution.

But the arguments of the two sides don't necessarily cancel each other out. The framers' *public* interest of building a strong nation and their *private* interest of protecting their property could work together. Like most people, they believed that what was good for themselves was good for society. That most of the population (workers, the poor, blacks, women) was not represented at Philadelphia was not surprising by the standards of the day. Nor should it be surprising that the delegates' ideas for a nation and a government not only did not work against their own economic interests but in many cases aided them.

Federalists versus Anti-Federalists

This is not to say that there were not divisions within this elite. Many of the debates during the writing and ratification of the Constitution divided the political elite into what were essentially conservative and liberal camps, the Federalists and Anti-Federalists.

The Federalists (conservatives) generally favored a strong federal (national) government, with protection of private property rights, and limits on popular participation in government. (Alexander Hamilton, a leader of the Federalists, once described the people as "a great beast.") In the debates over the Constitution, the Federalists pushed for high property qualifications for voting, an indirectly elected Senate modeled after the English aristocratic House of Lords, a lofty indirectly elected president, and a strong nonelected judiciary. The Federalists, being more pessimistic about human nature (including the nature of the rulers), wanted these "cooling-off" devices in the government to filter down the popular will and create guardians of the people's real interests.

The Anti-Federalists (liberals) were more optimistic about human nature, though just as suspicious about the nature of those in power. They favored strong state governments because they felt the states would be closer to the popular will than a strong central government would be. They wanted fewer limits on popular participation and pushed for the legislative branch to have more power than the executive and judicial branches. Believing that the majority was responsible (though agreeing that it might need cooling off), they wanted government to rest ultimately on public opinion.

The Constitution is a compromise between the conservative and liberal positions. It was designed to prevent tyranny both from the bottom (which the Federalists feared) and from the top (which the Anti-Federalists feared). Both sides generally believed that the government that governed best governed least.

RATIFICATION AND THE BILL OF RIGHTS

The struggle for ratification of the Constitution focused the debate between the Federalists and Anti-Federalists. Conventions in nine states had to approve the Constitution before it could go into effect. As a majority of the people were against the Constitution, the fight for ratification wasn't easy. The Anti-Federalists wanted a more rigid system of separation of powers and more effective checks and balances. Fearing that the president and Senate would act together as an aristocratic clique, they proposed compulsory rotation in office (as under the Articles of Confederation) to avoid this.

The Federalists chided the Anti-Federalists for their lack of faith in the popular selection process and for ignoring the advantages of national union. They mounted a propaganda campaign using pamphlets and newspaper articles. The best known of these was a series of essays in a New York newspaper written by Madison, Hamilton, and John Jay, later republished as *The Federalist Papers*. The book stands today as the most famous commentary on the nature of the Constitution and what the framers thought of it.

The debate over including the Bill of Rights (the first ten amendments) in the Constitution became a key issue in the struggle over ratification. The Philadelphia convention, dominated by conservatives, had failed to include a bill of rights in the original document. This was not due so much to opposition to the ideals of the bill as to a feeling that such a statement was irrelevant. (A proposed bill of rights was voted down unanimously near the end of the convention partly because everyone was worn out and wanted to go home.) The Federalists, from their pessimistic viewpoint, believed that liberty was best protected by the *procedures* (such as federalism and checks and balances) established by their constitutional government. No matter what ideals were written down, such as freedoms of speech, press, and religion, the Federalists argued that support for them would depend on the "tolerance of the age" and the balance of forces established by the Constitution.

For the Anti-Federalists the Bill of Rights was a proclamation of fundamental truths, natural rights due to all people. No matter whether another generation might ignore them, these rights were sacred. Any government resting on the consent of its people must honor them in its constitution. Although the Anti-Federalists had lost the battle in Philadelphia, they eventually won the war over the Bill of Rights. Massachusetts and Virginia agreed to accept the Constitution with the recommendation that such a proclamation be the first order of business of the new Congress. It was, and the Bill of Rights became the first ten amendments to the Constitution on December 15, 1791.

FOUR MAJOR CONSTITUTIONAL PRINCIPLES

In establishing a system of government the United States Constitution did three things. First, it *established the structure* of government. In setting up three branches of government within a federal system, it gave the country a political framework that has existed down to the present. Second, the Constitution *distributed certain powers* to this government. Article I gave legislative powers, such as the power to raise and spend money, to Congress. Article II gave executive powers to the president, including command over the armed forces and wide authority over foreign policy. And Article III gave judicial power, the right to judge disputes arising under the Constitution, to the United States Supreme Court. Third, the Constitution *restrained the government* in exercising these powers. Government was limited, by the Bill of Rights for example, so that certain individual rights would be preserved.

The Constitution, then, both *grants* and *limits* governmental power. This can be most clearly seen by looking closely at four major constitutional principles: *separation of powers and checks and balances, federalism, limited government,* and *judicial review.*

Separation of Powers and Checks and Balances

The first major constitutional principle is actually two: separation of powers, and checks and balances. But the two principles can't be understood apart from each other, and they operate together.

Separation of powers is the principle that the powers of government should be separated and put in the care of different parts of the government. Although never exactly stated in the Constitution, this principle had a long history in political philosophy and was in practice in the governments of the colonies. The writers of the Constitution divided the federal government into three branches to carry out what they saw as the three major functions of government. The *legislative function* — passing the laws — was given to Congress; the *executive function* — carrying out or executing the laws — was given to the president; and the *judicial function* — interpreting the laws — was given to the Supreme Court.

Though it is nice and neat, the principle is probably also unworkable. The purpose of the separation of powers was to allow ambition to counter ambition, to prevent any single authority from monopolizing power. Yet simply dividing the powers of government into these three branches would probably make the legislature supreme — as was the case in the colonies. As the starter of the governmental process, the legislature could determine how, or even if, the other branches played their role. Something else was needed to curb legislative power. That something was checks and balances.

Checks and balances create a mixture of powers that permits the three branches of government to limit one another. A *check* is a control one branch has over another's functions, creating a *balance* of power. The principle gives the branches constitutional means for guarding their functions from interference by another branch. The principle of checks and balances mixes together the legislative, execu-

---

MADISON ON GOVERNMENT

"... If men were angels, no government would be necessary. If angels were to govern men, neither external or internal controls on government would be necessary. In framing a government, which is to be administered by men over men, the great difficulty lies in this: You must first enable the government to control the governed; and in the next place, oblige it to control itself." — James Madison, *The Federalist Papers* (No. 51)

tive, and judicial powers, giving some legislative powers to the executive, some executive powers to the legislative branch, and so on, to keep any branch from dominating another.

There are a number of examples of checks and balances in the Constitution. The presidential veto gives the chief executive a primarily legislative power to prevent bills he dislikes from being passed into law by Congress. Congress can check this power by its right to override the veto by a two-thirds vote. The Senate is given an executive power in its role of confirming presidential nominations for major executive and judicial posts. Further, Congress can refuse to appropriate funds for any executive agency, thereby preventing the agency from carrying out the laws.

But the system of separation of powers and checks and balances is even more elaborate than this. The way each branch of government is set up and chosen also checks and balances its power. For example, Congress is divided into two houses, and both must approve legislation before it becomes law. Limited terms of office and varied methods of selection help keep any one person or branch from becoming too strong. The House of Representatives was to be popularly elected for two-year terms; Senators were elected for six years, originally by their state legislatures (changed by the Seventeenth Amendment to popular election); the president was elected for four years by an electoral college; and federal judges were to be appointed by the president, confirmed by the Senate, and serve for life during good behavior. All these procedures were designed to give government officials different interests to defend and varied bases of support.

This elaborate scheme of separation of powers and checks and balances was certainly not designed as the most efficient form of government. Rather, it was established "to control the abuses of government" — to oblige the government to control itself. It set up what historian Richard Hofstadter has called "a harmonious system of mutual frustration."

Four Major Constitutional Principles

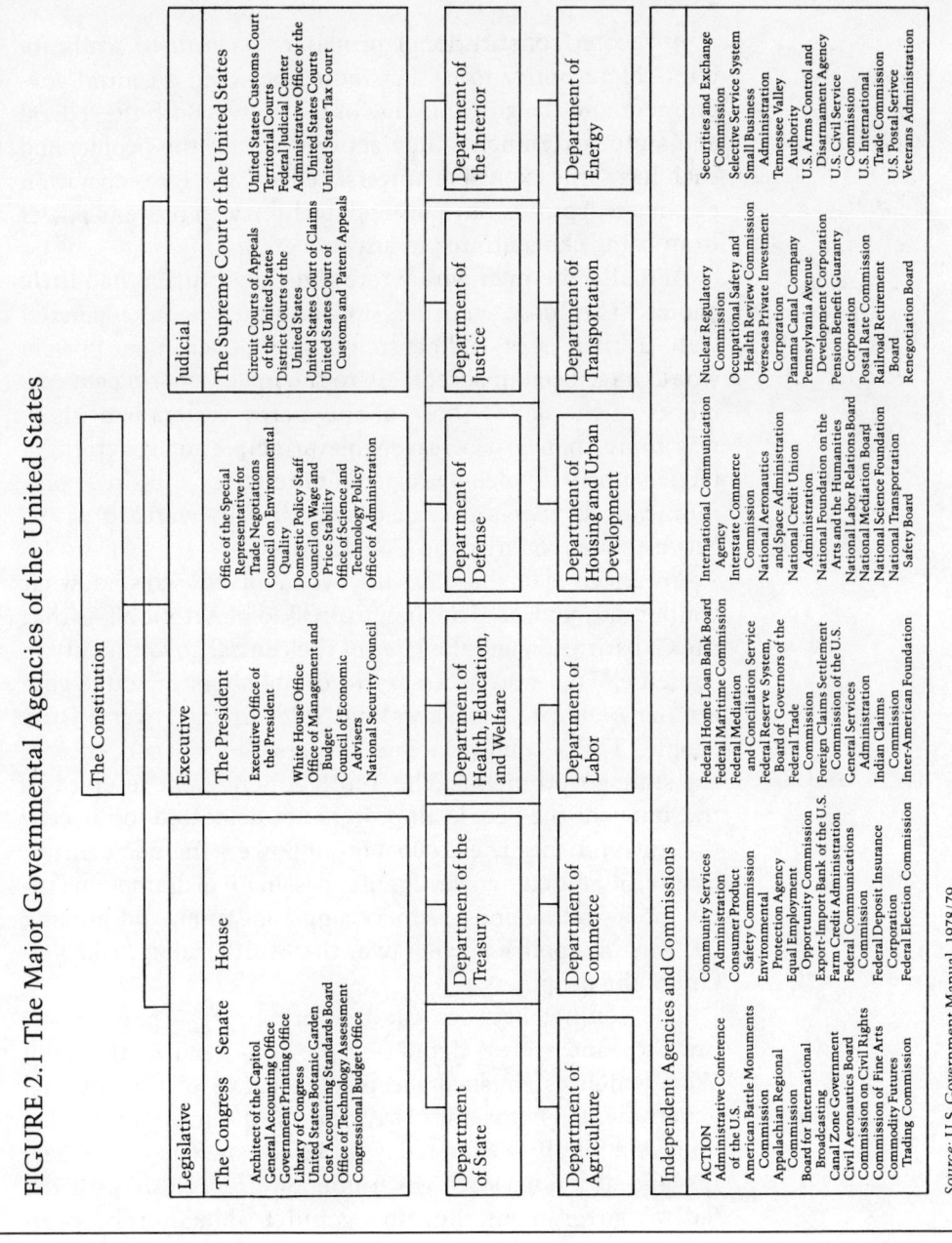

FIGURE 2.1 The Major Governmental Agencies of the United States

Source: U.S. Government Manual, 1978/79.

Federalism

A second constitutional principle, *federalism*, calls for political authority to be distributed between a central government and the governments of the states. Both the federal and state governments may act directly on the people, and each has some exclusive powers. Federalism, like separation of powers, spreads out political authority to prevent power from being concentrated in any one group.

Actually the men who wrote the Constitution had little choice. The loose confederation of states hadn't operated well, in their eyes, and centralizing all government powers would have been unacceptable to the major existing governments of the day — those of the states. Federalism, then, was more than just a reasonable principle for governing a large country divided by regional differences and slow communications. It was also the only politically realistic way to get the states to ratify the Constitution.

American federalism has always involved two somewhat contradictory ideas. The first, expressed in Article VI, is that the Constitution and the laws of the central government are supreme. This was necessary to establish an effective government, able to pass laws and rule directly over all the people. The second principle ensures the independence of the state governments: The Tenth Amendment reserved to the states or the people all powers not delegated to the central government. These substantial powers include controlling local and city governments, passing legislation governing labor and business, supervising education, and holding the general "police power" over the health, safety, and welfare of the people.

The conflict between the two principles — national supremacy and states' rights — came to a head in the Civil War, which established the predominance of the national government. That is not to say that the question was settled once and for all — even today, in issues such as school busing and abortion, state governments often clash with the federal government. But the conflict shouldn't be over-

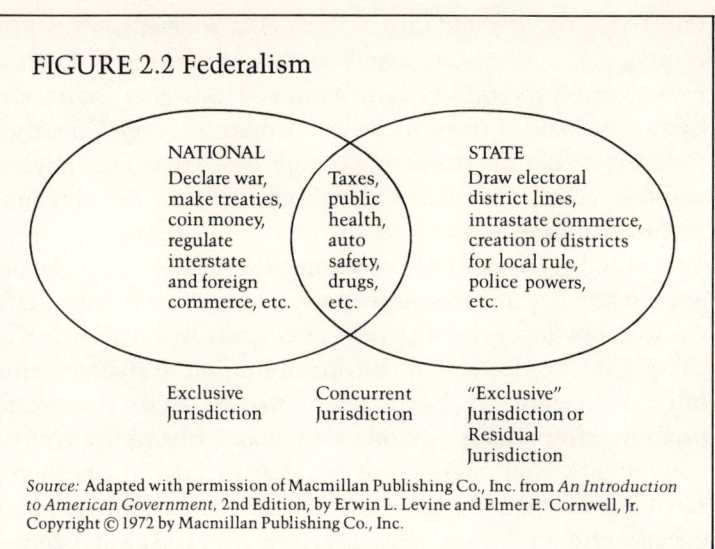

FIGURE 2.2 Federalism

Source: Adapted with permission of Macmillan Publishing Co., Inc. from *An Introduction to American Government*, 2nd Edition, by Erwin L. Levine and Elmer E. Cornwell, Jr. Copyright © 1972 by Macmillan Publishing Co., Inc.

stated. Even though the Constitution divided the powers of government by federalism, it also clearly set up the basis for national union. In the years since, the national government has grown far more important than state governments. (Urbanization, the trend for people to move to city areas, also may have reduced the importance of the states by focusing attention on local city governments.) As political issues — whether regulating the economy or protecting the environment — became national, so too did solutions come to center in the national government. This trend was not only consistent with the goals of the Constitution, it was actually an outgrowth of the foundations of union laid down by the document.

Limited Government

The principle of *limited government* means that the powers of government are limited by the rights and liberties of the governed. This principle is basic to the very idea of constitutional government: the people give the government certain listed powers and duties through a constitution, while reserving the rest to themselves. Government actions then must rest on the *rule of law*, approved, however indirectly, by the consent of the governed. Furthermore, the Constitution sets up certain procedures, such as separation of powers and federalism, to ensure that the government remains limited to its proper duties and powers.

Limited government guarantees citizens their *rights against* the government as well as *access to* the government. Civil rights guarantee the openness and competitiveness of the political process. This means not only the right to vote, but the freedom to dissent, demonstrate, and organize to produce alternatives, in order to make the right to vote meaningful. Civil rights also protect the citizen from arbitrary governmental power. Under civil rights would fall a citizen's right to a fair and speedy trial, to have legal defense, and to be judged by an impartial jury of his or her peers. Further, government cannot take life, liberty, or property without due process of law, nor interfere with a citizen's right to practice religion, nor invade his or her privacy. In short, the people who make the law are also subject to it.

Judicial Review

An important means of keeping government limited and of maintaining civil rights and liberties is the power of judicial review vested in the Supreme Court. *Judicial review*, the last constitutional principle, is the judicial branch's authority to decide on the constitutionality of the acts of the various parts of the government (state, local, and federal).

Although judicial review has become an accepted constitutional practice, it is not actually mentioned in the document. There was some debate in the first years of the Constitution over whether the Court had the power merely to give nonbinding opinions, or whether it had supremacy over acts of the government. Most people at that time agreed that the Court did have the power to nullify unconstitutional acts of the state governments, but opinion was divided over whether this extended to the acts of the federal government. In 1803, in the case of *Marbury* v. *Madison,* the Supreme Court declared that it did have the right to judge acts of Congress (see page 138). Since then, this power has become a firmly entrenched principle of the Constitution.

Judicial review has put the Court in the position of watchdog over the limits of the central government's actions, and made it the guardian of federalism. This latter function, reviewing the acts of state and local governments, has in fact been the Court's most important use of judicial review. Though relatively few federal laws have been struck down by the Court, hundreds of state and local laws have been held to violate the Constitution. As Justice Oliver Wendell Holmes said over fifty years ago, "The United States would not come to an end if we lost our power to declare an act of Congress void. I do think the Union would be imperiled if we could not make that declaration as to the laws of the several states."

HOW IS THE CONSTITUTION CHANGED?

To say that the Constitution has lasted some 190 years is not to say it is the same document that was adopted in 1789. The Constitution has changed vastly; in practical ways, it bears little resemblance to the original. Most of the framers would scarcely recognize the political process that operates today under their Constitution. Changes in the Constitution have been made by four major methods: formal amendments, judicial interpretation, legislation, and custom.

Amendments

Although the amendment process is the first way we usually think of for changing the Constitution, it is actually the least common method. Only twenty-six amendments (including the first ten amendments, which can practically be considered part of the original document) have been adopted. (A twenty-seventh, the Equal Rights Amendment, and a twenty-eighth, the Washington D.C. Voting Rights Amendment, have been proposed by Congress and not yet ratified by the needed three-fourths of the state legislatures.) This is largely because the process of adopting amendments is so difficult. Though the Constitution's framers recognized the need for change in any such document, no matter how farsighted, they wanted to protect it from temporary popular pressure. Hence they required unusually large majorities for adopting amendments.

Article V of the Constitution provides a number of methods for adopting amendments. Amendments may be *proposed* by a two-thirds vote of each house of Congress or (if requested by two-thirds of the state legislatures) by a national convention called by Congress. They must be *ratified* by conventions in three-fourths of the states, or by three-fourths of the state legislatures (the choice is up to Congress).

The national convention has never been used; all amendments have been proposed by Congress. Only the Twenty-

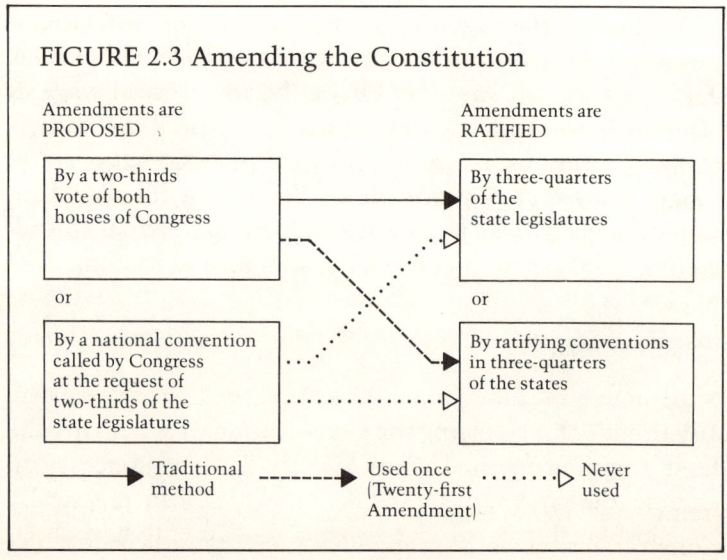

FIGURE 2.3 Amending the Constitution

first Amendment (repealing Prohibition) was ratified by state conventions. (The idea behind this one use of state conventions was that the state legislatures were still full of the same representatives who had passed Prohibition in the first place, and conventions seemed likely to be the fastest way to change it.) A major reason why the national convention method has never been used to propose amendments is Congress' jealousy toward another body trespassing on its powers. Another is worry over how many amendments might be proposed by such a convention. After all, the Constitution was written by an earlier runaway convention set up only to amend the Articles of Confederation.

Judicial Interpretation

If the amendment process is the least used method of changing the Constitution, interpretations by the Supreme Court are probably the most common. Practically every part of the Constitution has been before the Supreme Court at some time or another. In the process the Court has shaped and reshaped the document. Recent Court decisions have allowed Congress great scope in regulating the economy, prohibited legal segregation of races, allowed local communities to determine the limits of obscenity, and established "one man, one vote" as a constitutional principle governing election to the House of Representatives (see page 99). The Court has also given practical meaning to general constitutional phrases such as "necessary and proper" (Article 1, Section 8), "due process of law" (Amendments 5 and 14), and "unreasonable searches and seizures" (Amendment 4). No wonder the Supreme Court is sometimes called "a permanent constitutional convention."

Legislation

Congress has been largely responsible for filling in the framework of government outlined by the Constitution. Congress has established all the federal courts below the

Supreme Court. It has determined the size of the House of Representatives as well as the Supreme Court. The cabinet and most of the boards and commissions in the executive branch have been created by congressional legislation. And a large number of the regulations and services we now take for granted, such as social security, have come from measures passed by Congress.

Custom

Custom is the most imprecise way the Constitution has changed, yet one of the most widespread. Many practices that have been accepted as constitutional are not actually mentioned in the document. The growth of political parties and the influence of party leadership in the government, the presidential nominating conventions, the breakdown of the electoral college, and the committee system in Congress are just a few customary practices not foreseen by the Constitution.

Custom has also changed what, at least on the surface, seem to have been some clear intentions of the framers. The Eighth Amendment forbidding "excessive bail" has not prevented courts from setting bail in serious offenses that is too high for the accused to raise. Although Congress has the right to declare war (Article II, Section 8), presidents have entered conflicts that looked very much like wars (Korea, Vietnam) without such a declaration. Customs also have been broken and reestablished by law. The custom that a president only serves two terms was started by Washington and cemented by Jefferson. Broken with much debate by Franklin D. Roosevelt in 1940, the custom was made law in the Twenty-second Amendment adopted in 1951.

WHY HAS THE CONSTITUTION SURVIVED?

All these ways the Constitution has been changed to meet different needs at different times do not completely explain its survival. Various explanations have been put forth for why the Constitution has endured to become the oldest written constitution of any country.

The major reason it has lasted probably lies not in the Constitution itself but in the stability of American society. Disturbances like the Civil War, the Indian campaigns and massacres, and foreign wars all have been dealt with within the same constitutional structure. The Constitution has been adapted to integrate potentially disruptive groups, such as immigrants, former slaves, women, and the poor, that were originally excluded from political participation. The Constitution's emphasis on procedures has served it well through the wars and depressions as well as the peace and prosperity of various ages.

Other explanations for the Constitution's durability focus on the document itself. One maintains that it is a work of genius. William Gladstone, the nineteenth-century British prime minister, described it as "the most wonderful work ever struck off at a given time by the brain and purpose of man." Incorporating centuries of English political traditions as well as the framers' own experience, the Constitution set out the principles and framework of government in concise, well-written phrases.

The *shortness* of the document (only some seven thousand words with all the amendments) is another major reason for its durability. Although it sets out the basic principles and structures of a government, the Constitution leaves much only generally stated or not mentioned at all. In a word, the Constitution is *ambiguous*. Many of the most enduring Constitutional phrases ("freedom of speech," "due process of law," "all laws which shall be necessary and proper," "privileges or immunities of citizens") have been applied differently at various times in our history. Other principles, such as majority rule and individual liberties, sometimes may seem contradictory. It is left to the political players of each age to resolve the conflicts among various groups claiming constitutional support. This flexibility has been one of the Constitution's major strengths in adapting to new political pressures and allowing people to reach compromises under competing principles.

FREEDOM OF SPEECH

"I disagree profoundly with what you say, but I would defend with my life your right to say it." — Voltaire

"If all mankind minus one were of one opinion, and only one person were of the contrary opinion, mankind would be no more justified in silencing that one person than he, if he had the power, would be justified in silencing mankind." — John Stuart Mill

"The character of every act depends upon the circumstances in which it is done. . . . The most stringent protection of free speech would not protect a man in falsely shouting fire in a theater and causing a panic. . . . The question in every case is whether the words used are used in such circumstances and are of such a nature as to create a clear and present danger that they will bring about the substantive evils that Congress has a right to prevent." — Justice Oliver Wendell Holmes

"It shall be unlawful for any person with intent to cause the overthrow or destruction of any government in the United States, to print, publish, edit, issue, circulate, sell, distribute, or publicly display any written or printed matter advocating, advising, or teaching the duty, necessity, desirability or propriety of overthrowing or destroying any government in the U.S. by force of violence." — The Smith Act

"Overthrow of the government by force and violence is certainly a substantial enough interest for the government to limit speech. Indeed, this is the ultimate value of any society, for if a society cannot protect its very structure from armed internal attack, it must follow that no subordinate value can be protected." — Chief Justice Fred M. Vinson

"The vitality of civil and political institutions in our society depends on free discussion. . . . It is only through free debate and free exchange of ideas that government remains responsive to the will of the people and peaceful change is effected. The right to speak freely . . . is therefore one of the chief distinctions that sets us apart from totalitarian regimes.

Accordingly, a function of free speech under our system of government is to invite dispute. It may indeed best serve its high purpose when it induces a condition of unrest, creates dissatisfaction with conditions as they are, or even stirs people to anger." — Justice William O. Douglas

Case Study: The Evolution of a Constitutional Right, Freedom of Speech

The flexibility of the Constitution can be seen most clearly by looking at one important part of it: that section of the Bill of Rights guaranteeing freedom of speech. How differently the same words have been applied throughout United States history underlines the importance of political power in giving meaning to constitutional principles.

On the face of it the constitutional right of freedom of speech seems both obvious and absolute. The First Amendment reads:

> Congress shall make no law respecting an establishment of religion, or prohibiting the free exercise thereof; or abridging the freedom of speech, or of the press; or the right of the people peaceably to assemble, and to petition the Government for a redress of grievances.

Of the above rights, freedom of speech is probably the most vital. As one Supreme Court justice wrote, it is "... the indispensable condition of nearly every other form of freedom." But note, this constitutional right is really a negative guarantee: the First Amendment states what Congress may *not* do; it does not state what people *are* allowed to do. It also fails to deal at all with what the states are allowed to do. Does the Constitution prevent individual states from abridging First Amendment freedoms? These ambiguities as well as the political climate of the age led in the nineteenth century to what we would clearly see today as violations of freedom of speech.

Not many years after the ink had dried on the Bill of Rights, a Federalist-controlled Congress during the presidency of John Adams (a signer of the Constitution) passed the *Alien and Sedition Acts* of 1798. Aimed at the opposition Democratic-Republican party (the Anti-Federalists), these acts established heavy fines and imprisonment for those judged guilty of writing or speaking anything false, scandalous, or malicious against any government official. Such a broad prohibition today would stop many a political speech — and that was exactly the intent then. Although only one Vermont congressman was convicted under the law, the Acts caused a political uproar in the country. When the Federalists lost control of Congress their Republican opponents soon ended the acts.

The slavery issue brought more lasting controls on freedom of speech. Before the Civil War the southern states prohibited antislavery speeches within their borders. They also unofficially censored the United States mails to prevent the spread of antislavery literature. Congress wasn't much better. In 1840 Congress passed the "Gag Rule" preventing antislavery petitions from being received by Congress (thus violating a specific First Amendment right). Among others, John Quincy Adams was tried for violating this rule. President Andrew Jackson called on the northern states to suppress the abolitionists and on Congress to pass a bill prohibiting the use of the mails to encourage slave rebellions. The bill didn't pass — not on grounds of freedom of speech, but because the states concerned were already censoring the mails.

This suppression of rights continued into the twentieth century. Within five months after the United States entered World War I, every leading socialist newspaper had been suspended from the mails at least once and some permanently. Protecting the country's national security was also the motive behind the Espionage Act passed in 1917 which effectively outlawed Marxist parties. The constitutionality of the Act was challenged in the courts by Charles T. Schenck, general secretary of the Socialist party, who had been convicted under it for urging draft resistance. This case, *Schenck* v. *U.S.* (1919), marked the first time the Supreme Court was called on to resolve an important question of free speech. In its decision the Supreme Court upheld Schenck's conviction, basing its decision on a doctrine of "clear and present danger." The majority opinion was written by Justice Oliver Wendell Holmes. Under this ruling speech can be punished only when it may lead directly to illegal actions and when the connection between the speech and the actions is obvious. The doctrine illustrates the Supreme Court's preference for restricting the government to narrow limits in enforcing laws regulating speech rather than directly challenging the constitutionality of the laws themselves.

The Court's slowly expanding defense of freedom of speech continued. In a landmark case, *Near* v. *Minnesota* (1931), the Court used the Fourteenth Amendment ("... nor shall any state deprive any person of life, liberty, or property, without due process of law") to limit state governments in restricting freedom of speech. Here the Court began to establish that the Bill of Rights could be interpreted to apply to the states.

On questions of national security versus freedom of speech the Court was more uncertain. The *Smith Act* of 1940 put it to the test. A central aim of the law was to forbid any teaching or advocating of the violent overthrow of the American government. Surprisingly little used during the war, the Smith Act was employed in the late 1940s and 1950s when anticommunism was at its height. With Senator Joseph McCarthy whipping up unsupported fears of communists in government, and with relations between the Soviet Union and the United States at the coldest point of the cold war, supporting leftist ideas became a dangerous act. In 1951, eleven Communist party leaders were convicted of violating the Smith Act. Chief Justice Fred M. Vinson, supporting the convictions, charged that the party leaders were organizing a conspiracy which was "a clear and present danger." He wrote, "We reject any principle of governmental helplessness in the face of preparation for revolution..." (*Dennis* v. *U.S.*). The "preparation for revolution," as other dissenting justices pointed out, only involved the advocating and teaching of major works of Marxist thought, like *The Communist Manifesto* (books found today in any college library). All but one of the defendants was sentenced to five years in prison.

Other convictions followed. But as the nation swung away from McCarthyism and more liberal justices were appointed to the Supreme Court (such as Chief Justice Earl Warren in 1953), dissenting opinions were heard more clearly from the bench. Justice Hugo Black, a consistent defender of freedom of speech, warned that the government could not outlaw the Communist party ". . . without endangering the liberty of all of us." In the more liberal political climate of the 1960s the Court refused to enforce penalties against individuals who declined to answer questions by Congressional committees about their beliefs. The nation as a whole seemed willing to ignore the communists and other Marxist parties, to allow them to recruit members, and to circulate their publications. The Smith Act, however, remains on the books.

This protection of free speech was extended by the Court to the civil rights and anti-Vietnam War movements. The Supreme Court struck down the conviction of a black man accused of violating a Georgia law which said that any person ". . . who shall without provocation use . . . abusive language, tending to cause a breach of the peace . . ." was guilty of a crime. *Symbolic speech* (a token action to underline a message) was also given greater protection. The Court overturned the conviction of a man who put the peace symbol on a flag, and also struck down as unconstitutionally vague a Massachusetts law under which a person had been arrested for sewing a flag patch on the seat of his jeans.

In general a wide tolerance for freedom of speech seems to prevail today. Congress has disbanded the committees that most trampled on the Bill of Rights (such as the House Committee on Un-American Activities) and is more careful than in the past in its treatment of dissenters. The attempts by the executive branch in the 1970s to suppress its opponents led to exposure in the press, the downfall of numerous high officials in the Nixon Administration (including President Nixon), and recent charges brought against FBI officials for violating citizens' rights.

Nonetheless, critical questions of freedom of speech remain unresolved. Should pornography be considered an issue of free speech? Chief Justice Warren Burger thought not when he wrote, "... Obscene material is not protected by the First Amendment." Many others, like Justice William O. Douglas, disagreed with Burger. Should American Nazis be allowed to demonstrate in Skokie, Illinois, a town chosen by them because 7,000 Jewish survivors of German concentration camps live there? Even organizations dedicated to expanding the right of free speech, like the American Civil Liberties Union, have divided over this question. Does free speech mean the right of access to the mass media for citizens and groups to have their opinions widely heard? Does it mean that corporations should have the right to spend unlimited funds on issue campaigns, like nuclear energy, to support their point of view? These and other free-speech questions remain to be answered in future plays of the political game.

Clearly neither the Constitution, the courts, nor our political leaders will have the final word on freedom of speech. It is a principle which, as we have seen, has been supported by many in the abstract but few in the cases of unpopular opinions. This brief history may not tell us exactly what freedom of speech is. It does seem to say that it is only effective when enough people make it their duty to defend it, and exercise it.

WRAP-UP

We have covered quite a bit in this chapter. In looking at the writing of the Constitution we saw how the colonists drew from the tradition of English political thought, the models of colonial government, and experience with the Articles of Confederation in shaping the Constitution. But the framers were also influenced by who they were. As a wealthy elite they sought to establish a government which would further both the interests of the nation and their own economic concerns. They divided into conservative and liberal groups, known as Federalists and Anti-Federalists, over how strong the government should be and how personal rights would be protected best. Ratification and the addition of the Bill of Rights forged an uneasy agreement between the two groups.

The Constitution as it has developed centers on four major principles: separation of powers and checks and balances, federalism, limited government, and judicial review. Although these principles remain fundamental to the document, the Constitution has been changed vastly by four main methods: formal amendment, judicial interpretation, legislation, and custom. The changes it has undergone have enabled the Constitution to endure. Perhaps more important to its survival, however, has been the stability of American society and the ambiguity of the document itself.

But does the flexibility and vagueness of the document mean that the Constitution as a body of rules governing the American political game is meaningless? That essentially it serves the interests of those in power and its interpretations change only as those interests alter? Perhaps. Certainly any document which has presided in olympian indifference over a political system that imported and enslaved its black residents, placed its citizens of Japanese descent in detention camps, allowed sweatshops and child labor, looked away from tremendous concentrations of wealth alongside abject poverty, has much to answer for. Is the Constitution an unworkable grab-bag of obsolete principles used to rationalize domination by the few?

As we said in Chapter 1, politics is not primarily about words, it is about power and ideals. One cannot blame a body of principles and procedures for the power or lack of power, for the ideals or lack of ideals, of the players in the game. All great historical documents, from the Bible to the Constitution, have been given vastly differing applications by different people at different times.

More than the rules of the game, then, the Constitution stands as a symbol of the ideals of a people. But this symbol does influence behavior. That a president violates the law does make a difference in whether he remains in power. That people have a constitutional right to demonstrate against a war can change the outcome of that war. That the press has the right to publish government documents (and the courts, not the administration, decide this) does place limits on the bureaucracy. Even the hypocrisy of politicians in bowing to ideals they may wish to ignore shows the strength of the symbol.

Yet the substance of the principles of the Constitution must ultimately rest on the political relationships of each generation of players. The *right* to demonstrate is meaningless without the *will* to demonstrate. Freedom of speech means nothing if no one has anything critical to say. Freedom of the press, or judicial safeguards, or rights to privacy could be lost without anyone's necessarily changing a word of the Constitution. Power without principle may be blind, but principle without power is impotent.

The rules of this game, then, are not fixed or unchanging. Though rooted in the traditions of the past, they are supported by the politics of the present. They are not only guidelines but goals as well. Therefore they remain unfinished, as must any constitution setting out to "secure the Blessings of Liberty to ourselves and our Posterity."

THOUGHT QUESTIONS

1. Do federalism and separation of powers and checks and balances support or restrict democracy?
2. What were some of the issues that the framers of the Constitution agreed on almost from the beginning? On which did they have to compromise, and what have been the historical effects of those compromises?
3. What makes the Constitution a flexible document? Do you agree that it is really that flexible?
4. How efficient are the political structures set up by the Constitution in dealing with contemporary problems? Do the goals of efficiency and democracy in the Constitution work against each other?

SUGGESTED READINGS

Beard, Charles A. *An Economic Interpretation of the Constitution of the United States.* New York: Macmillan, 1935. Pb.
The famous criticism of the framers' economic motivations in writing the Constitution.

Brown, Robert E. *Charles Beard and the Constitution.* New York: Norton Library, 1965, 1961. Pb.
Refutes Beard's analysis.

Hamilton, Alexander, James Madison, and John Jay. *The Federalist Papers.* New York: A Mentor Book. Pb.
The classic work on what the framers thought about their Constitution.

Lipset, Seymour Martin. *The First New Nation.* New York: Anchor, 1963. Pb.
Compares the early America to a present-day developing country.

McDonald, Forrest. *E Pluribus Unum.* Boston: Houghton Mifflin, 1965.
A lively account of the early days of the republic.

Vidal, Gore. *Burr.* New York: Bantam, 1974. Pb.
An accurate though fictional account of the nation's early years, well told from the viewpoint of Aaron Burr.

The Executive Branch: The President and the Bureaucracy

3

If there is a superstar in the American political game, it is the president of the United States. Although the head of just one of the three branches of the United States government, the president is the only official (along with the vice president) elected by the entire nation. Often he stands as the symbol of not only the whole federal government but the country as well. To many people, the Vietnam War and the Watergate scandal indicated that the power of the president had grown so great as to be a threat to democracy.

This chapter is about the executive branch of government and its chief executive, the president. We will trace the history of the growth of the presidency from the limited powers granted to the office in the Constitution. We will discuss different approaches to being president and the various roles of the office. The departments of the federal bureaucracy under the president, and the problems he has in controlling the bureaucracy, will take up another part of the chapter. Finally, we will look at three cases of the uses of presidential power and then draw some conclusions.

THE PRESIDENT AND THE CONSTITUTION

Article II of the Constitution lists the president's powers. It grants a president far less power and far fewer duties than it gives Congress in Article I. Yet the opening sentence of the article ("The executive Power shall be vested in a President of the United States of America") and other vague phrases ("he shall take Care that the Laws be faithfully executed") have been used by presidents to justify enlarging their powers. As we will see, presidential practice has vastly expanded the Constitution's ideas of executive powers.

In setting requirements for the office, the Constitution states that the president must be at least thirty-five years old, fourteen years a resident of the United States, and a native-born citizen. The president is immune from arrest while in office and can be removed only by impeachment. His term of office is fixed at four years. Under the Twenty-second Amendment, passed in 1951, presidents are limited to two terms. During the last months of his final term the president is often called a *lame duck:* Because he cannot be re-elected, his influence — and his accountability — are lessened.

Presidents are not chosen by direct popular elections. All the votes across the United States are not added up on election day with the candidate receiving the most declared the winner. Rather, presidents are chosen through the *electoral college.* Each state is granted as many electors (members of the electoral college) as it has senators and representatives combined. On election day the votes *within each state* are added up, and the candidate with the most votes receives *all* that state's votes in the electoral college. When the counting has been done in each state, the number of electoral-college votes for each candidate is added up. If any candidate has a majority (fifty percent plus one) he becomes president. If no candidate wins a majority (because several candidates split the votes), the Constitution provides that the election be decided in the House of Representatives with each state delegation casting one vote.

The electoral college was created by the authors of the Constitution as another way of filtering what they feared might be the passions and prejudices of the mass of voters. It was hoped that the members of the electoral college would be cautious, sober people who would make a wise choice. The development of political parties (see Chapter 6) has undercut the purpose of the electoral college, since electors are now pledged to one party's candidate at the time of the elections. Although there have often been calls for replacing the "outmoded" electoral college with direct popular election (this would take a constitutional amendment), they have so far been unsuccessful.

The major official duty of the *vice president* is to preside over the Senate. Although in recent years the vice president has taken over more executive tasks, his main function is to succeed the president if the office should become vacant. (The Speaker of the House of Representatives and the president pro tem of the Senate are next in line.) The facts that thirteen vice presidents have become president, and that four of our last seven presidents were vice presidents at some point, has increased the political importance of the office. Vice President Walter Mondale has been given a unique amount of influence as a close advisor to the president. Jimmy Carter has termed him "the deputy president." Still, the vice presidency remains a limited and frequently frustrating position. As Harry Truman, Franklin Roosevelt's vice president, remarked, "Look at all the vice presidents in history. Where are they? They were about as useful as a cow's fifth teat."

HISTORY OF THE PRESIDENCY

Thirty-nine men have been president of the United States, from George Washington, who took office in 1790, to Jimmy Carter, who became president in January, 1977. Between Washington and Carter, the influence and powers of the president have expanded considerably.

Most members of the Constitutional Convention in 1789 did not see a *political* role for the president. They pictured the president as a gentleman-aristocrat, who would stand above politics as a symbol of national unity. He would be selected by an electoral college chosen by the states, to ensure that he wasn't dependent on party or popular support. Congress, not the president, was to be supreme. Yet strong presidents confronting various crises soon expanded these powers.

TABLE 3.1. Presidents and Vice Presidents of the United States

Year	President	Party	Year	President	Party
1789	George Washington		1888	Benjamin Harrison	Republican
1792	George Washington		1892	Grover Cleveland	Democratic
1796	John Adams	Federalist	1896	William McKinley	Republican
1800	Thomas Jefferson	Democratic-Republican	1900	William McKinley	Republican
1804	Thomas Jefferson	Democratic-Republican	1901	Theodore Roosevelt*	Republican
1808	James Madison	Democratic-Republican	1904	Theodore Roosevelt	Republican
1812	James Madison	Democratic-Republican	1908	William H. Taft	Republican
1816	James Monroe	Democratic-Republican	1912	Woodrow Wilson	Democratic
1820	James Monroe	Democratic-Republican	1916	Woodrow Wilson	Democratic
1824	John Quincy Adams	Democratic-Republican	1920	Warren G. Harding	Republican
1828	Andrew Jackson	Democratic	1923	Calvin Coolidge*	Republican
1832	Andrew Jackson	Democratic	1924	Calvin Coolidge	Republican
1836	Martin Van Buren	Democratic	1928	Herbert C. Hoover	Republican
1840	William H. Harrison	Whig	1932	Franklin D. Roosevelt	Democratic
1841	John Tyler*	Whig	1936	Franklin D. Roosevelt	Democratic
1844	James K. Polk	Democratic	1940	Franklin D. Roosevelt	Democratic
1848	Zachary Taylor	Whig	1944	Franklin D. Roosevelt	Democratic
1850	Millard Fillmore*	Whig	1945	Harry S Truman*	Democratic
1852	Franklin Pierce	Democratic	1948	Harry S Truman	Democratic
1856	James Buchanan	Democratic	1952	Dwight D. Eisenhower	Republican
1860	Abraham Lincoln	Republican	1956	Dwight D. Eisenhower	Republican
1864	Abraham Lincoln	Republican	1960	John F. Kennedy	Democratic
1865	Andrew Johnson*	Democratic (Union)	1963	Lyndon B. Johnson*	Democratic
1868	Ulysses S. Grant	Republican	1964	Lyndon B. Johnson	Democratic
1872	Ulysses S. Grant	Republican	1968	Richard M. Nixon	Republican
1876	Rutherford B. Hayes	Republican	1972	Richard M. Nixon	Republican
1880	James A. Garfield	Republican	1974	Gerald R. Ford*	Republican
1881	Chester A. Arthur*	Republican	1976	James E. Carter	Democratic
1884	Grover Cleveland	Democratic			

History of the Presidency

Year	Vice President	Party	Year	Vice President	Party
1789	John Adams	Federalist	1888	Levi P. Morton	Republican
1792	John Adams		1892	Adlai E. Stevenson	Democratic
1796	Thomas Jefferson	Democratic-Republican	1896	Garrett A. Hobart	Republican
1800	Aaron Burr	Democratic-Republican	1900	Theodore Roosevelt	Republican
1804	George Clinton	Democratic-Republican	1904	Charles W. Fairbanks	Republican
1808	George Clinton	Democratic-Republican	1908	James S. Sherman	Republican
1812	Elbridge Gerry	Democratic-Republican	1912	Thomas R. Marshall	Democratic
1816	Daniel D. Tompkins	Democratic-Republican	1916	Thomas R. Marshall	Democratic
1820	Daniel D. Tompkins	Democratic-Republican	1920	Calvin Coolidge	Republican
1824	John C. Calhoun	Democratic-Republican	1924	Charles G. Dawes	Republican
1828	John C. Calhoun	Democratic	1928	Charles Curtis	Republican
1832	Martin Van Buren	Democratic	1932	John N. Garner	Democratic
1836	Richard M. Johnson	Democratic	1936	John N. Garner	Democratic
1840	John Tyler	Whig	1940	Henry A. Wallace	Democratic
1844	George M. Dallas	Democratic	1944	Harry S Truman	Democratic
1848	Millard Fillmore	Whig	1948	Alben W. Barkley	Democratic
1852	William R. King	Democratic	1952	Richard M. Nixon	Republican
1856	John C. Breckinridge	Democratic	1956	Richard M. Nixon	Republican
1860	Hannibal Hamlin	Republican	1960	Lyndon B. Johnson	Democratic
1864	Andrew Johnson	Democratic (Union)	1964	Hubert H. Humphrey	Democratic
1868	Schuyler Colfax	Republican	1968	Spiro T. Agnew	Republican
1872	Henry Wilson	Republican	1972	Spiro T. Agnew	Republican
1876	William A. Wheeler	Republican	1973	Gerald R. Ford*	Republican
1880	Chester A. Arthur	Republican	1974	Nelson A. Rockefeller	Republican
1884	Thomas A. Hendricks	Democratic	1976	Walter F. Mondale	Democratic

* Not elected to office, but succeeding to it through the death or resignation of predecessor.

George Washington sent troops to put down a rebellion among farmers in western Pennsylvania, who were angered by a tax placed on whiskey. Washington's action in the Whiskey Rebellion was later claimed as the precedent for a president's *residual power* (also called inherent power) — powers not spelled out in the Constitution but necessary for the president to be able to carry out other responsibilities. The third president, Thomas Jefferson, had, as leader of the liberals, fought against establishing a strong executive in the Constitution. Yet as president he too expanded the powers of the office. By negotiating and signing the Louisiana Purchase, gaining the approval of Congress only after the fact (perhaps inevitable in an age of slow communication), Jefferson weakened the principle of checks and balances. Congress not only played a minor role in doubling the size of the country but also couldn't easily reverse the president's action once it had been taken.

Abraham Lincoln, the sixteenth president, disregarded a number of constitutional provisions when he led the North into the Civil War. Lincoln raised armies, spent money Congress had not appropriated, blockaded the South, suspended certain judicial rights, and generally did what he felt was necessary to preserve the Union. Congress later approved these actions, but the initiative clearly lay with the president. This pattern of crisis leadership continued into the twentieth century with strong presidents like Theodore Roosevelt and Woodrow Wilson.

Franklin D. Roosevelt's coming into office in 1933 in the midst of a depression resulted in the president's taking virtually full responsibility for the continual shaping of both domestic and foreign policy. FDR's programs (called the New Deal) in response to the depression, and his leadership of the United States into the international role it would play during and after World War II, firmly established the strong leadership patterns we find today in the presidency. Roosevelt thus is often called the first modern president. He probably influenced the shape of that office more than anyone else in this century.

TYPES OF PRESIDENTS

The seemingly inevitable growth of the presidency should not obscure the many different types of people who have occupied the office. To simplify matters, we will talk about three general approaches which various presidents have adopted toward the office and see which chief executives fit into each category.

Buchanan Presidents

The first category has been called *Buchanan presidents*, after James Buchanan, who is known mainly for his refusal to end southern secession by force in 1860. Presidents in this group view their office as purely administrative: The president should be aloof from politics and depend on leadership from Congress. Buchanan presidents adopt a *custodial* view of presidential powers: The president is limited to those powers expressly granted to him in the Constitution. Otherwise, they argue, there would be no limits on presidential power. Presidents who have followed this approach generally have been considered the less active chief executives. They include Warren Harding, Calvin Coolidge, and Herbert Hoover, Republican presidents in the 1920s and early 1930s.

Buchanan - Custodial

Lincoln Presidents

Secondly, there are the *Lincoln presidents*. In this approach, the president is an active politician, often rallying the country in a crisis. Abraham Lincoln did this in the Civil War; Theodore Roosevelt did it later when he moved against the large business monopolies called trusts. In this century the Lincoln president also originates much of the legislation Congress considers; he leads public opinion; and he is the major source of the country's political goals.

Lincoln presidents do not interpret the Constitution as narrowly as Buchanan presidents. In their view the presi-

Lincoln - Active

dency is a *stewardship;* its only limits are those explicitly mentioned in the Constitution. The president's powers then are as large as his political talents. Following this approach have been activist presidents such as Andrew Jackson, Theodore Roosevelt, Franklin Roosevelt, Harry Truman, and John Kennedy.

Eisenhower Presidents

The last two approaches to the presidency were outlined by Theodore Roosevelt, who as the twenty-fifth president did much to expand the influence of the office. Another category has been added since then, a combination of the other two called the *Eisenhower president.* Like Buchanan presidents, the Eisenhower president seeks to avoid political leadership and to keep out of party conflicts. But the Eisenhower president is not merely a chief administrator. He sees himself as a *chief delegate,* representing and organizing a national consensus rather than the special interests he believes Congress reflects. Believing that the people are basically good, and that government tends to corrupt, the Eisenhower president limits government on behalf of the people by intervening to veto ill-advised political measures passed by Congress.

Modern Presidents

Recent presidents have been hard to categorize, but they all have leaned toward the activist end of the scale. Lyndon Johnson combined an Eisenhower pose with the results of an activist president like Franklin Roosevelt. Unlike Eisenhower, Johnson sought not only to represent a national consensus but to create and guide this coalition as well. President Johnson was well-known for his midnight phone calls and political arm twisting to gain support for his proposals. Richard Nixon tried to create an image of the presidency above politics while using his own powers as president for partisan and, sometimes, unconstitutional ends. Gerald

Ford came to his brief presidency as the nation's only non-elected vice president. His calm tenure of low activity was marked by issuing more vetoes of congressional legislation in a shorter time than any president in history.

President Jimmy Carter, while gaining high marks as a manager of the bureaucracy, has been criticized for his lack of political leadership, especially in his deadlocks with Congress. Trained as an engineer, Carter has thoroughly, and usually privately, surrounded himself with the details of the policy decisions he has to make. He has been widely praised for having "depomped" the Imperial Presidency (with his inaugural stroll down Pennsylvania Avenue, his viewer call-in television shows, and his access to the press) but he has been just as widely criticized for being all things to all people (environmentalist, budget balancer, and southern populist) without effectively defining or leading the country toward his own vision of a just American society. In short, President Carter has shown himself to be a well-meaning inexperienced outsider working at what he accurately described as a "hopeless" job.

A Psychological Approach

A well-known modern attempt to categorize presidents has centered on their psychological makeup. Political scientist James D. Barber uses this personality approach to focus on the style and character of various chief executives.[1] A president's *style* refers to his ability to act and to the habits of work and personal relations by which he adapts to his surroundings. A style is either *active* or *passive*. *Character* refers to the way a president feels about himself (his self-esteem). Character is either *positive* or *negative*. Putting style and character together, Barber comes up with four categories of personalities in which he places some of our recent presidents (Active-Positive, Active-Negative, Passive-Positive, Passive-Negative).

[1] James David Barber, *The Presidential Character: Predicting Performance in the White House* (Prentice-Hall, 1972).

So, for example, because of their activism in office, as well as their ability to gain satisfaction from their accomplishments, John Kennedy and Harry Truman are labeled Active-Positive. (Jimmy Carter, Barber feels, may also fit under this personality type.) Not so fortunate are Active-Negative types like Presidents Johnson and Nixon, who, while being intensely active, suffered from a low opinion of themselves and gained little personal satisfaction from their efforts. Passive-Positive presidents, such as William Howard Taft, are easily influenced men searching for affection as a reward for being agreeable rather than being assertive. President Eisenhower fits into the final category, Passive-Negative, combining a tendency to withdraw from conflict with a sense of his own uselessness. Only his sense of duty leads the Passive-Negative type into the presidency.

This last category gives us a clue to some of the shortcomings of Barber's interesting approach. Having been Supreme Commander of the Allied Expeditionary Force during World War II and a five-star general, Eisenhower may have seemed Passive-Negative compared to other presidents but could hardly have achieved what he did if these characteristics dominated his entire career. It therefore seems inadequate to explain any shortcomings of his presidency solely in terms of his personality. The makeup of the executive bureaucracy, the strength of his party, the interests he represented, and the political mood of the country are just some of the factors needed to understand the direction of Eisenhower's presidency. Studying a president's personality will provide interesting insights into how and why he acts. It does not, and Barber would agree, give us the full picture of the staff, institutions, and political and economic interests that shape the behavior of the office of the presidency.

PRESIDENTIAL ROLES

The reasons the presidency has expanded lie not only in the history of the office and the personality of the occupant,

> **IF CARTER HAD DELIVERED THE GETTYSBURG ADDRESS**
>
> "Exactly two hundred and one years, five months and one day ago, our forefathers — and our foremothers, too, as my wife, the First Lady, reminds me — our highly competent Founding Persons brought forth on this land mass a new nation, or entity, dreamed up in liberty and dedicated to the comprehensive program of insuring that all of us are created with the same basic human rights.
>
> "At the present moment, our nation clearly seems to be gathered up in a period of great disharmoniousness, testing whether our country, or homeland, can achieve an increasingly stable relationship and at the same time balance the budget by the end of my first term, which is my present intention. . . .
>
> "I have taken a leadership role in strongly supporting initiatives for national survival that contain three basic elements and are fair. When my comprehensive reform proposals are adopted, and we have fruitful exchanges between North and South, then I think it is accurate to say that this government of the persons, by the persons, and for the persons shall not vanish in a highly erroneous display of incompatibility and disharmoniousness." — William Safire, "Carter's Gettysburg Address," *The New York Times* (December 5, 1977), p. 37.

but in the many roles the president fills today. When a specific national problem arises, whether it is aid to a foreign ally, racial discrimination, or inflation, the president is usually called on to respond. The president is also required by law to handle a number of important duties, such as drawing up and presenting the annual budget. In fulfilling these responsibilities the president plays six somewhat different roles which often overlap and blend into one another.

Chief of State

The president is the symbolic head of *state* as well as the head of *government*. (In England the two positions are separate: the queen is head of state, a visible symbol of the nation, and the prime minister is head of government, exercising the real power.) As chief of state, the president has many ceremonial functions, ranging from declaring National Codfish Week to greeting foreign dignitaries. Because of this role, many people see the president as a symbol of the nation, somehow more than human, a fact which also gives him a political advantage. The difficulty in separating his ceremonial from his political actions can be seen when President Carter makes television broadcasts and the Republicans ask for equal time. Is he speaking in his role as a nonpolitical chief of state, or as the head of the Democratic party?

Chief Diplomat

Much of the recent increase in presidential power has occurred because of the importance of the second role filled by the President — chief diplomat. The president has the power to receive foreign ambassadors, to appoint United States ambassadors, and to sign treaties which take effect with the consent of two-thirds of the Senate. Over the years, the president has become the chief maker and executor of American foreign policy. Despite the Senate's power to ratify treaties and Congress' power to appropriate money for foreign aid and to declare wars, there are fewer checks on the president's power over foreign affairs than there are on his conduct in domestic matters. After World War II, in an age of cold war when the United States and the Soviet Union seemed to be competing in every sphere, this authority over foreign policy extended the president's responsibility to almost all parts of society. Presidents argued that the health of the economy, the effectiveness of the educational system, and even racial discrimination affected our standing abroad and thus involved the president in how they should be resolved.

The Watergate and CIA investigations illustrated the dangers in this wide interpretation of the president's powers as chief diplomat. The Central Intelligence Agency, which is part of the executive branch, was created to protect American interests and security by gathering information in foreign countries. But instruments developed for influencing events abroad became threats to democracy at home. In the Watergate case, ex-CIA officials tapped the telephones of opponents of the Nixon administration. Similarly, investigations of the CIA discovered that the agency had violated its charter by spying on American citizens who opposed presidential policies.

The Senate's power to ratify or reject treaties also has been changed by practice. Since its refusal in 1920 to approve United States membership in the League of Nations, the Senate has seldom refused to ratify a treaty. However, most international agreements involving the United States never reach the Senate. Because *executive agreements* do not require the approval of the Senate, their use has increased to the point where a president may sign hundreds of them in a single year. Presidents argue that these agreements usually concern only minor matters, and that important issues, such as the Panama Canal Treaty in 1978, are still submitted to the Senate for ratification. Those who disagree have pointed to the many agreements kept secret from the public and Congress that involve matters of far-reaching importance. Both Wilson and FDR used executive agreements to aid the Allies in the two world wars, and by doing so involved the country in those conflicts before war was formally declared. Attempts by Congress to limit the president's use of executive agreements have all failed, although Congress can refuse to appropriate funds to carry out the agreements. For example, Congress has yet to provide funds for the reconstruction of North Vietnam as called for in the executive agreement to end the war.

Commander in Chief

Closely tied to his role as chief diplomat is the president's role as commander in chief of the armed forces. The idea

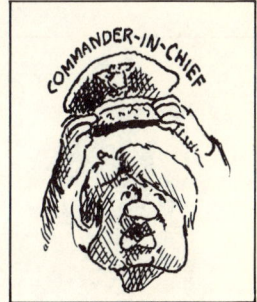

behind the president's acting as commander in chief is the principle of *civilian supremacy* over the military: an elected civilian official, the president, is in charge of the armed forces. In practice, this authority is given to the secretary of defense, who normally delegates his command to members of the military. This role, too, is not limited to actions abroad, as was shown by President Kennedy's use of federal troops in 1961 to enroll a black man, James Meredith, in the University of Mississippi. Its political importance is further reflected by the fact that national-security matters (including not only the armed forces but also the CIA, Veterans' Administration, and debts for past wars) use about one-half of the country's budget, and over forty percent of all government employees work in the defense establishment.

Although the Constitution gives Congress the power to declare war, Congress has not done so since December, 1941, when the United States entered World War II. Presidents, in their role as commander in chief, initiated the country's involvement in the Korean and Vietnam wars. Congress supported both actions by appropriating money for the armed forces. Criticism of the president's role in Vietnam led to the *War Powers Act* of 1973 to limit the president's war-making powers. The law, passed over President Nixon's veto, limited the president to committing troops abroad to a period of sixty days, or ninety at most if needed for a successful withdrawal. If Congress does not authorize a longer period, the troops must be removed.

Chief Executive

The president is, at least in theory, in complete charge of the huge federal bureaucracy in the executive branch. His authority comes from Article II of the Constitution, which states: "The executive Power shall be vested in a President of the United States of America." Executive power here means the ability to carry out or execute the laws. By 1978 this led to the president's heading a bureaucracy dispensing over $460 billion a year, employing three million civilians on a payroll of around $50 billion. The government's revenues are larger than those of the top forty United States corporations combined, and it ranks as the largest administrative organization in the world. We will take a closer look at the federal bureaucracy later in this chapter.

Chief Legislator

Although the Constitution gives the president the right to recommend measures to Congress, it was not until the twentieth century that presidents regularly and actively participated in the legislative process. The president delivers his "State of the Union" address to a joint session of Congress at the beginning of every year to present the administration's annual legislative program. He also gives an annual budget message and frequently sends special messages to Congress supporting specific legislation.

Most bills passed by Congress originate in the executive branch. Getting this legislation passed requires some presidential popularity in Congress and in the nation. The president may use tactics like social exclusion (not inviting those who oppose him to White House parties) and threats in order to block a member of Congress' local public-works project or to gain support for programs he favors. There were widespread reports in the fall of 1978 that President Carter promised research funds for nuclear reactors to states whose senators were key votes for passage of his energy bill.

The president's main constitutional power as chief legislator is the *veto*. If a president disapproves of a bill passed by Congress, he may refuse to sign it and can return it to Congress with his objections. Congress may override the veto by a two-thirds vote of each house, though this has happened in only three percent of vetoes. Because the president does not have an *item veto*, he cannot veto only the specific sections of the bill he dislikes. Rather he must approve or reject the whole bill that comes before him. The veto is most often used as a threat to force compromises in a bill while it is still being considered by Congress.

One recent conflict between the president and Congress has been the president's use of *executive privilege*. Under this doctrine presidents have claimed the right to withhold information about the activities of people in the executive branch from Congress and the judiciary. Although it is nowhere actually stated in the Constitution, the claim rests on the separation of powers of the three branches of the government. Former President Nixon used executive privilege to withhold White House tapes concerning the Watergate coverup from Congress and the courts. In the summer of 1974 the Supreme Court ruled against him, though it hedged on the issue of executive privilege.

Party Leader

A president is also head of his party. As party leader the president has a number of major duties: to choose a vice president after his own nomination; to distribute a certain number of offices and favors to the party faithful; and to demonstrate that he is at least trying to fulfill the *party platform*, the party's program adopted at his nominating convention. The president is also the chief campaigner and fund raiser for his party. He names the national chairperson and usually exerts a great deal of influence over the national party machinery.

However, the president's control over his party is limited by the decentralized nature of American political parties. Local party organizations are very strong. Often congressional members of the president's party refuse to support his programs and he has few sanctions to use against them. He has no power to refuse members of Congress the party's nomination, or to keep them from reaching positions of power in Congress through seniority. In the Ninety-fifth Congress, for example, senate democrats from oil-producing states opposed President Carter's efforts to increase the taxes on crude oil while keeping the prices regulated. Presidents also vary in how much they wish to be involved in their party's affairs. President Eisenhower often avoided Republican party politics, whereas President Johnson kept close control on the Democratic party organization.

THE PRESIDENT AND THE PUBLIC

A major result of the president's many powers and roles is his influence over mass opinion. His visibility, his standing as a symbol of the nation, and his position as a single human being compared to a frequently impersonal government, give the chief executive a great deal of influence in the political game.

Yet all this visibility may also work against him. After all, a president is chosen by election and has to keep the voters happy to keep himself and his party in office. Usually this means accomplishing his administration's goals as well as maintaining his own personal popularity. But these two aims are not always compatible. Two recent presidents, Lyndon Johnson and Richard Nixon, left office widely unpopular, Johnson because of the Vietnam War and Nixon because of Watergate. In both cases the public attention focused on them by the mass media probably hastened their decline. Even President Carter, who has enjoyed fairly good relations with the press, publicly complained about his coverage. He said the media had shown "some degree of complete irresponsibility and some absence of integrity, some deliberate distortion."

While keeping up his standing with other branches of the government and the public at large, the president must still try to carry out the tasks of his office and the goals of his administration. In doing this, his most central relationship is with the bureaucracy under him. What makes up this bureaucracy and how the president handles it are the focus of the rest of this chapter.

THE FEDERAL BUREAUCRACY

The federal bureaucracy carries out most of the work of governing. Despite the bad implications of the word, a *bureaucrat* is simply an administrator, a member of the large administrative organization — the bureaucracy — that carries out the policies of the elected officials of the government. The great growth of the national government, and the tasks it has confronted during this century, have produced an administrative system of unequaled size and complexity. Most of this bureaucracy is within, or close to, the executive branch. The structure of the bureaucracy can be broken down into the executive office of the president, the cabinet departments, the executive agencies, and the regulatory commissions.

The Executive Office of the President

The *executive office* was established in 1939 to advise the president and to assist him in managing the bureaucracy. It has grown steadily in size and influence until today it includes over a half dozen key agencies and some 1,700 people. Three of the most important agencies of the executive office are the White House staff, the National Security Council, and the Office of Management and Budget.

The *White House staff* is a direct extension of the president. Its members are not subject to Senate approval. In recent years the centralization of executive power has increased the authority of the White House staff at the expense of the cabinet officers. Henry Kissinger, as Nixon's assistant for national security affairs, played such a central role in foreign policy that his influence overshadowed the secretary of state's. President Carter has tried to avoid the growth of powerful White House aides by not appointing a chief of staff and by running the staff himself in a fairly unstructured manner. This has led to reports of disorganization and confusion within the White House.

The *National Security Council* (NSC) was established early in the cold war (1947) to help the president coordinate American military and foreign policies. These policies mainly involve the departments of State and Defense which are represented on the council. (The Central Intelligence Agency, though an executive agency, also falls under the authority of the NSC.) Presidents have varied on how much they wished to use the NSC. President Kennedy preferred more informal ways of getting advice on national security matters, but President Nixon restored the council to a more central role in formulating and executing policy.

The *Office of Management and Budget* (OMB) was created by President Nixon in 1970 to replace the Bureau of the Budget. Departments of the executive branch submit competing claims for shares in the federal budget to the OMB. Besides preparing the budget, OMB is also an important general-management arm of the president. It helps the president control the executive branch by overseeing all the agencies and their success in accomplishing their programs. Preparing and administering the annual budget (which is then submitted to Congress for approval) gives OMB tremendous power within the government.

The *Council of Economic Advisors* is another important unit of the executive office. It is a three-member council of economic experts, appointed with Senate approval, which helps the president form a national economic policy and gives him advice on economic developments.

The Cabinet Departments

The *cabinet departments* are the major agencies of the federal government. Originally there were only three (the departments of State, War, and the Treasury); today there are twelve. The expansion of the cabinet has been due largely to the growth of problems that people wanted the federal government to deal with. The raising to cabinet level of the departments of Housing and Urban Development in 1965, Transportation in 1966, and Energy in 1977, shows both the public's and the government's recent interest in these areas.

Each cabinet department is headed by a secretary who is appointed by the president with the consent of the Senate (which is usually given). Cabinet secretaries hold office as long as the president wishes. How much the president uses the cabinet as a whole is strictly up to him, for the cabinet

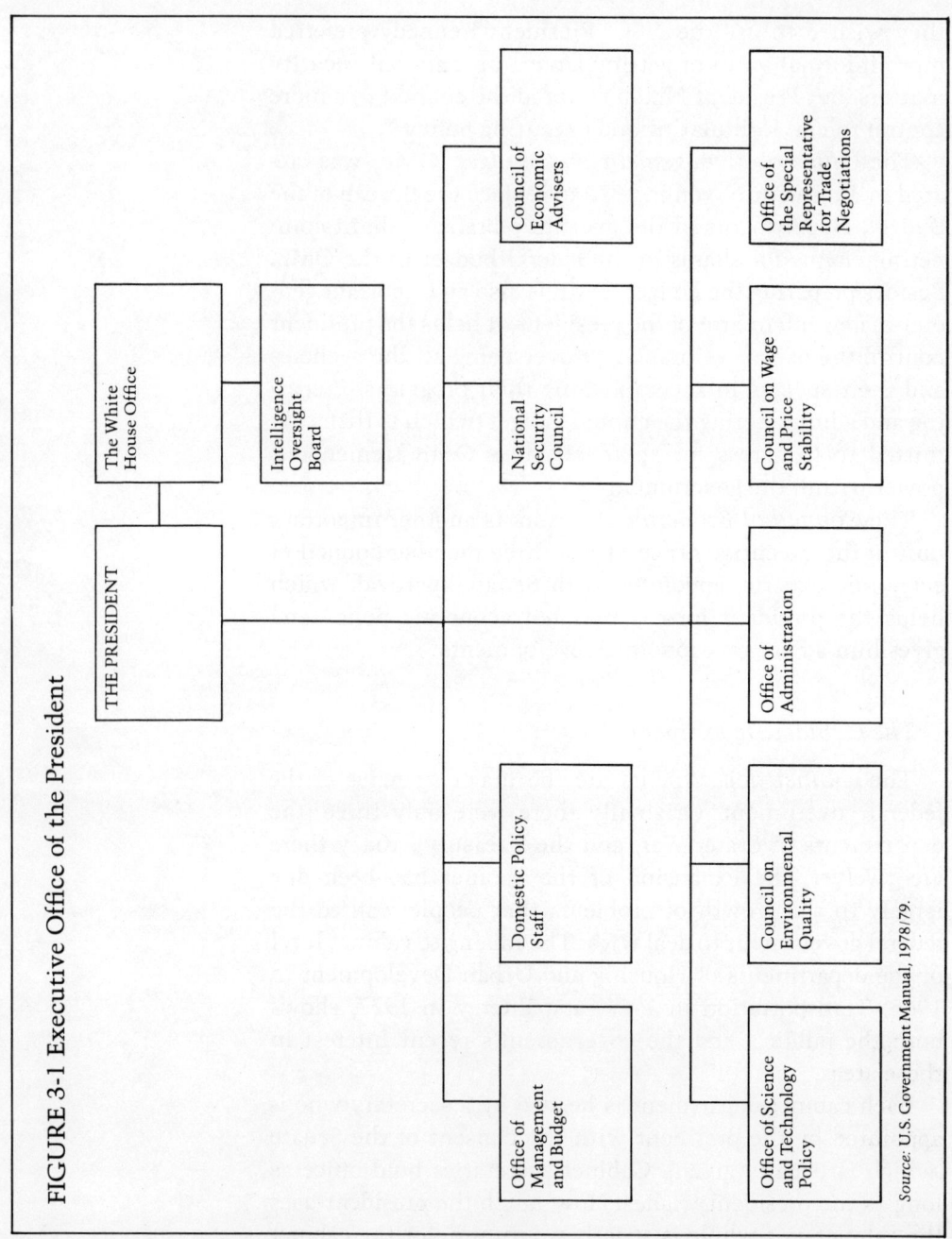

FIGURE 3-1 Executive Office of the President

Source: U.S. Government Manual, 1978/79.

has no power as a body. Although President Carter entered office promising to give cabinet members policy-making authority, one member of his cabinet after a year called this "lip-service." There's a story about President Lincoln being opposed by his entire cabinet on an issue and remarking, "Seven nays, one aye; the ayes have it."

The amount of control each cabinet head has over his or her own department varies greatly. Often a department may only be a loose structure containing strong, relatively independent groups. For example, although the attorney general has authority over the FBI, which is in the Justice Department, J. Edgar Hoover's reign as director of the FBI limited the cabinet secretary's influence. The Energy Department under James Schlesinger, on the other hand, appears to be much more tightly run by the cabinet head.

The Executive Agencies

Executive agencies are simply important agencies of the executive branch that are not in the cabinet. Their heads are appointed by the president with approval of the Senate, but they are not considered important enough to be part of the cabinet. Examples of executive agencies are the Veterans' Administration (VA), the National Aeronautics and Space Administration (NASA), and the Central Intelligence Agency (CIA).

Under executive agencies we might include *government corporations*, which were originally semi-independent but have come increasingly under presidential control. Government corporations, like private corporations, perform business activities such as operating a transportation system or developing and selling electricity. They are usually governed by a board of directors, have limited legislative control over them, and allow for flexible administration. The Tennessee Valley Authority (TVA) is a government corporation, set up in the 1930s to develop electricity for the Tennessee Valley. The United States Postal Service is another, established in 1970 when Congress abolished the Post Office as a

> ### THE PRESIDENT AND THE MOUSE
> The problems presidents have with their bureaucracy are not always limited to major policy matters. For example — "When a couple of mice scampered across the President's study one evening last spring, an alarm went out to the General Services Administration, housekeeper of Federal buildings. Some weeks later, another mouse climbed up inside a wall of the Oval Office and died. The President's office was bathed in the odor of dead mouse as Carter prepared to greet visiting Latin American dignitaries. An emergency call went out to G.S.A. But it refused to touch the matter. Officials insisted that they had exterminated all the "inside" mice in the White House and this errant mouse must have come from outside, and therefore was the responsibility of the Interior Department. Interior demurred, saying that the dead mouse was now inside the White House. President Carter summoned officials from both agencies to his desk and exploded: 'I can't even get a damn mouse out of my office.' Ultimately, it took an interagency task force to get rid of the mouse." — Hedrick Smith, "Problems of a Problem Solver," *The New York Times Magazine* (January 8, 1978), pp. 52 and 53.

cabinet department and set it up as a semi-independent government-owned corporation.

The Regulatory Commissions

Regulatory commissions are charged with regulating certain parts of the economy. Examples are the Interstate Commerce Commission (ICC), which regulates railroads, buses, and trucking, and the Federal Communications Commission (FCC) which oversees telephone, radio, and television operations. Although the president appoints the members of the commissions and chooses the chairmen, the commissions are relatively independent of all branches of the government. They are bipartisan (members come from both parties); the president has only a limited right to remove commissioners, who generally serve longer terms than the president; and there is no presidential veto over their actions. These commissions also have all three capacities of government: They can make rules that have the force of law (legislative), administer and enforce these regulations (executive), and conduct hearings and issue orders (judicial).

The reason behind these agencies is the commonly held view that private economic groups will not always act in the public interest unless they are forced to. However, the independence of these commissions from the rest of the government has meant that the public has little control over their activities. The commissions often come under pressure from the groups they are regulating, and the lack of governmental controls has led them to negotiate with, rather than regulate, some important economic interests. As Ralph Nader, a consumer advocate, has shown in the case of the Federal Trade Commission, some agencies actually have become pressure groups supporting the interests they are supposed to regulate. (See the discussion of the FAA and McDonnell Douglas on pages 14–15.)

THE PROBLEMS OF BUREAUCRACY

The word "bureaucracy" is often used nowadays to imply incompetence and red tape. The problems with bureaucracies seem to be related to their size rather than the nature of the public or private organizations they serve. Socialist bureaucracies don't appear to operate much better than bureaucracies in capitalist countries. The size and complexity of a large bureaucracy makes it hard to tell who is responsible for a particular action; this inhibits public scrutiny and control.

The fact that bureaucrats are experts in their own areas is a major source of their influence in government, but it also presents problems. A member of Congress or a president wanting information or advice on welfare policy, housing programs, or energy costs would probably go to the bureaucrat in charge of the subject. The problem is how to get these experts in the bureaucracy to see beyond their own narrow fields of expertise to the broader public interest. During the Vietnam War, bureaucrats often pursued their own departments' interests (the navy wanted more ships, the air force more planes, and the army more troops), rather than asking questions about whether the war could ever be won.

The Rise of the Civil Service

In the first century of the federal government, the usual method of choosing government bureaucrats was known as the *spoils system*. Taken from the phrase "To the victor belong the spoils," the spoils system meant that victorious politicians filled government positions with their supporters. This system of widespread patronage reached its high point during the administration of President Andrew Jackson (1828–1836) when bureaucrats did not even need to be knowledgeable in their fields. But as the tasks expected of bureaucrats became more complex and corruption grew, pressure for reform also increased.

In 1881 President James Garfield was assassinated by a disappointed (and slightly crazy) office seeker. The new president, Chester Arthur, backed by public outrage over the murder, supported the Civil Service Reform Act (also known as the Pendleton Act), which was passed by Congress in 1883. The act set up a bipartisan Civil Service Commission under which government employees were chosen by merit through examinations. At first only about ten percent of federal employees were covered by civil service, but the system has grown to where it now covers over eighty-five percent of the bureaucracy. This has considerably weakened the spoils system and has added an element of stability to government activity. The president today only fills about 6,500 patronage jobs, of which less than a third are at a policy-making level.

Controlling Bureaucracy

The rapid growth of the federal bureaucracy has led some people to ask whether it has become the master of government, rather than its servant. Both liberals and conservatives have proposed ways of making bureaucracy more responsive to the government and public. Stronger executive control by the president has been suggested, but many people fear the president is already too strong. Congress has been called on to watch the bureaucracy more closely. President Carter's Civil Service Reform Act of 1978 makes it easier to fire incompetent employees and creates a core of top civil servants (a senior executive service) who would exchange job security for large pay bonuses based on performance. Public involvement through consumer groups like Ralph Nader's "Raiders" have grown in popularity. Efforts to decentralize the bureaucracy and put parts of it under local control are another solution that has been only partly successful. This can only work where the community has adequate resources and awareness to both support and control the local bureaucracy. Existing political and bureaucratic interests have often halted all these attempts at reform.

Nevertheless, President Carter called for a major overhaul of the executive bureaucracy during his election campaign and, since being elected, has pushed two major initiatives: *zero-based budgeting* and *reorganization*. Zero-based budgeting means that all budget items are examined from zero up. Rather than just looking at the change in spending from last year's budget, every department must justify its existence and the existence of all its programs. In writing the budget, each department head starts at zero (no organization, no salaries, no people) and ranks in order of importance the activities of every level of their bureaucracy. This bottom-up process, it is hoped, will allow a close look at all government programs and the elimination of unnecessary ones. Although the president used zero-based budgeting as governor of Georgia, the greater complexity of the federal government and the long-term nature of many of its programs probably means the technique will be used only for certain categories in the budget.

Reorganization is another sticky problem. In 1977, the president persuaded Congress to pass a *reorganization authority bill*. This law re-establishes the president's traditional authority (which Congress during Watergate had refused to continue) to create, end, or merge independent agencies, unless these plans are vetoed by Congress within sixty days. The major accomplishments under this bill were the reduction of units and staff in the executive office of the president, and the elimination of some 500 advisory committees, including the very forgettable National Peanut Advisory Committee and the Board of Tea Experts. More important, and therefore more difficult to carry through, are the attempts to reduce and simplify the 70,000 pages of federal regulations, the reforms of the Civil Service designed to raise the efficiency of government workers, and the consolidation of the government's civil rights responsibilities. Other reorganization plans for local economic development, law enforcement, and a cabinet-level department of education have been proposed. Whether these reforms would prove to be effective remained a question of the administration's political will and the political strength of its bureaucratic opponents.

THE PRESIDENT AND THE BUREAUCRACY

The bureaucracy at his disposal is an important support of the president. The federal bureaucracy gives the president access to more information than his opponents are likely to have and allows him to initiate policies to which others must react. Curiously, though, the bureaucracy also provides the major limit on a president's actions. To carry out his policies the president must rely on the information, advice, and actions of subordinates. Keeping control over the three million employees of the executive branch is a full-time job in itself. As political scientist Richard Neustadt commented, the president spends much of his time finding out what his subordinates are doing in his name.

Members of the bureaucracy may work to protect their own interests or may respond to pressures from economic concerns threatened by presidential policies. Often these departments have long-standing rivalries with each other: Labor versus Agriculture on food prices, State versus Defense over foreign policy. The president must act as a judge over these conflicts yet maintain close ties with both sides. Even cabinet officials appointed by the president may represent their own departments' interests against those of the president. Does the secretary of defense represent the president to the Defense Department, or the department to the president? Clearly both, but conflict often results.

To operate in this bureaucratic jungle the president must know how to bargain. Presidential power thus often boils down to the power to persuade. The president both influences and reflects the existing interests and powers in the country. His ability to gain acceptance for his policies, be they actions against inflation or for foreign aid, depends on the interests he represents and his ability to bargain with the political elites. Examples of this can be seen in the following cases of presidential confrontations with the steel industry.

Case Study: Three Examples of Presidential Power

Outlining the powers and duties of the executive branch will not necessarily tell us what a president can do in real situations. How successfully a president plays the roles of his office and uses the bureaucracy depends partly on what political situations he faces. And of course it also depends on his own experience and skill. The following three cases, in which presidents Truman, Kennedy, and Carter faced similar conflicts with the steel industry, underline the difficulties and the advantages in using presidential power.

Truman and Steel (1952)

In 1952 the United States was involved in the Korean War, and both strikes and inflation were serious threats to the country. So when union and management leaders in the steel industry deadlocked over union wage demands, President Truman faced a crisis. The Wage Stabilization Board (WSB), which had been set up to hold down wages and prices so as to reduce inflation, recommended a proposal which was accepted by the union but strongly opposed by management. It was also opposed by Charles Wilson, who headed the Office of Defense Mobilization which oversaw the WSB. The president agreed with the WSB, and Wilson resigned.

Meanwhile, industry officials argued that a large price increase would be necessary to meet the union's wage demands. President Truman responded that if a price rise were needed "in the interest of national defense" it would be granted, but he refused to commit himself to any specific figure. The steel management then presented a wage offer less than the WSB had recommended. The union turned it down and prepared for a strike.

Given the wartime situation, the president's problem was to avoid a strike without causing a large rise in the price of steel. He saw three alternatives. (1) He could use the Taft-Hartley Law to seek an eighty-day cooling-off period in which no strike could occur. (But he disliked this antilabor law, which had been passed over his veto.) (2) He could grant both the union's wage demands and the industry's price increase. (But he saw this as increasing inflation.) Or (3) He could seize the steel mills and put them under government management. Two hours before the strike was due to start, Truman ordered the mills seized.

Some of what followed was predictable. On April 8, 1952, the president went after public support. He bitterly attacked a "few greedy companies" for demanding "outrageous prices" which would wreck the entire price-control program. A spokesman for the steel industry responded in kind, accusing the president of having "transgressed his oath of office" and "abused" his power. Congress and the press were generally upset by what they felt was the president's overstepping the limits of his office in seizing the mills. The industry brought a suit against the seizure, and the case went quickly through the lower courts to the Supreme Court.

Things began to go badly for the president for a number of reasons. Truman's seizure of the mills was designed only as a tactic to give him time and a way to informally force an agreeable wage and price settlement. Essentially the seizure was designed to be so unattractive to both union and management that they would come to an agreement. But Truman's own secretary of commerce, who was ordered to administer the mills, opposed the seizure. Though he did not refuse to follow the president's orders, the secretary did drag his feet. By the time the plan was ready to take effect it was too late. The Supreme Court ruled against the president's claim that as commander in chief he had the "inherent power" to seize the mills in the interest of national security. Such emergency powers rested only in Congress. Truman had lost.

Kennedy and Steel (1962)

Ten years later President Kennedy confronted the steel industry in a similar crisis. In this case, the Kennedy administration had persuaded the steel union to accept a moderate wage rise, under the impression that this would not mean a price increase. To the president's surprise, the leading steel company, United States Steel, then announced a sharp rise in price. This action was quickly followed by most of the other large steel corporations.

The next day, April 11, President Kennedy responded in a nationally televised press conference. He called the actions by the companies "a wholly unjustifiable and irresponsible defiance of the public interest." Referring to the "grave crises in Berlin and Southeast Asia," he stressed the need for "restraint and sacrifice" by every citizen. He charged that there was no economic reason for the increase because of the industry's already high rate of profit. He concluded that "a tiny handful of steel executives" had shown "utter contempt for the interests of 185 million Americans," adding, "Some time ago I asked each American to consider what he would do for his country. And I asked the steel companies. In the last twenty-four hours we had their answer."

But Kennedy did not merely use his position as chief of state to shame the steel executives with speeches. He backed up his statements with some pointed informal threats. The president warned the steel companies that the Department of Justice was exploring possible violations of antitrust laws in the way the companies set prices. The Department of Defense, a major steel buyer, might also decide to buy from those companies that had not raised their prices. Further, in his roles of chief legislator and party leader (the Democrats controlled Congress at the time), Kennedy hinted that Congress might change tax laws to the disadvantage of the steel industry.

After initial resistance, the steel corporations caved in. Two major companies announced they would not raise prices. The ones that already had quickly cancelled the increase. In concluding the conflict, President Kennedy remarked that his administration "harbors no ill will" against any industry of the American economy. It was easy for Kennedy to be graceful. He was a winner.

Carter and Steel (1977)

On May 6, 1977, two major steel companies raised the prices on their products by 8.8 percent. The price rise was widely expected. Steel workers had recently won an eleven percent increase in wages spread over three years, and five of the nine leading steel producers had lost money the previous year.

The Carter administration, while agreeing on the need for higher prices, thought that the increases were too large.

Steel prices had already risen twelve percent in the last year, and these new increases for an essential product threatened the administration's program of voluntary wage and price restraints to fight inflation. The president, in a written statement, called the rise "unwarranted" and his Council on Wage and Price Stability (which had no formal authority to lower the prices) announced an immediate investigation of the increase.

At the same time the administration offered the steel companies an attractive incentive for moderating their prices. For years the steel industry had complained that foreign steel manufacturers had been illegally "dumping" their product in the American market. ("Dumping" consists of selling steel in the United States at a lower price than steel is sold in the home country of the producer.) More detached observers have contended that the industry was inefficient and poorly managed, and that limiting foreign imports would free the American producers from competition and would thereby raise prices. The Carter administration had been generally against restrictions on imports. Nonetheless at a breakfast meeting with steel representatives, advisors to the president linked holding down prices by the companies to restricting imports by the administration.

The mutual back scratching seemed to have an effect. On May 10th, United States Steel, which had not raised its prices, announced a six percent price rise. A rollback to six percent in the prices announced by the other companies quickly followed. High administration officials stated they were "very happy" with this figure. At the same time, leaks in the press announced that the administration was considering opening negotiations with foreign countries over their steel-pricing policies. A deal had been made. Each side had gotten something they wanted, which may be the nearest thing in politics to a draw.

What Made the Difference?

Why did Truman lose, Kennedy win, and Carter play to a draw? What do these cases tell us about presidential power?

It is worth noting that Truman used *formal power* in challenging the steel industry whereas both Kennedy and Carter used the *informal influence* of their office. Employing his doubtful legal powers as commander in chief, Truman took direct action in seizing the steel mills. The companies responded by moving the playing field from the public arena to the courts. Here Truman, on weak legal ground, lost.

A major reason for Truman's taking such drastic action was his political weakness. He chose the formal action of seizure in order to increase his informal influence. But it didn't work. His own bureaucracy undercut his efforts. Wilson resigned and the secretary of commerce defied him. The reasons why he didn't fire the secretary probably lie outside the steel crisis. Truman in 1952 was an unpopular president, a lame duck nearing the end of his term. He had recently fired his attorney general and had dismissed the very popular General Douglas MacArthur for disobeying his orders. Truman felt he had to tolerate his secretary's delaying tactics.

Kennedy used both his symbolic position as representative of the national interest and the informal influence of his office to put pressure on the steel companies. Like Truman, he "wrapped himself in the flag," pointing to threats from overseas and hurling thunderbolts of national indignation at the companies. But it is doubtful whether hard-headed steel executives would have cut into their profits out of patriotism alone. It was the threats to restrict government buying, to start antitrust suits, and to use tax laws against the companies that were probably more central to their switch.

Carter's low-key approach avoided a confrontation. Perhaps remembering that Kennedy's win had marked him as "anti-business," Carter tried in a nonpublic, informal way to push the prices down. Although at first successful, skirmishes continued. Soon the industry had an apparently unanswerable argument for government opposition to price increases — mill closings. In early fall, 1977, some 20,000 steelworkers were put out of work. Labor united with industry to lobby for restrictions on steel imports. By the end of the year the industry had raised their prices another 5.5 percent and the administration announced a plan to limit low-priced foreign imports. Despite opposition from some of the bureaucracy to this plan (the independent Federal Trade Commission said in early 1978 that it would cost consumers $1 billion a year), President Carter seemed to be losing ground to an industry which could get its unemployed workers to symbolize its interests.

All three presidents had the same formal powers, yet their use of these powers differed. Kennedy combined the tools of presidential power with his political standing and smoothly used the media to bring his message to the public. Carter had more modest goals than either Kennedy or Truman, which may have led him to more moderate methods. Carter's methods of influence involved less conflict than the other two Democrats, and while his achievement was more limited than Kennedy's, his losses were less visible than Truman's. Both Carter and Kennedy also had an advantage in coming after Truman — they could learn from the other's mistakes.

But we should hesitate in drawing too many conclusions from these cases. The use of presidential power is always surrounded by politics. Similar political conflicts are not the same as identical chemistry experiments. The ingredients and procedures of the chemistry laboratory can be repeated exactly to prove conclusions. Political events cannot. Too much remains uncertain. Perhaps uncertainty over the results of the use of presidential power is the most central conclusion we can draw from these cases.

WRAP-UP

This chapter has introduced the executive players in the political game — the president and the bureaucracy. We have seen how the presidency has steadily grown in influence from a limited grant of constitutional powers, and we have looked at three different presidential styles as well as a psychological approach to a president's personality. The six major roles a president fills — chief of state, chief diplomat, commander in chief, chief executive, chief legislator, and party leader — show how broad his power has grown.

The bureaucracy within the executive branch generally reinforces the president's power. Yet its size and the complexity of its structures, from the executive office to the cabinet departments, executive agencies, and regulatory commissions, limit the president's control of the bureaucracy. As the steel cases made clear, a president's power in a real situation may be hindered as well as extended by the rest of the executive branch.

The president as both an individual and an institution is likely to continue to play a central role in the American

political game. The history of deceptions and arbitrary actions by presidents in Vietnam and at home has shown how powerful a president can be and how easily he can manipulate public opinion. More recent presidents have seemed weak and ineffective in managing the bureaucracy and getting their programs acted on by Congress. Yet people have tended to focus their dissatisfaction on individual presidents rather than on the institution of the presidency. Most of us still look for a presidential Moses to lead us out of the wilderness of economic and foreign troubles. We often fail to realize that it was largely these expectations of the public's that encouraged presidents' inflated powers and removed the presidency from the original limits of the office.

Presidents are people too. As political players they have performed neither better nor worse than most of the other players in the game. But the unrealistic expectations and powers given them have magnified their faults.

THOUGHT QUESTIONS

1. What are the major reasons for the growth in the power of the president? Do you think it has been inevitable?
2. How does the executive-branch bureaucracy both limit and support the power of the president?
3. Do you think the president and bureaucracy are too powerful or not powerful enough? Give some current examples to back up your argument.
4. What should a president do? Is it possible for any president to accomplish what people expect him to do?

SUGGESTED READINGS

Fellmeth, Robert. *The Interstate Commerce Omission.* New York: Grossman, 1970. Pb.
   A critical study of the cooperation between the ICC and the industries it is supposed to regulate.

Kearns, Doris. *Lyndon Johnson and the American Dream.* New York: Harper & Row, 1976. Pb.
   Tantalizing behind-the-scenes looks at the character and career of Lyndon Johnson.

Neustadt, Richard E. *Presidential Power.* New York: John Wiley & Sons, 1976. Pb.
The updating of a classic work on the presidency with an added look at Johnson and Nixon.

The New York Times. *The Pentagon Papers.* New York: Bantam, 1971. Pb.
The actual papers of the executive bureaucracy's planning for the Vietnam War.

Schlesinger, Arthur M., Jr. *The Imperial Presidency.* Boston: Houghton Mifflin, 1973. Pb.
A critical view of the growing powers of the modern presidency.

Washington Monthly (Charles Peters, ed.). *Inside the System.* New York: Praeger, 1973. Pb.
A collection of informative and often disturbing inside looks at government policy making.

White, Theodore. *Breach of Faith.* New York: Atheneum, 1975.
The best explanation yet of the decline and fall of Richard Nixon.

Wooten, James. *Dasher.* New York: Simon and Schuster, 1978.
A journalist's breezy story tracing the rise from peanuts to president of the puzzling Jimmy Carter.

The Legislative Branch: Congress 4

The framers of the American Constitution meant for the Congress to be the center of the American political game. Their experience with King George III of England and his often arrogant, dictatorial, or incompetent governors had left the colonists with a deep suspicion of strong executive authority. As a result, the Constitution gave many detailed powers and responsibilities to the Congress but far fewer to the president. And through its major function — lawmaking — Congress creates the ongoing rules that govern all the political players. Article I of the Constitution gives Congress the power to levy taxes, borrow money, raise armies, declare war, determine the nature of the federal judiciary, regulate commerce, coin money, and "make all Laws which shall be necessary and proper for carrying into Execution the foregoing Powers, and all other Powers vested by this Constitution in the Government of the United States, or in any Department or Officer thereof."

Many of the powers given to the president are limited by the powers of Congress. The president was named the commander in chief of the armed services, but he could not declare war or raise armies. If he wanted an army, the Congress had to provide it. The president was to be the chief administrative officer of the government, but there would be no government to administer if the Congress did not create it. He could appoint executive officials and negotiate foreign treaties only if the Senate agreed. Although the president could veto a bill passed by Congress, the Congress had the power to override his veto and make the bill a law in spite of the president's wishes. Both the raising of money through taxes and the spending of it by the government required the approval of Congress. Finally, Congress was given the power to impeach and remove the president, if in its judgment he was found guilty of "Treason, Bribery, or other high Crimes and Misdemeanors."

During the early years and through the nineteenth century, Congress often played the dominant role in shaping the nation's policies. Members of Congress such as Daniel Webster, Henry Clay, and John C. Calhoun molded the major issues of their times from within the legislature. As late as the end of the nineteenth century, Woodrow Wilson could proclaim, "Congress is the dominant, nay, the irresistible power of the federal system."

Wilson was later to change his mind, however, and most observers have gone along with him. During the twentieth century, and especially since the Great Depression and World War II, the executive branch of the government has greatly increased in influence compared to Congress. As we saw in the previous chapter, the increasing size and complexity of the problems facing the American government have caused remarkable growth in the president's staff and the federal bureaucracy. Because of the president's central role in foreign affairs, the importance of this area since World War II has increased presidential influence. Still, the Congress remains a vital part of the American government. In this chapter we will examine the structure of Congress, how it was designed to operate, and how it actually carries out its functions today.

MAKEUP OF THE SENATE AND HOUSE

The Congress of the United States is made up of two branches: the Senate and the House of Representatives. The Senate consists of two senators from each state regardless of the size of the state. House members are distributed according to population so that the larger the state's population, the more representatives it gets. The Constitution requires that each state have at least one representative, no matter how small it may be. These provisions are the result of a political compromise between the small states and the large states during the writing of the Constitution.

As the country has grown, so has the size of Congress. The first Congress consisted of twenty-six senators and sixty-five representatives. With each new state added to the union, the Senate has grown by two, so that it now has one hundred members. As the nation's population grew, the size of the House of Representatives grew also. In 1922 the Congress passed a law setting the maximum size of the House at 435 members, where it remains today. In the first House each member represented perhaps 50,000 citizens. The average representative now serves more than 500,000 constituents.

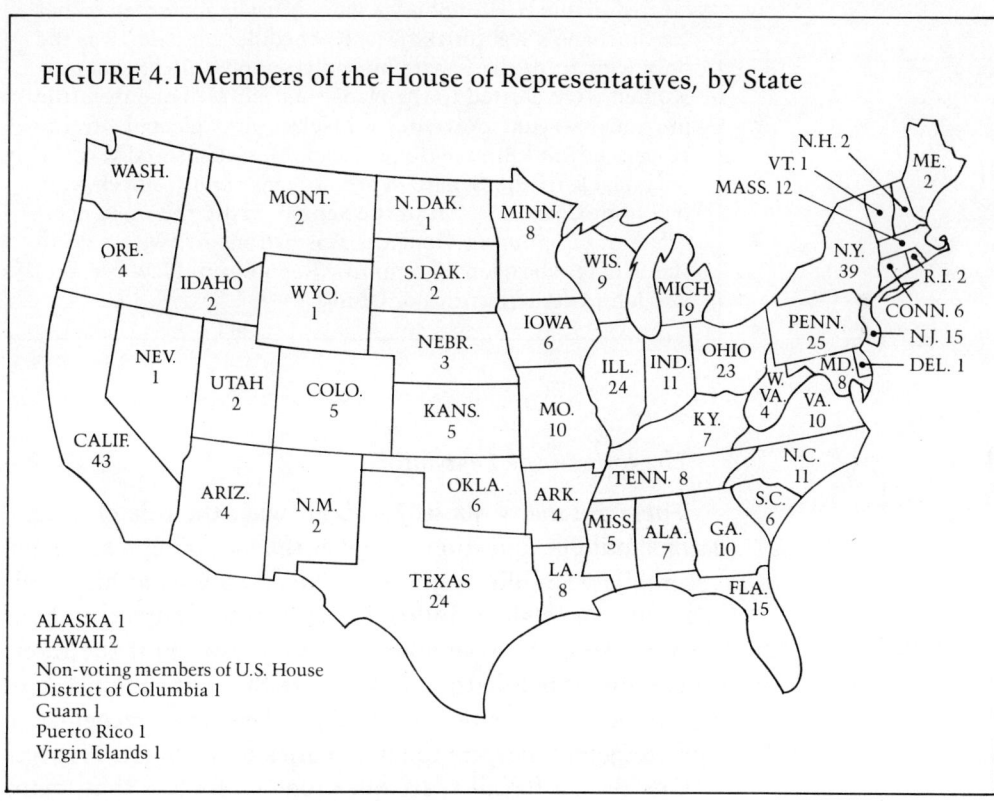

FIGURE 4.1 Members of the House of Representatives, by State

> THE NINETY-FIFTH CONGRESS
>
> The Ninety-fifth Congress was elected in the fall of 1976. The trend toward new and younger members of both Houses, begun with the Ninety-fourth Congress in the wake of the Watergate scandal and President Nixon's resignation, continued as sixty-seven freshmen entered the House and eighteen entered the Senate. The average age of members of the House was 46.8, the youngest group since World War II. Nick Joe Randall (Democrat, West Virginia) was the youngest legislator in the House at age twenty-seven, and Joseph Biden (Democrat, Delaware) was the youngest senator at age thirty-four. Texas Congressman W. R. Poage was the oldest House member at age seventy-seven. Milton Young (Republican, South Dakota) at eighty-one was the oldest senator.
>
> Although several women ran for the Senate, none was elected. (Hubert Humphrey's wife, Muriel, appointed to her late husband's seat until the next scheduled election, was the only woman in the Senate but only temporarily.) Seventeen women were elected to the House, a decline of one from the previous session. Seventeen blacks were elected to the House; Edward Brooke (Republican, Massachusetts) was the only black in the Senate. Three Asians, two from Hawaii, one from California, sat in the Senate. Easily the most over-represented group in Congress was astronauts, with two in the Senate, Harrison H. Schmitt (Republican, New Mexico) and John Glenn (Democrat, Ohio).

The Role of the Legislator

There are many questions about what the role of a legislator should be, questions as old as the idea of representative assemblies. Should a representative do only what his or her constituents wish, or follow his or her own judgment about what is best? What should a representative do if the interests of his or her district seem to conflict with the needs of the nation as a whole? Should a legislator recognize a "greater good" beyond the boundaries of his or her district?

One reason for all these questions is the fact that members of Congress are both *national* and *local* representatives. They are national representatives in that they make up one branch of the national government, are paid by that federal government, and are required to support and defend the interests of the entire nation. Yet they are elected by local districts or states. In running for election, legislators must satisfy local constituents that they are looking out not only for the national interest but for local interests as well. In controversial areas like cutting taxes, the legislator's view of the national interest may be very different from local popular opinion. But as an often-heard warning in Congress goes, "To be a good congressman you first have to be a congressman."

Who Are the Legislators?

A member of the House of Representatives must be at least twenty-five years old, a citizen of the United States for seven years, and a resident of the state in which he or she is elected. A senator must be thirty years old, nine years a citizen, and a resident of the state that elects him or her. State residency is a fairly loose requirement, however. Robert Kennedy rented a New York City apartment and declared it his prime residence just before entering the New York Senate race in 1964.

Senators serve six-year terms and are elected by the entire state's population. Every two years, during the national elections, one-third of the Senate seeks reelection. The other senators do not run because they are only one-third or two-thirds of the way through their terms.

The Constitution originally provided that members of the Senate would be elected by their respective state legislatures. The purpose of this was to remove the choice from the masses of citizens and try to ensure that more conservative elements would pick the senators. This procedure was changed by the Seventeenth Amendment, ratified in 1913. Senators are now elected by the voting public of each state just like other elected officials.

TABLE 4.1. Characteristics of the Ninety-fifth Congress (beginning in January, 1977)

	House (435 Members)	Senate (100 Members)	Total
Party Affiliation			
Democrat	291	62	353
Republican	144	38	182
Average Age	46.8	54.6	48.1
Religious Affiliation			
Roman Catholic	116	16	132
Jewish	28	5	33
Methodist	66	20	86
Episcopalian	48	16	64
Presbyterian	39	15	54
Baptist	48	9	57
Other/None	90	19	109
Race			
Black	17	1	18
White	416	96	512
Asian	2	3	5
Sex			
Male	418	99	517
Female	17	1	18
Occupation *(some members list more than one)*			
Agriculture	16	9	25
Business or Banking	118	24	142
Education	72	12	84
Engineering	2	0	2
Journalism	14	4	18
Labor	6	0	6
Law	223	68	291
Law Enforcement	7	0	7
Medicine	2	1	3
Ministry	6	1	7
Public service	60	26	86
Science	2	1	3

Source: *Congressional Quarterly Weekly Report* (1977), pp. 19–27.

TABLE 4.2. Characteristics of the Ninetieth Congress (beginning in January, 1967)

	House (435 Members)	Senate (100 Members)	Total
Party Affiliation			
Democrat	249	64	313
Republican	186	36	222
Average Age	50.8	57.7	52.1
Religious Affiliation			
Roman Catholic	95	13	108
Jewish	16	2	18
Methodist	68	23	91
Episcopalian	50	15	65
Presbyterian	63	12	75
Baptist	42	11	53
Other/None	101	24	125
Race			
Black	6	1	7
White	427	97	524
Asian	2	2	4
Sex			
Male	424	99	523
Female	11	1	12
Occupation (some members list more than one)			
Agriculture	39	18	57
Business or Banking	161	23	184
Education	57	15	72
Engineering	6	2	8
Journalism	39	10	49
Labor	2	0	2
Law	246	68	314
Medicine	4	1	5
Ministry	2	0	2

Source: *Congressional Quarterly Weekly Report* (1967), pp. 62–65.

Members of the House of Representatives (called "members of Congress," although Congress technically includes both the Senate and the House) serve two years. They are elected from congressional districts within the states. No congressional district ever crosses state borders.

Congress is composed overwhelmingly of white males, and it tends to reflect the values of upper-middle-class America. Over sixty percent of members of Congress are lawyers. Other common professions are business, banking, education, farming, and journalism. There are many reasons why women and blacks are underrepresented in Congress, including (for blacks at least) the effects of malapportionment and gerrymandering, to be discussed in the following pages. Some other reasons are the selection of candidates by party organizations, lack of voter organization, and voter apathy. Recent elections, however, have brought more women and minority group members into Congress, a trend which will likely continue.

Another recent change in the makeup of Congress has been the trend toward *careerism* — the tendency for legislators to see service in Congress as a lifetime career. This hasn't always been the case. Until the 1840s the average length of service in the House was less than two years, and in the Senate less than four, meaning that many members were resigning for better opportunities. By the 1960s the average length of service was ten years in the House, and twelve in the Senate, with sixty percent of the Senate and nearly ninety percent of the House being reelected members. This has lessened now due to the unusually large number of new members elected to the Ninety-fourth and Ninety-fifth Congresses, so that over half of the House has only been there since 1972. Nonetheless the leadership positions in both the House and Senate, because of custom and seniority, have tended to require long periods in office and an orderly climb up the ladder of lesser offices. Few legislators actually go on to higher offices in the executive or judicial branches. It seems ironic that while high administrators and judges may be appointed from outside fields, it's a lifetime career to become a leader in a representative assembly. The problem with careerism is that, although it may guarantee loyalty to their institution, it may also insulate members from a rapidly changing society.

Malapportionment and Gerrymandering

The drawing of House districts is up to the various state governors and legislatures, who have often used these powers to boost their own party and penalize the party out of power. In the past, *malapportionment* (large differences in the populations of congressional districts) was common in many areas of the country. Districts would be drawn up so that minority party districts included more voters than majority party districts. This way, each minority party voter would count for less. In 1960, Michigan's sixteenth district had 802,994 people, whereas the twelfth had only 177,431.

In addition, the art of *gerrymandering* was practiced. The name comes from Massachusetts Governor Elbridge Gerry, who, in 1812, helped to draw a long, misshapen district composed of a string of towns north of Boston. The story goes that one critic observed, "Why, that looks like a salamander!" and another retorted, "That's not a salamander, that's a gerrymander." The two most common forms of gerrymandering are "packing" and "cracking." *Packing* involves drawing up a district so it has a large majority of your supporters, to ensure a "safe" seat. *Cracking* means splitting up your opponents' supporters into minorities in a number of districts to weaken their influence.

Such practices have long been attacked by reformers. In 1964, a Supreme Court decision held that legislative districts at both the state and national levels must be as equal in population as possible. Many of the worst abuses of malapportionment were ended by the Court's decision. Urban areas in particular are now more equally represented. In 371 of the 435 current House districts, the 1970 population fell within the narrow range of 450,000 to 500,000 people. Congress is reapportioned every ten years, after each census,

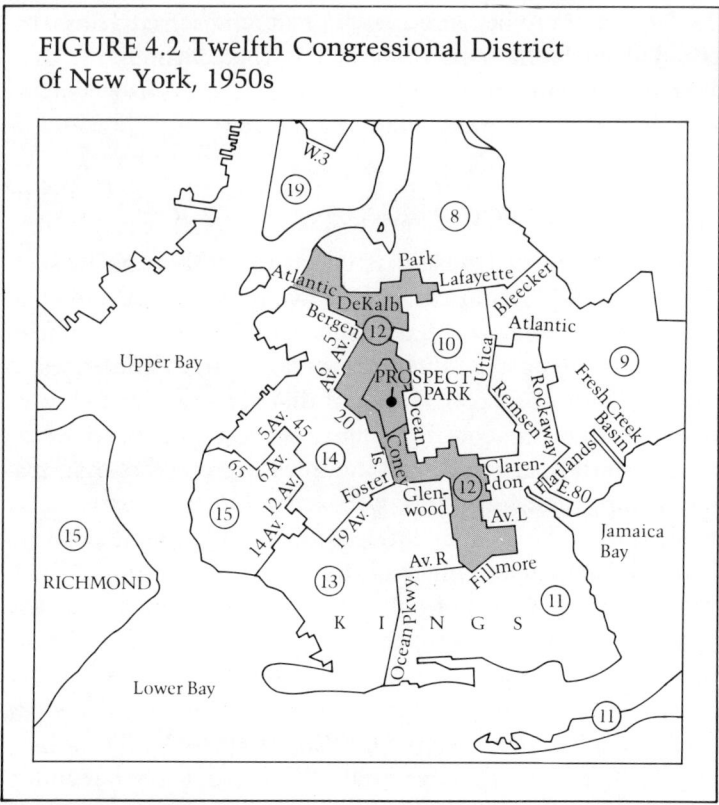

FIGURE 4.2 Twelfth Congressional District of New York, 1950s

"There are very few Republicans in Brooklyn, and distributed in ordinarily shaped districts they would never make a majority anywhere. But the Republican legislature strung G.O.P. areas into a district winding through the borough, and the result was Republican victories until this year." — Anthony Lewis, *The New York Times,* November 27, 1960.
Copyright © by The New York Times Company. Reprinted by permission

with the effect that some states may lose representatives while other states with growing populations may gain them. However, many of the injustices caused by biases in the shape of districts (gerrymandering) still remain.

Organization of the House of Representatives

The organization of both branches of Congress is based on political party lines. The *majority party* in each house is the one with the greatest number of members. Being the majority party is quite important because that party chooses the major officers of its branch of Congress, controls debate on the floor, selects all committee chairmen, and has a majority on all committees. For the past twenty years, the Democratic party has been the majority party in both the House and Senate; the Republicans are the *minority party*. It is possible for one party to hold the majority in the House and the other party in the Senate, but this is not the case at present.

In the House of Representatives, the majority party chooses from among its members the *Speaker of the House*. He does not have to be the oldest or longest-serving member, but he will certainly be well-respected and quite likely will have served a long apprenticeship in other party posts. In the past, the Speaker exercised almost dictatorial powers. This has changed in the twentieth century. However, the Speaker still retains considerable power. He presides over debate on the House floor, recognizes members who wish to

THE ADVANTAGES OF INCUMBENCY

During elections to Congress, the advantages of *incumbency* (being currently in office) are considerable. The incumbent is well-known, and by issuing "official" statements or making "official" trips to his district, he can get a lot of free publicity that his opponent has to pay for. Members of the House have office and staff budgets of approximately $200,000 a year; senators are given at least that and often considerably more if their states are large. Both receive thirty-two government-paid round trips to their districts each year. Facilities for making television or radio tapes are available in Washington at a low cost. And there is the *frank*, the privilege of free official mailing enjoyed by Congress. Two hundred million pieces of mail, much of it quite partisan, are sent free under the frank every year. Coupled with the usually low voter turnout in congressional races, it is no wonder that ninety percent of the incumbents who seek re-election are returned to office.

speak, votes in case of a tie, and interprets procedural questions. In addition, he influences the committee system, which we will look at later in this chapter. The present Speaker is Thomas "Tip" O'Neil, Democratic congressman from Massachusetts since 1952, and Speaker since 1977. The selection of the Speaker takes place every two years, at the beginning of Congress, in the majority party caucus.

The *caucus* of each political party in the House or Senate is simply a gathering of all the members of that party serving there. In recent Congresses the majority party caucus has grown more assertive. The House Democratic caucus has shown a willingness to influence committee and floor action on legislation, to remove committee chairmen from their positions, and to attempt to unite Democrats around the leadership of the Speaker.

The majority party caucus also chooses a *majority leader* who is second in command to the Speaker. The majority leader works closely with the Speaker and schedules legislation for debate on the House floor.

The Speaker and majority leader are assisted by *majority whips*. (The word "whip" comes from English fox hunting, where the "whipper-in" keeps the dogs from running away.) The whips help coordinate party positions on legislation, pass information and directions between the leadership and other party members, make sure party members know when a particular vote is coming, try to convince wavering representatives to vote with the leadership, and conduct informal surveys to check the likely outcome of votes. Being at the center of the congressional process, all these party leaders possess more information than other legislators, and this adds to their power.

The minority party in the House, currently the Republicans, select in their caucus a *minority leader* and *minority whips*. Like the majority party's leader and whips, their duties are to coordinate party positions. The minority leader is usually his or her party's candidate for Speaker should they become the majority party. (Gerald Ford was minority leader in the House before he was chosen vice president.)

The Democratic and Republican caucuses in the House

run their affairs in slightly different ways. The Democratic party chooses a *Steering and Policy Committee* to function as an executive committee of the caucus. The steering committee helps chart party policy in the House. It assigns Democratic members to committees, with the advice of the committees' chairmen and senior members. It also nominates committee chairmen, although the nominations must be approved by the full caucus. The approval used to be a formality, but in the Spring of 1975, at the beginning of the Ninety-fourth Congress, the House Democratic caucus rejected three nominees for chairmen; the incumbent heads of the Armed Services, Banking, and Agriculture committees. The increasingly important role of the Steering Committee has also enlarged the power of the House Speaker who, as leader of the Congressional Democrats, is chairman of the committee. On the other hand, it has also weakened the ability of committee chairmen to act independently of the wishes of their party caucus.

Republican party committee assignments in the House are made by a *Committee on Committees*. This group contains a member from each state with Republican party representation in the House, who has as many votes in the committee as his or her state's Republican delegation does in the House.

Organization of the Senate

The Senate has no Speaker. The *president of the Senate* is the vice president of the United States. He has the right to preside over the Senate Chamber and to vote in case of a tie. This is a largely ceremonial function, one he fills only on rare occasions when an important vote is scheduled. However, Vice President Mondale presided over several sessions of the Ninety-fifth Congress and made important procedural decisions, helping break a filibuster on the Senate floor. Former Vice President Spiro Agnew presided over the Senate during debates on the antiballistic missile system and the Nixon nominations to the Supreme Court.

The honorary post of *president pro tem* (from *pro tem-*

pore, meaning "for the time being") of the Senate is given to the senator from the majority party who has served longest in the Senate. His only power is to preside in the absence of the vice president, but he hardly ever does so. Because the vast majority of Senate work takes place in committees, the job of presiding over what may be a dull and nearly vacant Senate chamber usually falls to a junior senator, who is asked to do so by the Senate majority leader.

The *majority leader of the Senate* is the nearest equivalent to the Speaker of the House. He schedules debate on the Senate floor, assigns bills to committees, coordinates party policy, and appoints members of special committees. The position is currently held by Robert Byrd, Democratic senator from West Virginia since 1959, and majority leader since 1977. The Senate majority leader is assisted by one whip. The minority party in the Senate selects a *minority leader* and a *minority whip* who likewise coordinate party positions and manage floor strategy.

In the Senate the Democrats have a *Steering Committee* which makes committee assignments and a *Policy Committee* which tries to chart party positions and strategy. The Senate Democratic leader chairs the Democratic caucus, the Steering Committee, and the Policy Committee. Republican committee assignments are made by the Republican Steering Committee.

HOW DOES CONGRESS OPERATE?

Most legislation may be introduced in either the House or the Senate, or it can be presented in both houses at the same time. The only exceptions to this rule are money-raising bills, which the Constitution states must originate in the House, and appropriations (spending) bills which, by custom, also begin there. Approximately 20,000 bills are introduced in Congress each year. These may be part of the president's program, they may be drafted by individual senators or representatives or by congressional committees, or they may be the result of alliances between Congress and the executive bureaucracy or private interests.

When the president and both houses of Congress are of the same party, as at present, the president introduces the majority of all legislation finally passed by Congress. However, the Senate and House act separately, and may amend or revise bills as they see fit. For any bill to become law it must ultimately be passed by both branches of Congress in identical language and approved by the president or passed over his veto.

The Congress operates by division of labor. Most of the work of Congress goes on not on the House or Senate floor, but in committees. House committees may have anywhere from twenty to fifty representatives; Senate committees usually have ten to twenty senators. If they did not break down into committees, the Senate and House would move much more slowly and could deal with many fewer issues since they could consider only one subject at a time. It is almost impossible to imagine Congress operating without the committee system.

When a piece of legislation is introduced in either the Senate or House, it is assigned to a committee. The committee (or, often, one of its subcommittees) reviews the bill and decides whether to recommend it to the whole House or Senate. Between 80 and 90 percent of all bills introduced in Congress die in committee. Because the committee system is central to the operation of Congress, it will be discussed more fully later in this chapter.

Floor Debate in the House and Senate

Once a bill has been approved by committee (and in the House by the Rules Committee) it is sent to the House or Senate floor for debate. There it is placed on a calendar. *Calendars* are the business agendas or schedules in Congress. Certain calendars are for routine or minor legislation, others for more important bills, and one in the House, the "discharge calendar," can be used to try to force a bill out of committee against the committee's wishes. (It is rarely successful.)

In the House, floor debate is controlled by the Speaker. He schedules bills for consideration and then presides over the debate. House members are commonly restricted to a few minutes of talk each. The Senate, being smaller, is able to operate more informally. In general, power is more widely distributed in the Senate than in the House. Even junior (new) senators, for example, often chair subcommittees. The Senate majority leader schedules bills for debate, but his control during debate is much less than the House Speaker's.

When debate on a bill has ended, it is put to a vote. A simple majority of the legislators present is needed for passage. Whether a bill begins in the Senate or House, it must sooner or later be submitted to the other branch where the whole procedure of committee review and floor action will be repeated. Then, any differences between the House and Senate versions of a bill must be eliminated before it can be sent to the president for his signature (or veto).

Both in committees and on the floor of either branch of Congress, members of the same political party do not always vote together. Indeed, over the past several decades, the most common division in Congress has been between northern and western moderate to liberal Democrats joined by some liberal Republicans on one side with southern Democrats and moderate to conservative Republicans on the other.

Filibuster

In the Senate, except under very unusual circumstances, debate is unlimited. Senators may talk on a subject for as long as they wish and they will not be cut off. Never-ending talk by one or a number of senators designed to delay or block action in the Senate, is called a *filibuster*. (The original filibuster was a type of pirate ship. Its current meaning probably comes from the image of a lone individual defying

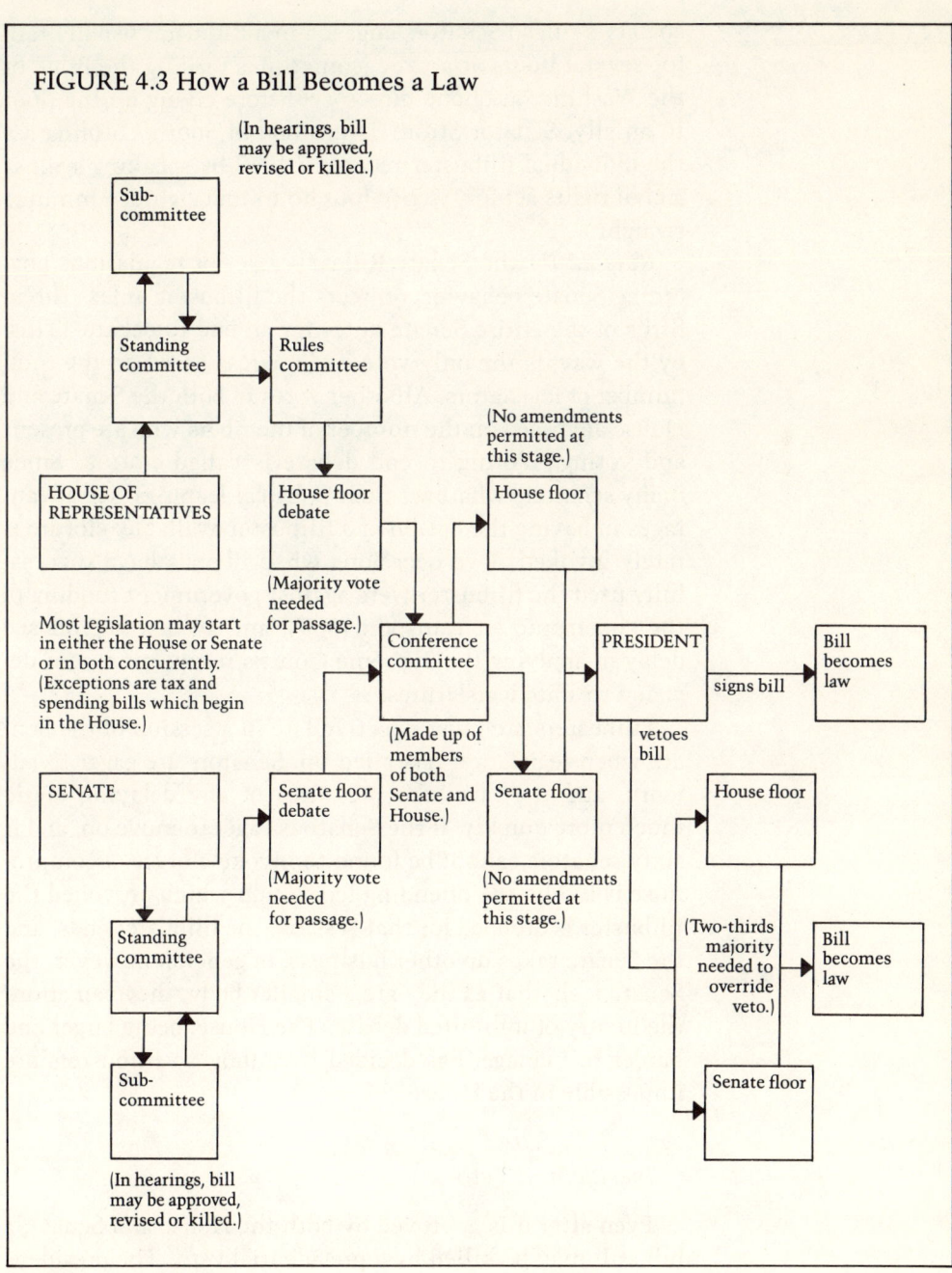

FIGURE 4.3 How a Bill Becomes a Law

society's rules.) Senators engaged in a filibuster usually talk for several hours at a time (sometimes reading the Bible or the Washington phone directory) before giving up the floor to an ally. Senator Strom Thurmond of South Carolina set the individual filibuster record in 1957 by speaking against a civil rights act for twenty-four hours and eighteen minutes straight.

Rule 22 (of the Senate Rules — a set of regulations governing Senate behavior) protects the filibuster unless three-fifths of the entire Senate votes for an end to debate. (This, by the way, is the only vote in Congress based on the total number of legislators. All other votes in both the Senate and House are based on the number of members who are present and voting.) Voting to end debate is called *cloture*. Since many senators, whatever their political leanings, see advantages in having the option of a filibuster available, cloture is rarely invoked. Two occasions when liberals have successfully used the filibuster were against government funding of the supersonic jet transport (SST), and against a proposed delay in applying the Supreme Court's reapportionment decision to state legislatures.

Filibusters are most effective late in a session of the Senate when legislation has piled up. Senators are eager to adjourn, and they feel the pressures of any delaying tactic much more quickly. If the Senate is eager to move on, and if sixty senators cannot be found to invoke cloture, a compromise is likely: the offending legislation which provoked the filibuster is dropped for that session, the filibuster ends, and the Senate takes up other business. In general, however, the Senate feels that as they are a smaller body, they can afford the luxury of unlimited debate. The House, being larger and harder to manage, has decided it cannot, so filibusters are impossible in the House.

Presidential Veto

Even after it is approved by both the House and Senate, a bill still may be killed by a presidential *veto*. The president may veto any legislation he wishes. He may not, however, veto only a piece of a bill (referred to as "item veto"). He must veto it all or accept it all. Still, the Congress has the last word: if Congress *overrides* a veto, the bill becomes law. To override a veto requires two-thirds approval of each house of Congress.

The president must act on a bill within ten working days. If he does not sign it within that period while Congress remains in session, the bill becomes a law without his signature. If Congress adjourns before the ten days are up, and the president does not sign the bill, it does not become law; this is called a "pocket veto."

The ban on "item vetoes" gives Congress an advantage in any confrontation with the president by allowing Congress to use *riders*. A rider is a piece of legislation attached as an amendment to another bill which may deal with a totally different issue. Commonly, the rider contains provisions which the president does not like, while the "parent" bill to which the rider is attached is strongly favored by the president. Since the president must veto all or none of the bill, he is faced with an unhappy alternative. Either he vetoes the rider he does not like and thus also the main bill which he desires, or he accepts the unwanted rider in order to get the rest of the bill.

Finally, it is important to realize that passing a legislative proposal does not automatically make anything happen. If money is needed for the government's wishes (as expressed in a bill) to be carried out, the entire legislative process must be gone through *twice* — once to pass the bill authorizing the activity, and a second time to pass an appropriations bill granting the money to do it. The goals of the bill will not come into being if the appropriations process does not provide the funds.

THE COMMITTEE SYSTEM

As we have mentioned, much of the work of both branches of Congress takes place within committees rather than on the "floor" of the House or Senate. Often, although not always, floor debate is little more than a formality designed to make a public record. On an average day, a visitor to the Senate or House chamber might find a dozen or fewer members listening inattentively to a colleague describing the superiority of Idaho potatoes or the reason Pennsylvania named the firefly its official state insect. At the same moment, many of the committee rooms would be filled with activity.

How Committees Work

There are four types of committees in Congress: standing, conference, select, and joint.

Standing committees are the basic working units of Congress. They were started early in the nation's history because Congress found it could do more work faster if it broke down into smaller, specialized groups. There are twenty-two standing committees in the House and eighteen in the Senate, most focusing on one or two general subjects. Representatives serve on one or two standing committees, senators on three or four. Usually these committees break down into subcommittees for a further division of labor. There are approximately 140 subcommittees in the House and a similar number in the Senate.

Before any bill can be sent to the floor for consideration by the entire Senate or House, it must be approved by a majority vote in the standing committee to which it is assigned. A committee's examination of a proposed bill may include holding public hearings in which interested parties, including the executive bureaucracies, are invited to testify. If the committee approves of the bill, it will be sent to the floor of the Senate or House with a report describing the committee's findings and the reasons the committee thinks the bill should be passed. If the bill is considered unnecessary or undesirable by the committee, it will be killed. The bill's sponsors may resubmit it in a later Congress, but if the committee involved continues to reject it, it will fail again.

Often the actual work on a bill assigned to a standing

committee goes on in one of its subcommittees. Subcommittees have become more powerful in recent Congresses. Because of the desire of the growing number of junior representatives and senators for a "piece of the action" more subcommittees have been created and given larger staffs and greater powers. Seniority has not been considered crucial in appointing subcommittee chairmen, especially in the Senate where first-term Democrats chair an average of two subcommittees. This increased reliance on subcommittees was also a revolt against the power of committee chairmen who have lost much of their influence over the activities and membership of the subcommittees to the party caucus. The result of this change, then, has been to spread out power away from committee chairmen to more junior (and liberal) members acting through the subcommittees and the party caucus.

A *conference committee* is a temporary body including both senators and representatives, created solely to iron out the differences between House and Senate versions of one particular bill. These differences come about because of amendments attached to the bill by one chamber but not the other or because the two houses have passed different bills dealing with the same subject. Before a bill can be sent to the president for his action, it must be passed in identical language by both houses.

House members of conference committees are appointed by the Speaker of the House, and Senate members by the Senate majority leader. They usually include senior members of the relevant committees. The conference committee engages in bargaining and trade-offs to reach a compromise; once this job is finished, it is disbanded.

When (and if) the conference committee reaches agreement, the new substitute bill is then sent back to the House and Senate floors for approval or disapproval. This bill cannot be amended; it must be accepted or rejected as is. (If this rule were not in force, of course, the bill might be amended again in different ways in House and Senate, thereby requiring another conference committee, and so on.)

LOBBYISTS

Many of the private individuals who help draft legislation and testify at committee hearings are *lobbyists*. The term lobbying originally came from the "lobby-agents" who waited in the lobbies of the legislature to catch legislators and pressure them for favorable treatment. A lobbyist is a representative of any private interest (a lobby) that tries to influence government policy. The common image of lobbyists is of people from private corporate interests looking for a tax break, and there are many of those. But groups such as the NAACP, Common Cause, or the Sierra Club also lobby Congress. Large labor unions maintain some of the most important lobbying organizations in Washington.

It is a fact of Washington life that special interests concentrate their campaign contributions on committee members who are in a position to help them. This sometimes results in scandals, like the recent one involving the Korean lobbyist, Tongsun Park. It is also true that constant contact between committee members and staff and interested private parties may lead to friendship and a sense of shared interests. Whether this familiarity is harmful to the public interest varies with the circumstances.

Select committees are set up to do specific, usually temporary, jobs, often to conduct an investigation. Recent examples include the Senate select committee charged with investigating the Central Intelligence Agency and the House Assassinations Committee investigating the deaths of the two Kennedys and Martin Luther King.

Joint committees are permanent bodies including both senators and representatives. Usually these committees coordinate policy on routine matters, such as printing or the congressional library. The Joint Committee on Atomic Energy and the Joint Economic Committee, however, have important tasks. Reformers often favor much greater use of joint committees in Congress to save time, money, and confusion. The two branches are jealous of their separate powers, however, and joint committees remain the exception rather than the rule.

Committee Chairmen and the Seniority System

Committee chairmen have considerable power within Congress. By the unwritten rule of *seniority*, the chairman of any committee is always the majority party member who has served longest (consecutively) on the committee. Some of the chairmen's power comes about naturally through the work of their committees, their understanding of congressional procedures, and their wide contacts within the government, results of long legislative service. But chairmen have formal power as well. They generally control the hiring and firing of majority party staff, schedule committee meetings and agenda, and have considerable informal influence over the appointment of new members to their committees.

The seniority system has been one of the most influential traditions in Congress, though it is not written down anywhere in the rules of the House or Senate. Still, for more than fifty years the custom was almost never broken. Then, in the fall of 1974, Wilbur Mills, chairman of the House Ways and Means Committee (which deals with taxation) was involved in several public incidents with a striptease dancer, Fanne Foxe. At one point Mills appeared on stage in a Boston burlesque house with Ms. Foxe. This greatly embarrassed other House members, and finally Mills was forced to resign his chairmanship, which then went to the next most senior Democrat on the committee. A similar sex scandal occurred two years later when Wayne Hays, chairman of the House Administration Committee, was accused by Elizabeth Ray of keeping her on the committee payroll for services above and beyond the call of duty. In spite of his seniority, the Democratic party caucus quickly acted to force Hays' resignation.

Hays' removal had been made easier by the successful challenge to seniority in early 1975 by the Ninety-fourth Congress. Under the pressure of the seventy-five newly elected freshman Democrats, the majority party caucus voted to remove three committee chairmen whom they felt were unqualified, too dictatorial, or unresponsive to the wishes of the party. This, and other reforms, underlined the increased power of the majority party caucus and its unwillingness to always follow the seniority system in appointing chairmen. It also served as a warning to other committee chairmen that the caucus and the House leadership would increasingly call the legislative tune to which they would be wise to dance.

Nonetheless, the seniority system (often called the "senility system") remains more or less in place. Attacked as out of date and undemocratic, it has favored conservatives from one-party regions like the Deep South where the same person is returned to Congress time after time. In spite of its rigidity and unresponsiveness, seniority ensures that an experienced, knowledgeable person will become chairman. More importantly, it has provided a predictable system of succession which has prevented constant fights over control of the chair. But clearly the newer members of Congress no longer feel the need to automatically follow a custom which limits their own influence. The hold of the seniority system is likely to continue to weaken, at least until the time when the now junior members of Congress themselves gain seniority.

Specialization and Reciprocity

Two other informal rules support the power of committees in Congress. The first, *specialization,* is closely related to the second, *reciprocity. Specialization* means that once assigned to a committee or subcommittee, a member of Congress is expected to specialize in its work and become expert in that area. Particularly in the House, members are not expected to follow all legislation in Congress equally, or to speak out on widely varying issues. Rather, the accepted pattern is to work hard and seriously on committee business and leave unrelated issues to other committees designed to deal with them. The result of this system is that committees and their individual members develop close and extensive knowledge of their own work but may not know much about other areas.

This potential problem is resolved through the informal rule of *reciprocity*. Under this rule, members look for guidance in voting on legislation outside their committee's or subcommittee's field to members of committees that do specialize in it. Legislators tend to vote the way the most closely concerned committee tells them to vote, because that committee knows most about the legislation and because the members want the same support and respect when their committee's business is involved. Specialization and reciprocity, then, are two sides of the same coin. You develop expertise in an area and other members follow your lead in that area. You in turn follow the lead of others more knowledgeable than you in areas outside your expertise.

This process has been slightly diluted in the Senate and recently in the House. Because senators commonly serve on three or four committees, their areas of specialization are more varied and less intense. The rise in importance of the House majority party caucus has meant that in some cases (such as the limits on tax advantages to oil companies in 1975) the caucus will help defeat committee recommendations on the floor. Still the general pattern operates both in the Senate and House. Indeed, were it not for specialization and reciprocity, the work of Congress would proceed much more slowly, with more confusion, and probably with much more conflict.

Members of Congress who do not abide by these informal rules are called *mavericks*. Mavericks may be popular in the media and in their home districts, but they are unlikely to be popular in Congress. They may receive unattractive committee assignments or generally be shunned by the majority of their colleagues. As Speaker Rayburn was fond of saying to the new members of Congress, "To get along you've got to go along." When former Representative Herman Badillo, an outspoken liberal, was first elected to Congress from a poor, urban district in New York, he was assigned to the Agriculture Committee, an area far from his and his constituents' interests. After many protests, and after having been taught the penalties for being too outspoken, he was finally given a more attractive spot on the Education and Labor Committee.

Because of the importance of committee and subcommittee work and the existence of specialization and reciprocity, these assignments are vital to a legislator's power and effectiveness. This tends to keep committees stable and discourage "hopping" from one to another. Once members of Congress have been assigned to a committee, they will not be removed against their wishes unless the party balance in Congress should shift so much as to change the total number of Democrats and Republicans on the committee. Of course, the result of representatives from rural areas preferring some committees while urban representatives prefer others is that some committees reflect a rural conservative bias (Agriculture) and others reflect an urban liberal bias (Education and Labor).

Major Committees in the House

Of the standing committees in the House of Representatives, the most important are Rules, Appropriations, and Ways and Means. Almost all legislation approved by committees in the House must pass through the Rules Committee before reaching the House floor. (Exceptions are bills coming from Ways and Means or Appropriations.) The Rules Committee's name comes from its function: If the committee approves a bill for transmission to the House floor, it assigns a "rule" to that bill setting the terms of debate. The Rules Committee can, for example, assign a "closed rule" which forbids any amendments and forces the House into a "take it or leave it" position. Or the committee may specify what portions of a bill may be amended and what may not, or even the exact wording of permissible amendments. Thus the Rules Committee acts as a "traffic cop." It has the power to delay or even kill legislation; it can amend bills or send them back to committee for revision.

These are formidable powers. They were originally granted to the Rules Committee in the interests of efficiency and coordination. The Rules Committee commonly screens out legislation that might be embarrassing, foolish, or too costly. For example, a proposal to publicly televise all House proceedings is unpopular with the House members (because they are often absent, tongue-tied, tired, or wrong and they prefer not to have this revealed), but it is difficult to vote against since the public might conclude the members have something to hide. By killing such legislation without a floor vote, the Rules Committee performs a useful function for House members.

Of course, the Rules Committee also has the power to stall or kill legislation supported by a House majority. In the past, this has often happened, particularly in the areas of civil rights and social welfare. A long history of such obstruction finally led to a revolt in the House in 1961, led by Speaker of the House Sam Rayburn and President John Kennedy. As a result, the Rules Committee was enlarged, with new members added to create a liberal majority on the committee. In early 1975 the majority caucus gave the Speaker the power to nominate the Democratic members and the chairman of the Rules Committee. This clearly brought the committee more under the control of the Speaker and the party.

The *Ways and Means Committee* is concerned with tax legislation, or the *raising* of revenue for the government. Because all money-raising bills begin in the House, any tax legislation goes first to the Ways and Means Committee. If approved by that committee, it then normally goes to the House floor under a "closed rule" (forbidding amendments). This keeps members of Congress from giving in to the temptation to attach amendments for special interests. Ways and Means also deals with social security legislation, medicare, unemployment insurance, and import tariffs.

In early 1975 an important change occurred in the Ways

and Means Committee similar to that made in the Rules Committee in 1961. The incidents with the striptease dancer that led to Wilbur Mills' resignation as chairman of Ways and Means were also used as an opportunity to enlarge the committee, create four new subcommittees, and fill the new positions with more liberal members. The Democratic members of the Ways and Means Committee also lost their right to make House Democratic party committee assignments, which had been an important part of their power. (As noted, committee assignments are now made by the Steering and Policy Committee of the Democratic caucus.)

The Ways and Means Committee handles tax bills to raise money; the *Appropriations Committee* deals with how government *spends* that money. When the federal budget is presented to Congress by the president each year, it is sent to the House Appropriations Committee and its thirteen subcommittees as the first stage in congressional review. Since the power to tax and spend is the power to make or break policies, programs, industries, areas, and individuals, and since specialization and reciprocity ensure that Congress will tend to follow the lead of its committees, the importance of the Ways and Means and Appropriations committees and their subcommittees is clear.

Major Committees in the Senate

The most important committees in the Senate are Appropriations, Finance, and Foreign Relations. The Senate *Appropriations Committee* receives appropriations bills after they have been passed by the House. Its procedures are very much like those of its House counterpart, with the important distinction that the Senate committee tends to act as a "court of appeals," adding money to the amounts granted by the House. If passed by the House, tax legislation then goes to the Senate *Finance Committee*, the Senate's equivalent of House Ways and Means.

The Senate *Foreign Relations Committee* is a watchdog over the president's dominant position in foreign policy. Its importance comes from the Senate's role in confirming appointments of ambassadors and approving or disapproving of treaties. These issues are reviewed by the committee before the full Senate votes on them. It is also considered a helpful publicity forum for senators with presidential ambitions.

The Senate also has a Rules Committee, but it is much less important than its House counterpart. The Senate has fewer than one-fourth as many members as the House. Thus, the problems of organization, coordination, and efficiency are not as great. Since each branch of Congress sets its own procedures, the Senate simply decided that it did not need to set up a strong "traffic cop" to screen legislation between committees and the Senate floor.

THE OTHER POWERS OF CONGRESS

So far we have discussed the *legislative* powers of Congress. Congress also has several *nonlegislative powers*. Among these are *oversight* of the executive branch and *investigation*. Through legislation, Congress created the various executive agencies and departments and specified their duties and powers. It can change them at any time. In addition, Congress appropriates the funds those agencies need to perform their jobs. These powers give Congress both an interest in what the executive branch is doing and the means to find out. For example, Congress can determine whether the government will regulate mail-order firms or not, decide who will and who will not receive food stamps and at what price, and judge whether environmentalists or oil drillers will decide on the location of the Alaska pipeline. In short, the annual appropriations process gives Congress the chance to ask what the bureaucracies are doing, tell them what they ought to be doing, and finally give money for what Congress wants and withhold money for what it doesn't want.

The *General Accounting Office* (GAO) and the new *Congressional Budget Office* are agencies created by Congress to help with its oversight function. Congress uses the GAO to examine certain government programs or departments. The Budget Office is intended to serve as a congressional counterweight to the president's Office of Management and Budget.

In addition, the Congress has the power to *investigate.* If Congress, or a particular committee (or committee chairman) decides that something is being done wrong, or not being done that should be, an investigation may be launched. The subject might be foreign-policy decision making in the executive branch, or price fixing by private industry, or the power and influence of organized crime. In other words, Congress can investigate whatever it wishes.

Congressional investigations are not welcomed by executive departments, for they allow Congress to influence executive behavior. The Senate Foreign Relations Committee's public hearings on the Vietnam War and the special Watergate Committee's investigation illustrated this power. Done for the wrong motives, however, congressional investigations can be dangerous. In the 1950s, for example, Senator Joseph McCarthy's Permanent Investigations Subcommittee and the House Un-American Activities Committee ruined the reputations of many innocent people, forced able persons out of government service, and whipped up fear and hatred throughout the country with their often unfounded charges of disloyalty and communist sympathies.

Just as the Constitution gives the president the right to make foreign treaties only with the approval of two-thirds of the Senate (illustrated by the close approval of the Panama Canal Treaty in 1978), the Senate also has the power to approve or reject most presidential appointments, including ambassadors, cabinet members, military officers, and other executive branch officials. The two-thirds majority needed for treaties and the simple majority for executive appointments are based on those members of the Senate present and voting when the issue arises, not on the entire hundred-person Senate.

Many presidential appointments within the executive branch are routine, and there is a tendency in the Senate to agree that the president has a right to have whomever he wishes working with him. Still, President Eisenhower once had a cabinet nomination rejected, and the "behind the scenes" pressure of Senate dissatisfaction undoubtedly causes presidents not to make certain unpopular nominations in the first place. In addition, the Senate often takes a more active role in presidential appointments to the independent regulatory commissions and the Supreme Court, as when it rejected two of President Nixon's nominations to the Supreme Court.

Congress also has certain judicial functions. The House of Representatives can *impeach* (bring charges against) a federal official by a simple majority vote. Then, the Senate holds a trial on these charges. If two-thirds of the Senate votes to uphold the charges and to convict the official, that official is thereby removed from office.

Impeachment is a difficult, slow, and cumbersome process. Several federal judges have been impeached and convicted in the past, but only one president was ever impeached, Andrew Johnson in 1868, and he was not convicted by the Senate. Richard Nixon resigned the presidency (the only president ever to do so) in the face of almost certain impeachment by the House and conviction by the Senate. Despite the difficulty of impeachment, the process does remain an ultimate power over the executive.

Case Study: Congress and the Campaign Finance Reform Bill[1]

On June 17, 1972, five burglars hired by the Nixon reelection committee broke into Democratic party headquarters in the Watergate office complex in Washington, D.C.

---

[1] For more detailed analysis, see *Congressional Quarterly Weekly Reports*, 1974, pp. 1003, 2233, 2691, 2865–70, and 2927–28; 1977, p. 1294.

They were caught by police while planting illegal listening devices in the office telephones. The investigations triggered by the Watergate break-in revealed the greatest scandal in American political history. Finally, more than two years after the Watergate break-in, faced with almost certain impeachment by the House and conviction by the Senate, Richard Nixon resigned the presidency in disgrace. Nixon's resignation did not, however, eliminate public anger and suspicion. Calls for large-scale reform of campaign practices were widespread.

Before 1972, there were few limits on American campaign practices, and the ones that existed were never effectively enforced. In 1972 Congress passed the Federal Election Campaign Act, which required candidates to report their campaign fund raising, and set limits on the amounts they could spend on radio and TV advertising. Although these disclosure provisions turned out to be helpful in unravelling the Watergate mess, the scandal itself showed up a need for further reform.

It was public pressure that did the most to force change. By 1974 Congress was looking at public opinion polls that showed it had even less public respect than President Nixon. Groups like Common Cause, calling itself a "people's lobby," and newspapers from across the country joined in criticizing the role private money had come to play in politics.

As the Watergate scandal continued to unfold, Congress began to act. As early as November of 1973, the Senate passed a new campaign financing bill that would have provided federal funding for both presidential and congressional races. But the House refused to accept it, and action was stalled.

After Congress reconvened in January, 1974, the Senate Rules Committee again began work on public campaign funding legislation. The bill they came up with called for partial public financing of primary campaigns and full public funding of general elections for both president and Congress, and placed limits on private contributions and spending. When the bill reached the Senate floor, it touched off a filibuster of southern Democrats and conservative Republicans who opposed the public financing sections. This was partly because southern Democrats often face little electoral opposition from the weak Republican party in the South, and thus do not need such funding, and conservative Republicans in general have little trouble raising private funds. Thus, public funding of campaigns was more likely to benefit their opponents than themselves. They also argued that the bill was unfair to taxpayers, one more instance of big government getting into areas that ought to be left alone. Nevertheless, the filibuster was defeated and the bill passed.

In the House, the Administration Committee had been working on a similar bill. It moved slowly, no doubt reflecting the fact that many conservative members of the House, who have little trouble getting reelected, preferred to leave things alone. The continuing Watergate revelations and the increasing likelihood of Nixon's impeachment, however, kept up the public pressure on Congress. The bill cleared the Rules Committee and reached the House floor in late July. Public financing of congressional elections had been eliminated, however, and on the floor spending limits for House candidates were lowered. (Low spending limits may sound like an obvious reform; but in reality they may help incumbents, if challengers are kept from spending enough to make their names known or to keep up with the free publicity an officeholder gets.)

Now the bill was sent to a conference committee, where members were deadlocked for three weeks over the issue of public funding of congressional races. The Senate demanded it, but the House refused. Finally the senators gave in, in exchange for higher spending limits in House and Senate elections and a tougher, more independent elections board to administer and enforce the law. No overall limit on campaign contributions from organizations was included in the bill. This appeared to be a victory for organized labor, but since the law's passage, many new "voluntary" organizations, particularly of businessmen, have been created.

Another interesting feature of the bill was the "Common Cause amendment," which requires any organization attempting to influence the outcome of a federal election to file reports with the new elections commission. As part of its lobbying, Common Cause had run an ad in the *Washington Post* that was critical of House Democrats. Later it held a news conference devoted to special interests and the Senate and House members who had substantially benefitted from them in the past. Wayne Hays, chairman of the House Administration Committee, had not appreciated Common Cause's pressure on the campaign financing bill, and the requirement that the group disclose its spending and contributions was Hays' revenge. The conference committee also settled on an annual limit of $15,000 on the fees members of Congress can accept for speeches or articles. This was a blow mainly to the better known and more popular senators. House conferees may have pushed this provision to make liberal Senate sponsors of the bill pay for their public image as reformers.

The final bill included public financing of presidential, but not congressional, elections. Private individuals were limited to $1,000 per candidate per election and $25,000 total per year. Organizations may spend $5,000 per candidate with no overall limit. A House candidate may spend $70,000 plus certain added expenses in each primary, runoff, and general election. Senate candidates may spend more, depending on the state's populations. Presidential candidates may spend a maximum of $10,000,000 in all primary elections combined. After a certain minimum is reached, all contributions under $250 will be matched by the federal treasury. In the general election, federal funding up to $20,000,000 is available in which case no private money is allowed. An elections commission will oversee the law, although it must refer possible criminal violations to the Justice Department.

President Ford signed the campaign finance bill (formally titled the Federal Elections Campaign Act Amendments of 1974) into law on October 15. Former President Nixon had earlier threatened to veto the bill (Nixon, who had raised more than $50 million for his 1972 race, some of it illegally, called the bill a "raid on the public treasury"). Ford also expressed doubts about using federal money for campaigns as well as possibly violating First Amendment rights by limiting contributions. However, Ford's pardon of Nixon on September 8 had drawn widespread criticism, and the congressional elections were less than a month away. As he said, "the times demand this legislation."

But passage of the law did not end debate. The bill's opponents (led by two former senators, James Buckley on the right and Eugene McCarthy on the left) simply moved to the courts where they challenged it on grounds of unconstitutional restriction on free speech, favoritism to incumbent members of Congress, and bias against all unknown challengers.

In its January, 1976, decision (*Buckley* v. *Valeo*) the Supreme Court upheld most of the bill, including the public financing section, but struck down several provisions. Perhaps the most controversial loophole created by the Court's decision was its removal of the limits on candidates' own contributions to their campaigns. The advantage this gave to wealthy candidates was shown by H. John Heinz (of the H. J. Heinz food company family), who contributed $2.5 million of his personal fortune to his successful campaign to become Republican Senator from Pennsylvania in 1976. Apparently, despite the law and the Court's decision, the influence of private money in public affairs will be with us for quite a while yet.

WRAP-UP

The United States Congress consists of two houses, the Senate and the House of Representatives. Two senators are selected from each state, and they serve for six years. Representatives are allocated to states according to population;

they serve for two years. The Senate, with 100 members, is smaller, more informal, more prestigious, and less hierarchical than the House, with its 435 members.

The House and Senate operate separately, but before any legislation can be sent to the president for signing it must be passed in identical language by both branches. In the House, floor debate is controlled by the Speaker of the House, who is elected by the majority party. The Speaker works closely with the House majority leader and whips. The Senate has no speaker; floor debate is managed by the Senate majority leader. Each branch also has minority leaders and minority whips. Both the House and Senate rely heavily on committees and subcommittees, and members in both branches tend to follow the lead of their committees. The pattern of specialization and reciprocity supports the committee system. Although this gives committee chairmen (who are always of the majority party) considerable power in Congress, the recent increased uses of the majority party caucus and of subcommittees has cut into their influence. Chairmen are almost always chosen on the basis of seniority — longest consecutive service on the committee.

All legislation other than revenue raising and appropriation bills (which must start in the House) can be introduced first in either the House or Senate. It is then assigned to the relevant committee for examination. Witnesses may be called to testify, and the bill may be revised. If approved by committee, the bill is sent to the floor of the House or Senate (going in the House through the Rules Committee). If approved there, the bill goes to the other branch for a similar process. Any differences between the House and Senate versions will be ironed out by a conference committee. When both branches of Congress have approved the same bill, it is sent to the president. He may sign it, veto it, pocket veto it, or allow it to become law without his signature. If he vetoes it (other than by a pocket veto), Congress may try to override the veto by a two-thirds vote in each house.

Congressional procedures seem complex and confusing

because they are complex and confusing. The Congress has often been criticized for being slow, unresponsive, and even unrepresentative. Certainly the procedures discussed in this chapter often involve much time-consuming duplication of effort. But these procedures also help to prevent a rash or unwise response to a momentary crisis or public passion. The seniority system, the filibuster in the Senate, and the overall fragmentation of power between committees and the floor may sometimes frustrate majority wishes, but they can also protect minority rights.

The Congress has remained an arena for national debate since it began. Although many would say its accomplishments have been too slow in coming, Congress has produced social security reforms, civil service reforms, voting rights bills, and measures designed to protect the environment and conserve energy. If Congress is sometimes slow to respond to apparent national needs, it may be because the country itself does not agree on the nature of the problem or the need to fix it. If Congress sometimes bogs down in partisan disputes or struggles to reach a watered-down compromise solution, it may be because a country as large as the United States includes strongly opposing interests and attitudes which the Congress merely reflects. If special interests sometimes seem to receive special treatment from Congress, this may simply be an accurate reflection of the political power of these players.

Congress was not set up to make government run more efficiently. It was established to reflect the wishes of the people governed, to be the democratic centerpiece among the institutions of government. In many ways Congress is "representative"; it does accurately reflect the distribution of political power in the country. The ease of gaining tax breaks for large corporations and the difficulty of passing legislation guaranteeing full employment, for example, mirror the influence of the political players affected by these congressional actions. Congress has, in recent years, shown an independent willingness to limit presidential abuses and to reform some of its own outdated procedures. The question whether Congress will show a similar independence in resisting the powerful few in order to represent the not-so powerful many remains for this vital player in the political game to answer.

THOUGHT QUESTIONS

1. In recent years, many commentators have argued that Congress is in decline relative to the executive branch. In what ways is Congress adequately organized and equipped to perform its role? What changes would you recommend?
2. Think about the "unwritten rules" of seniority, specialization, and reciprocity. How do these rules help Congress to operate? What are their drawbacks?
3. To what extent do political party leaders control what goes on in Congress? What factors encourage party leadership? What factors limit it?
4. Congress has been described as an arena of widely dispersed power centers faced with the constant threat of stalemate. Is this accurate? Are there any advantages to such a system?

SUGGESTED READINGS

Dodd, Lawrence C., and Bruce Oppenheimer, eds. *Congress Reconsidered.* New York: Praeger, 1977. Pb.
 Articles by scholars on recent reforms and changes in Congress.
Fiorina, Morris P. *Congress: Keystone of the Washington Establishment.* New Haven: Yale University Press, 1977. Pb.
 A brief study of how Congress operates — and for whom.
Harris, Richard. *Decision.* New York: Dutton, 1971. Pb.
 A fascinating account of the struggle in the Senate over the Nixon nomination of G. Harrold Carswell to the Supreme Court.
Mayhew, David R. *Congress: The Electoral Connection.* New Haven: Yale University Press, 1974. Pb.
 A very readable study whose central theme is that a member of Congress' principal motivation is re-election. Mayhew's book is also one of the best concise surveys available of the political science literature on Congress.
Radler, Don. *How Congress Works.* New York: Signet, 1976. Pb.
 A short, balanced introduction to Congress.

Suggested Readings

Redman, Eric. *The Dance of Legislation.* New York: Simon and Schuster, 1973. Pb.
An insider's engaging account of the messy realities of the legislative process, written by a twenty-one year old staff aide to Senator Warren Magnuson, chairman of the Commerce Committee.

Riegle, Donald. *O'Congress.* New York: Popular Library, 1972. Pb.
A year in the life of a young representative from Michigan.

5 The Judicial Branch: The Supreme Court and the Federal Court System

The Constitution is brief and to the point in providing for the judicial player: "The judicial Power of the United States shall be vested in one supreme Court, and in such inferior Courts as the Congress may from time to time ordain and establish" (Article III, Section 1). What Congress set up were two major levels of federal courts below the Supreme Court — federal district courts and courts of appeals. It has also set up several special federal courts as the need for them has arisen. The federal court system is responsible for judging cases involving the United States Constitution and federal laws.

Parallel to this is the state court system. Each state has its own judicial system to try cases that come under state law (though it may also deal with cases under the United States Constitution and laws). Issues involving the Constitution may be appealed to the United States Supreme Court. In this chapter we will focus on the federal court system and particularly the Supreme Court; state courts are set up in much the same way.

THE FEDERAL COURT SYSTEM

United States District Courts

At the base of the federal court system are the *United States district courts*. These are the courts of *original jurisdiction*. This means that except in a few special instances, all cases involving federal law are tried first in the district courts. There are ninety-four district courts in the United States and its possessions, with at least one federal district court in each state. The larger, more populated states have more district courts. New York, for example, has four. Each district has between one and twenty-four judges, for a total of four hundred district judges in the country. These judges preside over most federal cases, including civil rights, controversies involving over $10,000, antitrust and counterfeiting cases. The large volume of cases they handle (over 171,000 in 1976) has led to long delays in administering justice. For example, at one point it took an average of almost four years to complete a civil case in the Southern District of New York.

Courts of Appeals

Above the district courts are the *courts of appeals* (sometimes called by their old name, *circuit courts of appeals*). These courts have only appellate jurisdiction; that is, they hear *appeals* from the district courts and from important regulatory commissions, like the Interstate Commerce Commission. For example, if you took a civil rights case to your district court and lost, you could protest the decision and have the case brought before a court of appeals. The United States is divided into eleven *circuits* (ten plus one in Washington, D.C.), each with one court of appeals. Each of the eleven courts has from three to fifteen judges, depending on the volume of work. Usually three judges hear each case. In 1975 there were ninety-seven circuit court judges handling almost 20,000 cases. They are the final courts of appeal for most cases, but a few cases they consider are appealed further to the Supreme Court.

Special Federal Courts

Special federal courts have been created by Congress to handle certain cases. The *United States Court of Claims* deals with people's claims against government seizure of property or claims for income tax refunds. The *United States Court of Military Appeals* (often called "the GI Supreme Court"), composed of three civilians, is the final judge of court-martial convictions. (The United States Supreme Court can only review certain types of military cases.)

The Judges

All federal judges, including Supreme Court justices, are nominated to the bench by the president and must be approved by the Senate. Although it is usually given, confirmation by the Senate is not merely an empty ritual. In 1969 and 1970 two federal judges, Clement F. Haynesworth and G. Harrold Carswell, nominated to the Supreme Court by President Nixon, were rejected by the Senate.

Under the Constitution, all federal judges hold office for life "during good behavior" and can be removed only by

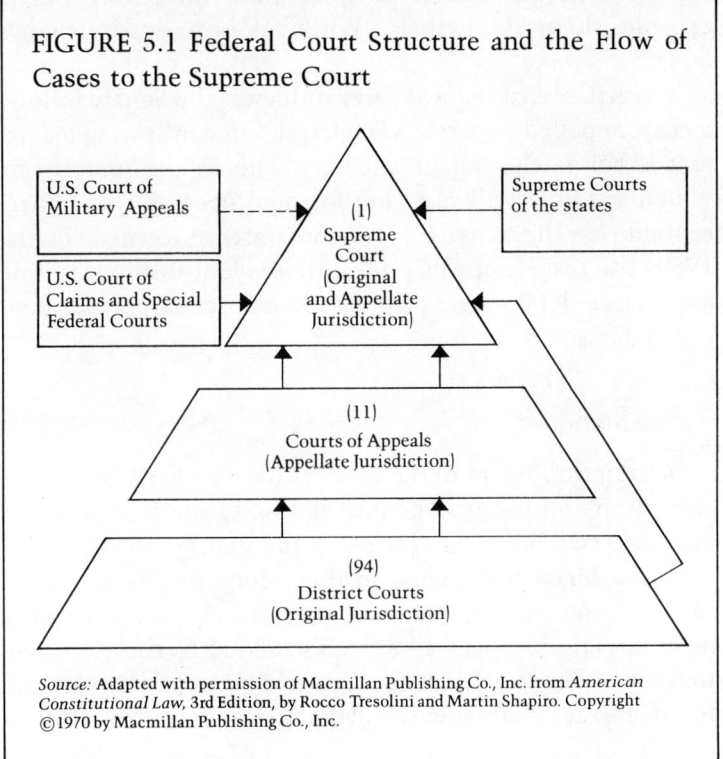

FIGURE 5.1 Federal Court Structure and the Flow of Cases to the Supreme Court

Source: Adapted with permission of Macmillan Publishing Co., Inc. from *American Constitutional Law*, 3rd Edition, by Rocco Tresolini and Martin Shapiro. Copyright © 1970 by Macmillan Publishing Co., Inc.

impeachment, which has happened only ten times. To further protect them from political pressures, judges' salaries cannot be reduced during their time in office.

Despite these protections, the appointment of judges is a very political matter. Judges are almost always selected on a party basis and usually as a reward for their political services to the party. One professor of law commented that the judiciary was "the place to put political workhorses out to pasture." In this partisan spirit ninety-three percent of Lyndon Johnson's appointments to federal judgeships were Democrats, while ninety-three percent of Richard Nixon's were Republicans. This power of the president to influence the makeup of one of the three major branches of the government is extremely important. Some observers feel that President Nixon's most lasting political impact may have been his appointment of four Republican judges to the Supreme Court. Remembering the justices' life tenure, others console themselves that "While there's death, there's hope."

To further ensure local party influence the Senate follows a custom called *"senatorial courtesy"* in confirming federal judges below the Supreme Court. This is the practice by which senators will not vote for nominees who are unacceptable to the senator from the state concerned. In the 1960s the results of this procedure made it difficult to find southern federal judges who would enforce unpopular civil rights decisions.

Jurisdiction

Jurisdiction refers to the matters over which a court may exercise its authority. The jurisdiction of the federal courts falls into two broad categories: in the first group it depends on the *subject of the case*, in the second on the *parties to the case*, no matter what the subject. The federal courts have jurisdiction over all subjects related to the Constitution, and over treaties of the United States. (Admiralty and maritime cases involving international law are also included.) Jurisdiction determined by parties includes cases involving ambassadors and other foreign representatives; controversies in which the United States is a party; and controversies between two or more states or between a state or citizen of the United States and a foreign citizen or state. The federal court system's last and largest source of cases is suits between citizens of different states.

This does not mean that the federal courts have the *only* jurisdiction over such cases. Federal courts have *exclusive jurisdiction* in some cases, such as cases involving crimes against the laws of the United States. But in other cases they have *concurrent jurisdiction*, shared with state courts. For example, some suits between citizens of different states may be heard by both federal and state courts.

THE UNITED STATES SUPREME COURT

The *Supreme Court of the United States*, composed of a chief justice and eight associate justices, stands at the head of the federal court system. (Congress can set by law the number of justices on the Supreme Court. Although the number has varied from time to time, it has remained at nine since 1869.) Although the Supreme Court has some *original jurisdiction* (some cases can be presented first to that court), most of the cases it hears are appeals of lower court decisions, which involve its *appellate jurisdiction*. If your civil rights case lost in both the district court and the court of appeals, you might be able to get it heard by the Supreme Court.

Actually very few cases ever reach the Supreme Court. Of more than ten million cases tried every year in American courts (federal and state), less than 2,000 petitions for review make it to the Supreme Court. In the 1976 term the Court heard oral arguments in 102 cases. The rest of the petitions were affirmed or reversed by written "memorandum orders."

Many cases that reach the Supreme Court involve consti-

TABLE 5.1. The Supreme Court, 1978

Justice	Appointed by	Date Appointed
William J. Brennan, Jr.	Eisenhower	1957
Potter Stewart	Eisenhower	1959
Byron R. White	Kennedy	1962
Thurgood Marshall	Johnson	1967
Warren E. Burger (Chief Justice)	Nixon	1969
Harry A. Blackmun	Nixon	1970
Lewis F. Powell, Jr.	Nixon	1971
William H. Rehnquist	Nixon	1971
John Paul Stevens	Ford	1975

tutional issues. The majority of these cases come to the Court in the form of petitions (written requests) for a *writ of certiorari* (certiorari means to be informed of something). A writ of certiorari is an order to the lower court to send the entire record of the case to the higher court for review. Someone who has lost a case in a lower court may petition for this writ. It is granted when four justices of the Supreme Court feel that the issues raised are important enough to merit a review. The Court denies between eighty-five and ninety percent of all such applications. This procedure keeps control over the appeal process in the hands of the Supreme Court, allowing it to keep a maximum of decisions in the lower courts. It also enables the Court to influence the actions of lower court judges by establishing guiding decisions on certain crucial cases.

The Final Authority?

The Supreme Court has been prominent in American political history because it has been thought to have "final" authority over what the Constitution means. Historically, however, a ruling of the Court has not always been the "final" word. The Court itself has reversed its decisions, as will be shown in the case study, "Separate but Equal" (page 146–152). Basic changes in the document accomplished by amendments to the Constitution also have reversed decisions by the Court. The Court's pre–Civil War *Dred Scott* decision supporting ownership of slaves in all parts of the country was reversed by the Thirteenth Amendment outlawing slavery. An 1895 Court decision striking down the federal income tax was overcome by the Sixteenth Amendment in 1913 which allowed such taxes. More recently there was an unsuccessful attempt to reverse the Supreme Court's ruling severely restricting anti-abortion laws by an amendment to the Constitution.

The strength of the Court's "final" authority is also affected by the other branches of government. Congress and the president, as well as the Supreme Court, have taken their turn in interpreting vague parts of the Constitution to meet the demands of the time and the needs of those in power. The president's right to involve the country in the Korean and Vietnam wars without a declaration of war would seem to fly in the face of the war-making powers given to Congress by the Constitution. Yet without a challenge by the courts and Congress (until recently), the president's interpretation of the Constitution stood.

Despite this shared role in changing the Constitution, the Supreme Court, by its constant interpretation and reinterpretation of the Constitution through its rulings, breathes life into two-hundred-year-old words. A brief history of the Court will show how this has been done.

Early Years of the Court

The Supreme Court has undergone many changes in the nearly two hundred years it has existed. For its first fifty years or so, surprising as it seems today, there was little interest in the Court. No cases at all were brought to the Supreme Court in its first three years. Many leaders, such as

> **CHIEF JUSTICE JOHN MARSHALL**
> John Marshall, the fourth chief justice of the Supreme Court (1801–1835), was a conservative and a federalist. Although he only attended two months of law school, Marshall is often considered the Court's greatest chief justice. Two of the cases he presided over became landmarks. *Marbury* v. *Madison* (1803) established the principle of judicial review. *McCulloch* v. *Maryland* (1819) established the supremacy of the federal government within its constitutional limits, and in doing so confirmed the role of the Court in judging disputes between the states and the federal government.

Patrick Henry and Alexander Hamilton, refused appointments to serve as judges; and court sessions were held in such places as basement apartments.

Two landmark decisions greatly increased the influence of the court during its initial period. The first established *judicial review*, the power not only to declare acts and laws of any state and local government unconstitutional but also to strike down acts of any branch of the federal government. The second major decision established the principle of *national supremacy*, that the United States laws and Constitution are the supreme law of the land and the existence of states does not limit the powers of the national government.

Judicial Review and National Supremacy

The principle of judicial review was established in the case of *Marbury* v. *Madison* (1803) in which the Supreme Court invalidated an act of Congress for the first time. The case also illustrates how shrewd Chief Justice John Marshall was as a politician. Shortly before leaving office, President Adams (who had nominated Marshall to the Court) appointed a number of federal judges in order to maintain the influence of his party in the coming administration of his opponent, Thomas Jefferson. When Jefferson took office, he discovered that one of the commissions, that of William Marbury, had not actually been delivered. Jefferson ordered his secretary of state, James Madison, to hold it up. Under a section of the Judiciary Act of 1789, Marbury sued in the Supreme Court to compel the delivery of the commission. Marshall was then confronted with deciding a case between his political allies and his enemy, Jefferson, who was not only president but also intent on undercutting the power of the conservative Supreme Court. What Marshall did was to dismiss Marbury's case, ruling that the section of the Judiciary Act under which he had sued was unconstitutional (the Act allowed the Supreme Court original jurisdiction in a case not mentioned by the Constitution). By doing this he clearly asserted that the Supreme Court, on the basis of *its* interpretation of the Constitution, could set limits on the actions of Congress. The Court also supported Jefferson's argument that he did not have to deliver the commission. How could the president object?

Another early decision established clearly that states could not interfere with the functioning of the federal gov-

---

ON JUDICIAL REVIEW: JEFFERSON VS. MADISON
"Why should an undemocratically constituted body of nine elitists, who are not responsible to the people via the ballot box, be accorded the overriding power to strike down what the people want? Is not Congress, and is not the Executive equally capable of judging and interpreting the constitutionality of a proposed measure or course of action? Are they not equally devoted to the principles of government under law?"
— Henry J. Abraham, on Jefferson's views, *The Judiciary*, 3d ed. (Boston: Allyn & Bacon, 1973), p. 128.

"Judiciary is truly the only defensive armor of the Federal Government, or rather for the Constitution and laws of the United States. Strip it of that armor and the door is wide open for nullification, anarchy, and convulsion." — James Madison, ibid., p. 129.

ernment. In this case, *McCulloch* v. *Maryland* (1819), the state of Maryland attempted to tax the Baltimore branch of the unpopular Bank of the United States, established by the federal government. Chief Justice John Marshall, speaking for a unanimous court, ruled that the federal government "... though limited in its powers, is supreme within its sphere of action." He also found that although the Constitution did not specifically allow Congress to create a bank, Article I, Section 8, gave Congress the power to make all laws "necessary and proper" for carrying out its authority. This statement of *implied powers* based on this clause was to be used later in broadly expanding the duties that Congress could undertake.

Then in 1857 came the famous *Dred Scott* case (*Dred Scott* v. *Sanford*). Here the Court ruled that a slave, Dred Scott, was not automatically free merely because his owner had taken him to a state not allowing slavery. Congress, the Court said, had no right to interfere with property rights guaranteed by the Constitution. The Court went on to say that the *Missouri Compromise* (1820), which had attempted to resolve the slavery issue by dividing the new western territories into slave and free parts, was invalid. In terms of constitutional development, this unpopular decision was the first time an act of Congress of any great importance was struck down by the Courts. As such, the *Dred Scott* case marked a critical expansion of judicial powers.

The Court since the Civil War

The end of the Civil War was also the end of the major political conflict which had dominated the first seventy-five years of the republic — *states rights* versus *federal powers*. With unity achieved, rapid national growth began. The resulting economic expansion, and the unrestrained growth of giant monopolies, created a new demand for government regulation of the economy. The Supreme Court became more active, and judicial power was greatly enlarged. In just nine years (1864–73), ten acts of Congress were struck down, as opposed to only two acts in the previous seventy-four years.

Not only was the Court more active, it was also more conservative. In the view of many, the Court became an instrument for protecting the property rights of the rich and ignoring popular demands for government regulation.

In the twentieth century, the Court began to find itself up against the growing power of the executive branch. The presidency was widely felt to be the most effective place in the government to regulate the social and economic changes brought about by the post–Civil War industrialization. But the Supreme Court continued to resist the expansion of state and federal regulatory power, even though much of the legislation it struck down (such as minimum wage and child labor laws) was demanded by the American people. Between 1890 and 1936, the Court declared forty-six laws unconstitutional in full or in part.

It was President Franklin D. Roosevelt who caused the Court's policy to change. He countered the Court's opposition to his New Deal measures with a threat to pack the Court with new judges of his own choosing, the so-called *court-packing* bill. Although Roosevelt's plan was unsuccessful and aroused a storm of public and congressional opposition, in 1937 the Court nevertheless backed down and turned away from the arena of economic policy making.

The Modern Court

Since 1937, Supreme Court decisions have shown three major trends. First, the Court has invalidated much less federal legislation than in the previous fifty years. Since 1936 only a handful of federal laws have been held unconstitutional, and in most of these cases the legislation struck down was not very significant. In a second area, the Court has avoided protecting private property rights. Generally the Court in the present era has not been greatly concerned with guarding economic interests from government policy making.

A third area, one in which the Court has shown more positive interest, is increased judicial protection for civil liberties. While reducing property rights in importance, the Court has sought to preserve and protect the rights of individuals against the increased powers of the government. First Amendment freedoms of speech, press, religion, and assembly have been developed and expanded by recent Supreme Courts. With Earl Warren as chief justice (1953–69), the Supreme Court moved in areas of reapportionment, racial discrimination, and the rights of defendants in criminal cases.

In decisions dealing with *reapportionment,* beginning with *Baker* v. *Carr* (1962), the Warren Court established the principle of "one man, one vote" for election districts. The Court ruled that districts should be drawn based on equality of population so that each citizen's vote would count as much as another's. In moving to eliminate *racial discrimination,* the Court has been a leading force in cutting away racism in schooling, voting, housing, and the use of public facilities.

A third major concern of the Warren Court's decisions, the rights of criminal defendants, has seen the Court throw the protection of the Bill of Rights around people accused of crimes by state and federal authorities. The Court has insisted on an impoverished defendant's basic right to a lawyer; declared that illegally seized evidence can not be used in criminal trials; and held that a suspect must be advised of his or her constitutional right to silence, and to have a lawyer, before questioning. This last area summed up as the *Miranda decision* (*Miranda* v. *Arizona,* 1966) is familiar to all fans of TV detective series.

The Supreme Court under Warren Burger, appointed chief justice by President Nixon in 1969, has been less activist than the Warren Court but not as conservative as some had expected. On the liberal side, the Burger Court has legalized abortions except in the last ten weeks of pregnancy, declined to stop publication of the Pentagon Papers, and severely limited capital punishment. The Burger Court has also outlawed wiretapping of domestic groups without a court warrant and declined to interfere with massive busing designed to integrate schools in cities like Boston and Los Angeles.

This is not the whole story of the Burger Court. In more conservative directions, the Court has allowed local communities, within certain limits, to define obscenity and ban those works considered pornographic. It has also been rather sympathetic to states' rights, as shown when it struck down a 1974 law extending federal minimum wage standards to millions of state and local government employees. Perhaps the most important changes the Burger Court has made in the precedents set under Chief Justice Warren are in the area of the rights of the accused. Here the Court has allowed the police broader powers in searching without a warrant — deciding, for example, that persons detained on minor charges (like traffic violations) may be searched for evidence of more serious crimes (like drugs). The Court has also permitted some illegally obtained information to be used at a trial and the police to continue their questioning after a suspect has claimed the right of silence. The Miranda decision still remains partly in effect.

PRESIDENTS AND THE COURT

Supreme Court justices have a way of disappointing the president appointing them. President Eisenhower was so angered at Chief Justice Earl Warren's rulings that he called Warren's appointment "the biggest damn-fool mistake I ever made." The controversy set off by the Warren Court's activism led President Nixon to appoint Warren Burger as chief justice to replace Earl Warren when he retired in 1969. Nixon hoped Burger would inspire greater judicial restraint in the Court. But President Nixon was certainly not pleased by the Burger Court's rulings making laws against abortion unconstitutional and ordering Nixon to give up the notorious White House tapes to the special Watergate prosecutor.

Many of these rulings by the Warren and Burger Courts have aroused fierce opposition. But much of today's widespread concern with human rights may have started with the decisions of this supposedly most conservative of American political institutions — the Supreme Court.

The Court as a Political Player

This brief history should make it clear that the Supreme Court is a *political institution* that sets national policy by interpreting the law. In applying the Constitution to the cases before it, the Court clearly makes political choices. In arriving at decisions on controversial questions of national policy, the Court is acting in the political game. The procedures may be legal, the decisions may be phrased in lawyers' language, but to view the Court solely as a legal institution is to ignore its important political role.

"We are under the Constitution, but the Constitution is what the judges say it is," declared former Chief Justice Charles Evans Hughes. In interpreting the meaning of the Constitution, each Supreme Court must operate within the political climate of its time. Clearly the judges not only read the Constitution, they read the newspaper as well. The Court has no armies and must rely on the executive branch to enforce its rulings. The Court cannot ignore the reaction to its decisions in Congress or in the nation, because, as a political player, its influence ultimately rests on the acceptance of these decisions by the other political players and public opinion. Nor, generally, are the Court's opinions long out of line with the dominant views in the legislative and executive branches.

Judicial Activism versus Judicial Restraint

The question of how the political and legal power of the Court should be applied has centered on the use of judicial review. Should judicial authority be active or restrained? How far should the Court go in shaping policy when it may conflict with other branches of the government? The two sides of this debate are reflected in the competing practices of *judicial activism* and *judicial restraint.*

Judicial restraint is the idea that the Court should not impose its views on other branches of the government or the states unless there is a clear violation of the Constitution. Judicial restraint (often called self-restraint) calls for a passive role in which the Court lets the other branches of the government lead the way in setting policy on controversial political issues. The Court intervenes in these issues only with great reluctance. Felix Frankfurter and Oliver Wendell Holmes, Jr., are two of the more famous justices of the Supreme Court identified with judicial restraint. Frankfurter often argued that social improvement should be left to more appropriate parts of the federal and state government. The Court, he declared, should avoid conflicts with other branches of the federal government whenever possible.

Judicial activism is the view that the Supreme Court should be an active, creative partner with the legislative and executive branches in shaping government policy. Judicial activists seek to apply the Court's authority to solving economic and political problems ignored by other parts of the government. In this view the Court is more than an umpire of the American political game: It is an active participant as well. The Supreme Court under Earl Warren for the most part practiced judicial activism. In its rulings on reapportionment, school desegregation, and the right to counsel, the Warren Court broadly and boldly changed national policy.

It is important not to confuse judicial activism versus restraint with liberal versus conservative. Although most of the recent activist justices, such as Earl Warren and Thurgood Marshall, have taken liberal positions on issues like school integration and toleration of dissent, this wasn't always so. John Marshall's court was both activist (in establishing judicial review) and conservative (in protecting private property rights). And it was the activist, *conservative*

Supreme Court during the 1930s that attempted to strike down most of Franklin D. Roosevelt's New Deal program as unconstitutional. On the other side, justices Frankfurter and Holmes were political liberals. Yet both believed it was not wise for the Court to dive into the midst of political battles to support policies they may have personally backed.

Case Study: Separate But Equal?

An example of the Supreme Court's role as a political player is the evolution of the "separate but equal" doctrine. In first approving this doctrine of racial segregation in the late nineteenth century and later abolishing it in the mid-twentieth century, the Court played a central role in establishing the national policy that governed relations between the races. The changing but always powerful position of the judiciary in the history of racial segregation shows how influential the Court's political role can be.

The Political Background of Segregation

The end of the Civil War and the emancipation of the slaves did not give blacks the full rights of citizenship. Nor did the passing of the Thirteenth Amendment in 1865 (which outlawed slavery), or the Fourteenth Amendment in 1868 (which extended "equal protection of the laws" to all citizens), or the Fifteenth Amendment in 1870 (which guaranteed the right to vote to all citizens regardless of "race, color, or previous condition of servitude").

Between 1866 and 1877 the "radical Republicans" controlled Congress. "Reconstruction" governments were established in the South to put through reforms in the former Confederate states, and also to bring in votes for the Republicans. Although the rather corrupt period of Reconstruction partly deserves the bad name it has gotten in the South, it was a time when blacks won a number of both civil and political rights. The radical Congress passed five civil rights and Reconstruction acts aimed at granting blacks immediate equality and preventing states from curbing these rights.

Then in 1875 Congress passed a civil rights act designed to prevent any public form of discrimination — in theatres, restaurants, transportation, and the like — against blacks. Congress's right to forbid a *state* to act contrary to the Constitution was unquestioned. But this law, based on the Fourteenth Amendment, assumed that Congress could also prevent racial discrimination by private individuals.

The Supreme Court disagreed. In 1883 it declared the Civil Rights Act of 1875 unconstitutional. The majority of the Court ruled that Congress could only pass legislation to correct *states'* violations of the Fourteenth Amendment. Congress had no power to enact "primary and direct" legislation on individuals; that was left to the states. This decision meant the federal government could not lawfully protect blacks against most forms of discrimination. In other words, white supremacy was beyond federal control.

With this blessing from the Supreme Court, the southern states passed a series of laws restricting the freedom of black people. The so-called *Jim Crow laws* included all-white primary elections, elaborate tests to qualify for voting, and other laws and customs legitimizing segregation. When in 1877 the radicals lost control of Congress, the Reconstruction Era had come to an end. White southern political power in Congress increased, which meant that most of the post–Civil War civil rights laws were gradually removed.

Separate But Equal

Segregation was given judicial approval in the landmark case of *Plessy* v. *Ferguson* (1896). Here the Court upheld a Louisiana law requiring railroads to provide separate cars for the two races. The Court declared that segregation had nothing to do with the superiority of the white race, and that segregation was not contrary to the Fourteenth Amendment as long as the facilities were equal. The doctrine of "separate but equal" in *Plessy* v. *Ferguson* became the law of the land.

In approving segregation and establishing the "separate but equal" doctrine, the Court was undoubtedly reflecting the temper of the time. To restore the South to the union, the new Congresses were willing to undo the radicals' efforts to protect blacks. It was the southern black who paid the price — exile halfway between slavery and freedom. And just as the Court was unwilling to prevent these violations of civil rights, so too were the executive and legislative branches.

Can Separate Be Equal?

Plessy v. *Ferguson* helped racial segregation continue as a southern tradition. For some forty years the "separate but equal" doctrine was not seriously challenged. "Separate" was strictly enforced; "equal" was not. Schools, government services, and other public facilities for blacks were clearly separate from tax-supported white facilities, but just as clearly inferior to them. One can argue that the Court did not even support its own doctrine during this period.

HARLAN'S OPINION ON *PLESSY* V. *FERGUSON*
Justice John M. Harlan, dissenting in the Plessy case (1896), wrote prophetically.
"The destinies of the two races in this country are indissolubly linked together, and the interests of both require that the common government of all shall not permit the seeds of race hate to be planted under the sanction of law. What can more certainly arouse hate, what more certainly create and perpetuate a feeling of distrust between these races than state enactments which in fact proceed on the ground that colored citizens are so inferior and degraded that they cannot be allowed to sit in public coaches occupied by white citizens."
— *Plessy* v. *Ferguson* 163 U.S. 537 (1896).

By the late 1930s, the Court began to look more closely at so-called equal facilities. In *Missouri ex. rel. Gaines* v. *Canada* (1938), the Court held that since the state did not have a law school for blacks it must admit them to the white law school. Missouri's practice of paying the tuition of black law students at law schools in other states did not provide equal treatment for residents of the same state, the Court ruled. In *Sweatt* v. *Painter* (1950), a black (Sweatt) was denied admission to the University of Texas Law School on the grounds that Texas was building a law school for blacks. The Court carefully compared the facilities of the existing law school with those of the one being built. The Court found the new school would in no way be equal to the white one and ordered Sweatt admitted to the existing school. In other important rulings in the 1940s, the Court outlawed racial discrimination in political primaries and refused to uphold contracts with racial or religious restrictions.

Thus the Plessy doctrine of "separate but equal" was increasingly weakened by judicial decisions. By stressing the "equal" part of the doctrine, the Court was in fact making the doctrine impractical. (Texas was not likely to build a law school for blacks equal to its white one.) These decisions also reflected the Court's change in emphasis after 1937 from making economic policy to more fully protecting individual rights.

Still, the Court did not overrule Plessy in this period. The Court was following precedent, a policy often called *stare decisis* ("to stand by the decisions"). Stare decisis is a common practice in which a court follows previous decisions made by other courts in cases involving the same issue.

We have noted that Supreme Court rulings tend to reflect the temper of the time. Paralleling the rulings of the Court in this case were the actions of the executive branch and some northern states that were increasingly critical of racial segregation. In 1941 Roosevelt issued an executive order forbidding discrimination in government employment, and in 1948 Truman abolished segregation in the army. By 1953 eight northern states had passed fair-employment laws outlawing racial discrimination in hiring. In contrast to these developments, Congress, dominated by a conservative-oriented seniority system and blocked by southern filibusters, was unable to pass a number of civil rights measures which came before it. Nonetheless, political attitudes toward segregation in the public at large were changing, and the Supreme Court's rulings were reflecting that change.

The End of Separate but Equal

In 1954 the Supreme Court finally reversed *Plessy* v. *Ferguson* in *Brown* v. *Board of Education.* Here the Court held that segregated public schools violated the "equal protection of the laws" guaranteed in the Fourteenth Amendment. "Separate but equal" had no place in public education, the Court declared. Drawing on sociological and psychological studies of the harm done to black children by segregation, the Warren Court's unanimous decision stated that in fact separate was "inherently unequal." This was the beginning of the end of *legal segregation.*

The Court backed up its new equal protection stand in other areas besides education. In the years following the *Brown* decision, it outlawed segregation in interstate transportation, upheld legislation guaranteeing voting rights for blacks, reversed convictions of civil rights leaders, and often protected civil rights demonstrations by court order. These decisions, though they stirred up opposition to the Court (including demands to impeach Earl Warren), helped a larger political movement apply pressures to wipe out racial discrimination. The NAACP's Legal Defense Fund was very active in these cases, which shows how results sometimes can be gotten from one part of government (the courts) if another part (the Congress) is unwilling to act.

Congress finally joined in by passing civil rights acts in 1957, 1960, and 1964. The 1964 act, coming after continuing pressure and agitation by blacks, was the first comprehensive legislation of its kind since 1875. The act prohibited discrimination in those public accommodations (hotels, restaurants, gas stations) involved in interstate commerce, and in most businesses, and more strictly enforced equal voting rights for blacks. The 1964 act also gave the attorney general the power to start desegregation suits, an important provision that was later removed by southern pressure.

In most of these areas the Court acted both to encourage and to force all levels of the government — federal, state,

---

THE BAKKE CASE

"It is far too late to argue that the guarantee of equal protection to all persons permits the recognition of special wards entitled to . . . protection greater than that accorded others."
— Justice Lewis F. Powell, Jr.

"The dream of America as the great melting pot has not been realized for the Negro; because of his skin color he never even made it into the pot." — Justice Thurgood Marshall

On June 28, 1978 the Supreme Court ruled on the controversial "reverse discrimination" Bakke case (*Regents of the University of California* v. *Bakke*). Allan Bakke, a white engineer, had charged that he was denied admission to medical school, while minority applicants less qualified than he were admitted because a quota of places had been set aside for them. Bakke challenged the University's affirmative action program as a violation of his constitutional right under the Fourteenth Amendment to equal protection of the laws.

In a complicated 5-4 ruling with many justices giving separate opinions the Court ordered the University to admit Bakke. The Court ruled that universities may not establish a quota for minorities denying whites the opportunity to compete for those places. However, the Court held, the Constitution does allow race to be considered as one of the factors in deciding who is to be accepted and who rejected. In other words, the Court seemed to say, strict quotas are unconstitutional, while affirmative action programs encouraging groups that have suffered from past discrimination are allowed. The divisions within the Court and the public controversy surrounding the case, make it clear that the Bakke ruling is far from the last word on government policies on race.

and local — as well as the private sector, to move toward full equality. The Court's support of busing to end segregation of schools caused by housing patterns has aroused opposition in northern cities like Boston. Affirmative action programs, requiring institutions to recruit minorities and women, also have produced conflict as shown by the Bakke case.

Yet white racism and black subordination remain. And for this the Supreme Court as well as the rest of the political system must share some responsibility. For it was the Supreme Court that struck down civil rights acts of the Reconstruction Era, and that failed to protect the rights of black people between 1883 and 1937 when they were most trampled on. And it was the Court that made "separate but equal" the legal justification for white supremacy and refused for far too long to reverse it. The Court's effort in the late 1950s to put equal rights before the eyes of the nation was in many ways merely an undoing of its past mistakes.

Throughout this history of the "separate but equal" doctrine, the Court has acted politically as well as morally. At times the Court held back efforts at social and political reform; at other times it confused the efforts; and at still others it forced political and social changes more rapidly than some would have preferred. Most recently the Court has stood as the one part of the government most responsive to the arguments of dissenters and minorities. Yet as the history of "separate but equal" makes clear, whether the Court's stand appears moral or immoral to us, it is never removed too far or for too long from the positions dominating the political game as a whole.

STRENGTHS AND WEAKNESSES OF THE SUPREME COURT

The United States Supreme Court has been often called "the least dangerous branch of government." Despite its great power of judicial review, the Court is clearly the weakest of the three branches. It must depend on the other parts of the government to enforce its decisions. Its authority to cancel actions of the other branches of the federal government is in fact seldom used and strictly limited. These limits are found both within the Court and in the political system as a whole.

Internal Limits on the Court

Most of the limits on the power of the Court are found within the judicial system, in the traditional practices of the Court. For one thing, a long-held interpretation of the Constitution requires that an *actual case* be presented to the Court for it to exercise judicial review. The Court cannot take the lead in declaring laws unconstitutional. It cannot give advisory opinions. It must wait for a real controversy brought by someone actually injured by the law to make its way through the lower courts. This means that years may pass after a law is put on the books before the Court can rule on it. (The Supreme Court's *Dred Scott* decision struck down the Missouri Compromise passed thirty-seven years before.)

Another important limit on the Court's actions is the practice that the Court will not attempt to resolve *political questions.* A political question is an issue on which the Constitution or laws give final say to another branch of government, or one the Court feels it lacks the capability to solve. Political questions often crop up in the field of foreign relations. The justices of the Court lack important secret information; they are not experts in diplomacy; and they recognize the dominance of the presidency over the conduct of foreign affairs. Consequently the Court has generally rejected attempts to involve it in resolving disputes such as those over the Vietnam War.

The Court has narrowed or expanded its definition of a political question at various times. For example, the Court used this doctrine of political questions for many years as grounds for refusing to consider reapportionment of state legislatures and congressional districts. However, in 1962 the Court reversed its position and forced state legislatures to draw boundaries to create districts with more equal populations. A political question, then, can be whatever the Supreme Court says it is.

Just as the Court attempts to avoid political questions, so it often *avoids constitutional issues.* The Court will not decide a case on the basis of a constitutional question unless there is no other way to dispose of the case. The Court usually will not declare a law unconstitutional unless it clearly violates the Constitution. In general, the Court will assume that a law is valid unless proved otherwise. Al-

---

THE SUPREME COURT AND OBSCENITY

"The Justices take their obligation to research opinions so seriously that in one area of law — obscenity — the result has led to a lot of snickering both on and off the bench. Since 1957, the Court has tried repeatedly to define obscenity. The subject has become so familiar at the Supreme Court building that a screening room has been set up in the basement for the Justices and their clerks to watch the dirty movies submitted as exhibits in obscenity cases. Justice Douglas never goes to the dirty movies because he thinks all expression — obscene or not — is protected by the First Amendment. And Chief Justice Burger rarely, if ever, goes because he is offended by the stuff. But everyone else shows up from time to time.

"Justice Blackmun watches in what clerks describe as 'a near-catatonic state.' Justice Marshall usually laughs his way through it all.... The late Justice Harlan used dutifully to attend the Court's porno flicks even though he was virtually blind; Justice Stewart would sit next to Harlan and narrate for him, explaining what was going on in each scene. Once every few minutes, Harlan would exclaim in his proper way, 'By George, extraordinary!' " — Nina Totenberg, "Behind the Marble, Beneath the Robes," *The New York Times Magazine* (March 16, 1975), p. 66.

though we have stressed the role of the Court in applying the Constitution, it is important to remember that the vast majority of cases it decides deal with the interpretation of less important federal and state laws.

A final internal limit on the Court is that of *precedent* and *stare decisis*. As we have seen, the Court generally follows previous Court decisions in cases involving the same issue. However, the Court has reversed past decisions in a number of cases.

What these and the other limits on the Court's power mean is that the Court actually avoids most of the constitutional questions pressed upon it. Both for political and legal reasons the Court will often duck an issue that is too controversial, on which the law is uncertain or no political consensus has formed. It may simply not hear the case, or it may decide it for reasons other than the major issue involved. Knowing the difficulty of enforcing a ruling against strong public opinion, the Court seeks to avoid such a confrontation. This may make the use of judicial review scattered and often long delayed. But one can argue that the Court has maintained its great authority by refusing in most instances to use its power of judicial review.

External Limits on the Court

The Court is also limited by the duties the Constitution gives to other parts of the government, especially to Congress. Congress has the right to set when and how often the Court will meet, to establish the number of justices, and to limit the Court's jurisdiction. This last power frequently has been used to keep the Court out of areas in which Congress wished to avoid judicial involvement. For example, the bill establishing the Alaska pipeline excluded the Court from exercising jurisdiction (on possible damage to the environment) under the Environmental Protection Act. Also Congress may pass legislation so detailed that it limits the Court's scope in interpreting the law. Finally, the Senate has

the duty of approving the president's nominations to the bench, and Congress has the seldom-used power to impeach Supreme Court justices.

These limits on the Court reflect the very real weaknesses of that body. With no army or bureaucracy to enforce its decisions, the Court must depend on other parts of the government and all the political players to accept and carry out its decisions. (President Andrew Jackson, violently disagreeing with a Supreme Court decision, once remarked: "John Marshall has rendered his decision; now let him enforce it!") Yet with few exceptions, the Court's decisions have been enforced and accepted. And when opposed, this weak and semi-isolated branch of government has been able to overcome resistance. Why?

Strengths of the Court

The major political strengths of the Court lie in its enormous prestige; the fragmented nature of the American constitutional structure; and the American legal profession, which acts in many ways as the Court's constituency.

The Court's *prestige* is unquestionable. Public opinion polls have shown repeatedly that the position of a judge is one of the most respected in our society. This is due not only to the generally high quality of the people who become judges, but to the judicial process itself. Anyone who has seen a court in action is aware of the aspects of theatre in the legal process: the judge sitting on a raised platform dressed in robes; the formal speeches addressed to "your honor"; the use of Latin phrases; the oath on the Bible. All create a heavy impression of dignity and solemnity which often masks the fact that a judge is simply a public administrator judging controversies. The Supreme Court, which presides over this judicial system, has added prestige because it is seen as the guardian of the Constitution and often is equated with that document in people's eyes.

Another strength of the Court lies in the *fragmented nature of the American system of government.* With separation of powers dividing up power among the branches of the federal government, and federalism dividing power between the states and federal government, conflict is inevitable. This creates a need for an umpire, and the Court largely fills this role.

However, in acting as an umpire the Court is hardly neutral. Its decisions are political (they determine who gets what, when, and how), and to enforce them it needs political support. The other political players might not give this support to decisions they strongly disagree with. Consequently, the Court's rulings generally reflect the practices and values of the country's dominant political forces. As an umpire the Court enforces the constitutional rules of the game as practiced by the political game's most powerful players, of which it is also one.

A final source of support for the Court is the *legal profession*. There are over 300,000 lawyers in the United States. Although this is less than 0.5 percent of the work force, lawyers occupy all of the major judicial positions and more than fifty percent of the executive and legislative offices in the national, state, and city governments. The American Bar Association (ABA), with about half the lawyers in the country as members, represents the legal profession. The ABA reviews nominees to the bench, and its comments on a candidate's fitness have a great deal of influence on whether he or she is appointed. The legal profession through the ABA has generally supported the Court. For example, it opposed bills to curb the Court for its liberal civil liberties decisions. Because of their own commitment to law, as well as some similarity in educational and social backgrounds, members of the legal community generally back the Court.

WRAP-UP

The federal court system consists of United States district courts, courts of appeals, special federal courts, and the

United States Supreme Court. Although very few of the cases tried in the United States ever reach the Supreme Court, it has a unique position as the "final authority" over what the Constitution means. Yet the Court's decisions often are changed over the years, usually by the Court itself, in part reflecting the changing political climate. Our brief history of the Court showed this, as did the case study of "separate but equal," where the Court first allowed racial segregation and then gradually reversed its position.

The practices of judical activism and judicial restraint are two sides of the debate over how far the political involvement of the Court should go. The Court is limited by a number of its own practices and, most importantly, by its dependence on other parts of the government to enforce its decisions. The Court's respect for these limits as well as its own great prestige have given it the strength to overcome most resistance. In recent years there have been frequent calls for reforms of the Court. Critics of its decisions on civil liberties and desegregation have attempted to restrict the Court's involvement in these areas. All the attempts have run up against solid support for the Court and have failed.

Secure within its limits and resting on its supports, the Supreme Court of the United States remains a unique political player. No other government in the world can boast of a long-held tradition which gives "nine old men," nonelected and serving for life, the duty of overturning the acts of popularly elected legislative and executive branches. Through this power of judicial review, the Court is deeply involved in influencing national policy, setting limits on how the political game is played, and bringing pressing social issues to the attention of the people and their leaders. Whether the Court continues to protect the rights of groups threatened by the most powerful players will depend on who the justices are and which political forces prevail in the country as a whole.

THOUGHT QUESTIONS

1. How is the Supreme Court protected from too much political pressure from the other political players? Why was it partly detached from the rest of the national government?
2. Is the Supreme Court too influenced or not influenced enough by the executive and legislative branches of government and by public opinion?
3. Do the courts, rather than popularly elected officials of the government, generally appear to be more interested in defending constitutional rights? If so, why?

SUGGESTED READINGS

Cox, Archibald. *The Role of the Supreme Court in American Government.* New York: Oxford, 1976. Pb.
   A brief scholarly treatment of the Supreme Court by a distinguished lawyer.
Epstein, Jason. *The Great Conspiracy Trial.* New York: Random House, 1970. Pb.
   A lively narrative of the antiwar "Chicago Seven."
Goulden, Joseph C. *The Million Dollar Lawyers.* New York: Putnam, 1978.
   These are behind-the-scenes stories of high-level lawyers involved in multimillion dollar cases, practicing the kind of law that was never taught in law school.
Lewis, Anthony. *Gideon's Trumpet.* New York: Vintage, 1966. Pb.
   A short, readable story that traces the development of a case from a Florida jail to the United States Supreme Court.
Simon, James F. *In His Own Image.* New York: McKay, 1973. Pb.
   A revealing account of the politics surrounding the Nixon nominations to the Supreme Court.
Woodward, C. Vann. *The Strange Career of Jim Crow.* 2d ed. Oxford: University Press, 1966. Pb.
   One of the best studies of segregation laws in the South.

Voters and Political Parties 6

Now that we have looked at the formal constitutional players in the political game, it's time to look at some important players who were not established by the Constitution. The next two chapters will examine voters, political parties, interest groups, and the media, to see what they do and how they influence American politics. A case study of an election at the end of the next chapter will bring all these players together in an actual game. This chapter will first look at voters — who they are, how they vote, and why many others don't. Then we will look at the political parties that organize voters and provide the link between them and the government. The history, the functions, the structures, and the consequences of our party system provide the bones of the story.

VOTERS

Who Votes?

The answer to "who votes?" may seem like an obvious one. Citizens who are eighteen years or older (because of the Twenty-sixth Amendment) and who have satisfied the residency requirements of their states *can* vote, but an increasing number of them do not. In the 1976 presidential election only fifty-five percent of the voting age population cast ballots (i.e., eighty-two million people voted and sixty-eight million did not). This figure, the lowest in almost thirty years of electing presidents (see Figure 6.1), is even lower in nonpresidential elections. In 1974, after the furor of Watergate, only thirty-nine percent of eligible voters turned up at the election booths. The questions grow. What influences whether people become voters? What influences how they vote? And what has led to the increasing numbers of people who don't vote?

Political Socialization

Political socialization provides part of an answer to how, or if, people participate in politics. *Political socialization is the process of learning political attitudes and behavior.* The gradual process of socialization takes place as we grow up in settings like the family and the schools. In the home children learn about participating in family decisions — for example, the more noise they make, the more chance they have of staying up late. Kids also learn which party their parents favor, how they generally view politics and politicians, and what are their basic values and outlook toward their country. Children of course don't always copy their parents' political leanings, but they are influenced by them. Most people, for example, stay with the party of their parents. Schools have a similar effect. Students salute the flag, obey their teacher, take civics courses, participate in student politics, and learn that democracy (us) is good and dictatorship (them) is bad.

People's social characteristics also have an influence on their participation in politics. Although it is difficult to weigh how important they are on each individual, whether a person is young or old, black or white, rich or poor, northerner or southerner will affect his or her political opinions and behavior. The views of a person's peer group (friends and neighbors), of political authorities ("The president knows what he's doing"), and of one's political party, influence how people vote as well.

An example of the influence of religion and ethnic background can be seen in most large cities where parties run "balanced tickets" with Irish, Italian, and Jewish candidates — and, more recently, blacks and women as well. Besides the well-known tendency for people to vote for "one of their

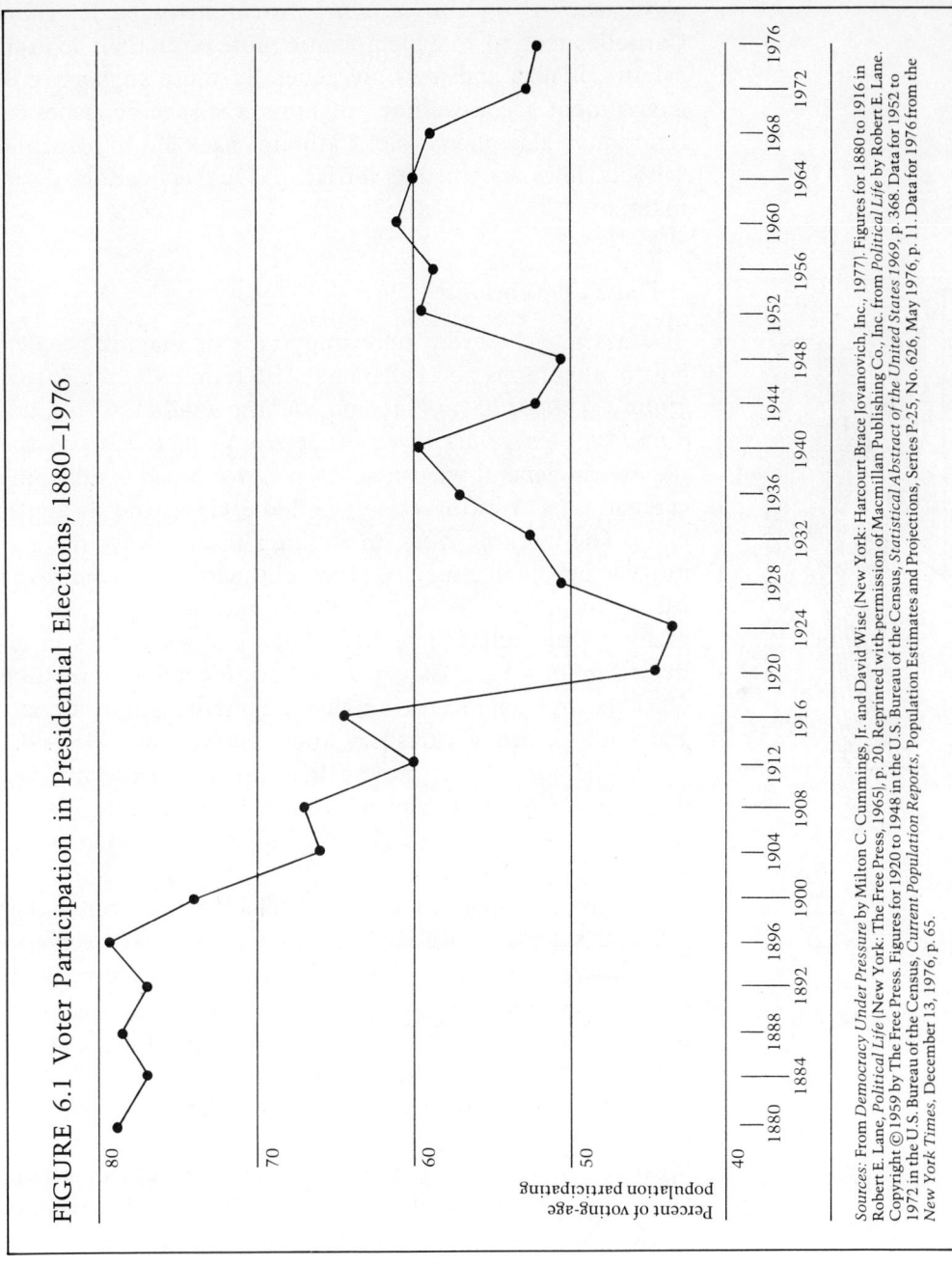

FIGURE 6.1 Voter Participation in Presidential Elections, 1880–1976

Sources: From *Democracy Under Pressure* by Milton C. Cummings, Jr. and David Wise (New York: Harcourt Brace Jovanovich, Inc., 1977). Figures for 1880 to 1916 in Robert E. Lane, *Political Life* (New York: The Free Press, 1965), p. 20. Reprinted with permission of Macmillan Publishing Co., Inc. from *Political Life* by Robert E. Lane. Copyright © 1959 by The Free Press. Figures for 1920 to 1948 in the U.S. Bureau of the Census, *Statistical Abstract of the United States 1969*, p. 368. Data for 1952 to 1972 in the U.S. Bureau of the Census, *Current Population Reports*, Population Estimates and Projections, Series P-25, No. 626, May 1976, p. 11. Data for 1976 from the *New York Times*, December 13, 1976, p. 65.

own," they also share certain political attitudes. Jews and Catholics tend to vote Democratic more often than do Protestants. Blacks and Jews are generally more supportive of government social-welfare programs. On specific issues religion may also play a role: Catholics back aid to parochial schools, Jews support jets for Israel, Quakers call for disarmament.

Class and Voting

Class may be even more important in shaping peoples' political opinions and behaviors. The term *class* refers to *a group's occupation and income, and the awareness this produces of their relations to other groups or classes in the society*. In general we can speak of three broad overlapping categories: a working class, a middle class, and an upper class. The *working class*, including almost always the majority of people in a society, receives the lowest incomes and fills "blue-collar" jobs in factories and farms, as well as many "white-collar" jobs like clerks and secretaries in offices. The *middle class* consists of most professionals (like teachers and engineers), small businessmen, bureaucrats, and some skilled workers (say, those earning over $15,000 a year). The *upper class* (often called the elite or ruling class) is composed of those who run our major economic and political institutions and receive the highest incomes for doing so.

At least as important as these "objective" categories that political scientists use are the "subjective" way people in these classes view their own position. Whether union members or teachers or housewives see themselves as members of the working class or middle class will also influence their political attitudes. An important fact about class in the U.S. is that class identification is quite weak. People either don't know what class they are in or don't think it's important. Most Americans see themselves as members of the middle class no matter what "objective" class they may be put into.

However class as reflected in income and occupation does

influence people's attitudes on a variety of issues. Studies have shown that people in the working class tend to be liberal in wanting greater economic equality and more social-welfare programs. This liberalism on economic issues contrasts strongly with their ideas on civil liberties. Here people of lower income and education tend to be intolerant of dissenters and not supportive of minority views and new styles of behavior (i.e., homosexual rights). Members of the middle class tend to be more conservative in their economic views and more liberal on issues such as free speech and respect for civil liberties. Class attitudes on political questions, then, tend to be both liberal and conservative depending on the type of issue.

The problem with figuring out how these various characteristics — race, class, religion — influence a person's political behavior is that so many of them overlap. For example, if we say that blacks are more likely not to vote than whites, are we sure that race is the key category? We also know that poorer people, those with less education, and those who feel they have less effect on their government also vote less. All these categories include the majority of blacks. But we don't know which is more important in influencing behavior. So even the "true" statement that blacks vote less may conceal as much as it reveals. We would also have to examine whether blacks with more income or education also vote less before we could conclude that race was a more important factor than, say, class.

Who Doesn't Vote?

The problems outlined above illustrate the difficulty of answering the question of why people increasingly don't vote. Studies have shown that nonvoters are most often from the less educated, nonwhite, rural, southern, female, poor, blue-collar, and very old or very young segments of the American population. Voters most often come from the white, middle-aged, male, college educated, city or suburban, affluent, white-collar groups. These are only broad tendencies, with a great many exceptions in each case. However, one result of these tendencies is a middle- and upper-class bias in voting. Another consequence is that although many more Americans are registered Democrats than Republicans, Republicans tend to vote in higher percentages, thus lessening their disadvantage.

There are some other things, gathered from various opinion polls, of which we are sure. (1) Americans, in general, are poorly informed about politics. Surveys have shown that only about half the voters know the name of their representative in Congress and only twenty percent know how he or she has voted on major bills. (2) Distrust of government and dissatisfaction with its leaders has grown in recent years. For example, in 1958 only eighteen percent of the public agreed with the statement that the government is run for the benefit of the few. Fifteen years later, sixty-seven per-

---

ON VOTING

"The existence of the vote does not make politicians better as individuals; it simply forces them to give greater consideration to demands of enfranchised and sizeable groups who hold a weapon of potentially great force.... The ability to punish politicians is probably the most important weapon available to citizens." — Gerard Pomper

"I never vote. It only encourages them." — a woman polled by CBS news

"Nobody will ever deprive the American people of the right to vote except the American people themselves." — Franklin D. Roosevelt

"Even *voting* for the right is *doing* nothing for it." — Henry D. Thoreau

"We regard the man who takes no interest in politics not as harmless, but as useless." — Pericles

cent agreed with the statement. (3) People feel they have less influence on their government. In 1960 seventy-two percent felt that people have some say about what government does. By 1973 less than half of those surveyed felt this way.[1] There has, then, been an increasing dissatisfaction with and detachment from politics and government, as shown by peoples' decreasing voting.

Part of the reason for these trends undoubtedly lies in the turmoil of the late 1960s and early 1970s. Vietnam and Watergate, with the demonstrations and scandals they led to, stood as symbols of government bungling, corruption, and unresponsiveness. As more was revealed about how the government operated, from the Pentagon Papers to the Nixon tapes, less respect and confidence were given to political leaders. Politicians became the butt of TV jokes, and cynicism became an accepted approach to political analysis.

Another explanation for voter apathy goes back to the question of class. There is no doubt that members of the working class vote and participate the least in politics. One study found that in a recent presidential election sixty-eight percent of working people reported no activity (such as attending a meeting or wearing a campaign button). Only thirty-six percent of those identifying themselves as "upper middle class" said they had done nothing. Voting figures say the same thing. In 1976, forty-six percent of those with incomes below $5,000 voted, while seventy-seven percent with incomes above $25,000 voted.

There are a number of reasons for these class differences. The most obvious is that low-income people with immediate personal problems like finding a job or paying bills will be more likely to view politics as a luxury they can't afford. Class differences in political socialization also have an effect. Working-class children, whether because of their more rigidly structured families or because of the poor education they receive are brought up with a more passive view of politics ("You can't fight City Hall"), stressing harmony

---

[1] Data from University of Michigan Survey Research Center studies.

rather than conflict. They are led to believe that they can have little influence on politics. At the same time, because of the disadvantaged reality they and their parents face, they tend to have a not-so-favorable image of political leaders like the president. These children, then, end up being both more resentful and more passive toward politics. Middle and upper-class children have a higher regard for political leaders and are taught in their schools to value participation in politics. They are encouraged to participate and led to believe that the political system will respond favorably to their participation.

The political game itself is shaped to limit the participation of lower-income citizens. A belief in equality has always been central to American political thought. This myth of "a classless society" leads to class being downplayed as a basis for participating in, or even understanding, politics. The United States is the only developed democracy without a socialist or labor party to represent and organize the working class. As we will see later in the chapter, the two-party system that does exist tends to push both parties toward the moderate center in seeking support. The lower class, living in a society not recognizing class differences and not providing organizations to voice its interests, tends to have its issues ignored and is given little encouragement to participate politically. Of course, the less that low-income groups participate, the less they will find the political process responding to their interests, and vice versa. The way out of this vicious circle was pointed to by two leading scholars who studied political participation: "If there were more class-based ideologies, more class-based organizations, more explicit class-based appeal by political parties, the participation disparity between upper and lower-status citizens would very likely be less."[2]

From another viewpoint nonvoting can also be seen as representing a basic satisfaction with how things are going. Supposedly, if people were upset enough by a depression or

---

[2] Sidney Verba and Norman Nie, *Participation in America* (New York: Harper and Row, 1972), p. 340.

a war they would vote. This argument, however, assumes that people see voting as an effective means of changing things. As seen by the growth of nonvoting and of dislike of politicians, many people no longer hold out this hope. Nonvoting has become both a sign of apathy and protest toward what many view as an unresponsive political process.

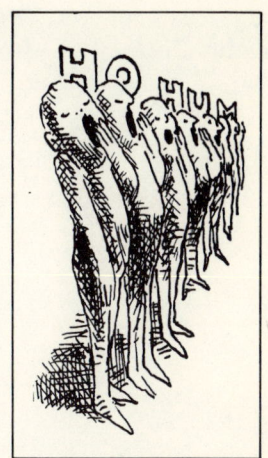

POLITICAL PARTIES

The major established structures for organizing people to determine the makeup of the government through elections are political parties. The history of their development in America, how they are structured to seek political power, and how well they do it, are the major themes for the rest of the chapter.

The national government, as we have seen, is based on a system of dividing or *decentralizing* power. Political parties, on the other hand, are a means or organizing or *centralizing* power. The framers of the Constitution decentralized power in separate branches and a federal system partly to avoid the development of powerful factions that could take over the government. This very decentralization of power, however, created the need for parties that could pull together or centralize that power.

A *political party* is an organization that runs candidates for public office under the party's name. Although the framers seemed more concerned with factions and interests than with parties, they were well aware of the probability that parties would soon develop. George Washington, in his famous farewell address, warned against "the baneful effects of the spirit of party." Nevertheless, the development of parties continued.

The Origin of Today's Parties

The *Federalists* and *Anti-Federalists*, the factions that supported and opposed the adoption of the Constitution, were not organized into actual political parties. They did not run candidates for office under party labels, but they were networks of communication and political activity struggling on opposite sides of a great dispute, ratification.

After the Constitution was ratified, the Federalist faction grew stronger and more like a political party. Led by Alexander Hamilton, secretary of the treasury under President George Washington, the Federalists championed a strong national government that would promote the financial interests of merchants and manufacturers. After Thomas Jefferson left President Washington's cabinet in 1793, an opposition party began to form under his leadership. The new *Democratic-Republican* party drew the support of small farmers, debtors, and others who did not benefit from the financial programs of the Federalists. Under the Democratic-Republican label, Jefferson won the presidential election of 1800, and his party continued to control the presidency until 1828. The Federalists, without power or popular support, gradually died out.

During this twenty-eight-year period of Democratic-Republican control, the party splintered into many factions. Two of these factions grew into new parties, the *Democrats* and the *Whigs* (first called the National Republicans). Thus our Democratic party, founded in 1828, is the oldest political party in the world. The early Democratic party was led by Andrew Jackson, who was elected president in 1828. It became known as the party of the common people. The Whigs, more like the old Federalists, were supported by the wealthier and more conservative classes in society: bankers, merchants, and big farmers.

In 1854, a *coalition* (a collection of groups that join together for a specific purpose) of Whigs, antislavery Democrats, and minor parties formed the *Republican* party. One of the common goals of the party supporters was to fight slavery. The Republicans nominated a "dark horse" (a political unknown), Abraham Lincoln, on the third ballot for president in 1860. The Democrats were so deeply divided over the slavery issue that the southern and northern wings of the party each nominated a candidate. Against this divided opposition, Lincoln won the election with less than a majority of the popular vote but more than any other candidate.

Maintaining, Deviating and Realigning Elections

The Democratic and Republican parties have dominated American politics for the past 120 years. Their relative strength, and the nature of their support, however, have shifted back and forth over time. We can see this shift by looking at three types of presidential elections: maintaining elections, deviating elections, and realigning elections. *Maintaining elections* keep party strength and support as they are. *Deviating elections* show a temporary shift in popular support for the parties, usually caused by the exceptional popular appeal of a particular candidate of the minority party. *Realigning elections* show a permanent shift in the popular base of support of the parties, and usually a shift in the relative strength of the parties so that the minority party emerges as the majority party.

Most presidential elections between 1860 and 1932 were maintaining elections. The Republicans kept the support of a majority of voters, and controlled the executive branch, for all but sixteen of those seventy-two years. When the Democrats did gain control of the presidency, they held office only for short periods. The two Democratic elections of Woodrow Wilson in 1912 and 1916, for example, were caused by temporary voter shifts, or deviations in party support, and splits within the Republican party.

The great social and economic impact of the Depression of the 1930s destroyed the majority support Republicans had enjoyed for so long, and caused a realignment in the two-party system. Under Franklin Delano Roosevelt, the Democrats became the majority party, and were known as the party of labor, the poor, minorities, urban residents, immigrants, eastern liberals, and the white South. Since 1952, however, the Republican party has gained substantial support in presidential elections among white voters in the once "solid South."

Some political analysts felt that Republican victories in

1968 and 1972 indicated a new realignment of voters. If this new realignment had taken place, it would have given the Republicans the support of the white South and the suburban middle classes, and would have made the Republican party the majority party. Despite these predictions, however, the Democrats maintained the support of the majority of voters in nonpresidential elections and won the presidency with the support of the South in 1976. With forty-six percent of the voters identifying themselves as Democrats, twenty-two percent as Republicans, and the rest as Independents in the 1976 election, it now looks like the 1968 and 1972 Republican presidential victories were deviating elections rather than realigning ones.

Tweedledee and Tweedledum?

Is there a real difference between the Republican party and the Democratic party? To answer this question we should look at both party image and party reality. The image of the parties is usually based on a stereotype of people who support the parties. A "typical" Republican is white, middle class, Protestant, has a college education, and lives in the suburbs. He or she supports big business, law and order, limited government intervention in the economy and in our private lives, and an "America first" policy in foreign affairs.

The "typical" Democrat is a member of a minority ethnic or racial group, working class, non-Protestant, and lives in an urban area. He or she supports social welfare measures to improve the status of the poor at home, government regulation of big business, more equal distribution of wealth and privilege, and an aggressive foreign policy. It is these differences in image that help support the commonly held myth that Republicans get us into depressions and Democrats get us into wars.

Of course, the reality is much more complex than the image. It has been found that leaders of the Democratic and Republican parties do disagree fairly consistently on major issues. But party followers (people who vote for the party but are not actively involved with the party in other ways) tend to be much more moderate than leaders on these issues. Democratic and Republican party followers, in fact, often agree more with each other than with their party leaders.

Another complicating factor in party differences is that each party is deeply divided within itself. The Democratic party includes, for example, liberal, black, urban, working-class supporters from the northern industrial cities, and conservative, white, wealthy planters from the South. The Republican party includes moderate-liberal business or professional people from the East, and small-town conservative shopkeepers or farmers from the Midwest.

One recent trend has been the increase of voters identifying with neither political party. These *independents* com-

---

ON PARTIES

"The spirit of party . . . serves always to distract the public councils and enfeeble the public administration. It agitates the community with ill-founded jealousies and false alarms; kindles the animosity of one part against another; foments occasionally riot and insurrection. . . ." — George Washington

"It should be stated flatly at the outset that this volume is devoted to the thesis that the political parties created democracy and that modern democracy is unthinkable save in terms of the parties." — E. E. Schattschneider

"Politics is as much a regular business as the grocery or the drygoods or the drug business." — George Washington Plunkitt

"When a leader is in the Democratic Party he's a boss; when he's in the Republican Party he's a leader." — Harry S Truman

"I don't belong to any organized political party. I'm a Democrat." — Will Rogers

pose about one-third of the voters, as opposed to one-fifth of the electorate twenty-five years ago. They also tend to be less well-informed and less active in politics than those voters belonging to a party. Since their opinions are more likely to change during elections, most presidential campaigns are aimed at holding onto the party base and winning over the independent voter. The rise of independents has led some analysts to predict the further decline of political parties. Despite the 1974 election of an independent governor in Maine, this trend has not yet developed.

PARTY FUNCTIONS

What do political parties do? Political parties throughout the world try to organize power in order to control the government. To do this, American political parties (1) contest elections, (2) organize public opinion, (3) bring interests together (often called *aggregating* interests), and (4) incorporate changes proposed by groups and individuals outside the party system and the government.

First, parties *contest elections.* This means that they organize in order to compete with other parties for electoral victory. To contest elections, parties or, more usually, their candidates *recruit* people into the political system to work on campaigns and run for office. Parties *provide people with a basis for making political choices.* In fact, most people vote for a particular candidate because of the party he or she belongs to. In addition, when parties contest elections, they must *express policy positions* on important issues. To some extent this serves to *educate* voters about the political process. Most people are not ordinarily involved in governmental politics. They often rely on electoral contests to keep them informed and active.

Second, parties organize *public opinion.* Despite the wide variety of opinion within them, parties give the public a limited channel of communication to express their desires about how government should operate. At the least, voters can approve the actions of the party that has been holding office by voting for it. Or they can show disapproval by voting for the opposition.

Third, the two major parties bring together or *aggregate various interests*. The Democratic and Republican parties aggregate the special interests of groups and individuals in society into large coalitions for the purpose of winning elections. Gathering special interests under the broad "umbrella" of a party label is an important function of American political parties.

Finally, the two major parties *incorporate changes* or reforms proposed by third parties or social protest movements. If third parties or political movements show that they have considerable support, their programs are often adopted, though usually in more moderate form, by one of the major parties. In the 1978 elections, for example, candidates of both parties supported tax cut referenda in response to the passage of Howard Jarvis' Proposition 13 in California.

VIEW FROM THE INSIDE: PARTY ORGANIZATIONS

American parties are weak organizations. They tend to be most formally organized on a local and state level, and become even weaker as they approach the national level. Powerless parties have not always been the rule in this country.

Historically, particularly in the last half of the nineteenth century, American parties at the local level were so rigidly organized that they were often called political *machines*. Party machines have a party *boss* (leader) who directly controls the political party workers at lower (usually city district or ward) levels. Local leaders obey the boss because he controls party nominations, patronage positions (jobs that can be given to loyal supporters), political favors, and party finances. Machines lost much of their leverage in the early twentieth century when three things happened: 1) local, state, and federal agencies took over distributing material benefits to the poor; 2) civil service reforms made most city jobs dependent on results of competitive examinations; and 3) direct primaries made competition for party nomination a contest anyone could enter.

American Party Structure

Today, we can picture American party structure as a pyramid. Local political organizations or clubs are at the bottom; county committees are above them; state committees are above the county; and the national committee of each party is at the top. Though the strength of the party is at the bottom in most localities the foundation is not very strong.

As a result of the welfare, civil service and primary reforms, most local party organizations have few goodies with which to maintain a strong organization. Local parties range from virtual disorganization to still powerful machines, with most parties falling closer to the pole of disorganization. In much of America, especially the rural areas, a handful of officials meet occasionally to carry out the essential affairs needed to keep the party alive. They are largely without influence, raise little money and create little public attention. The party comes alive only around elections to support a candidate who was generally selected by his or her own efforts. On the other end of the pole of organization, some party machines still exist. Until his death in 1976, Richard Daley, mayor of Chicago for over twenty years, kept firm control of a strong Democratic party machine. Daley's machine acted as an informal government and social service agency, meeting the immediate needs of urban citizens. This type of party organization, however, seems to be a leftover from the past.

State party organizations tend to be weaker than county or city organizations. State party committees run the party organization, but generally the state chairperson dominates party activity. In many cases the state governor is chairperson of his or her party. State party organizations have some patronage to distribute, and can give essential backing to candidates for state office.

National Party Organization

Between presidential elections, each party is governed by its *national committee*. The national committee consists of one man and one woman chosen from each state party organization. The committee is led by the *chairperson* who is chosen by the party's presidential nominee every four years. Most of the important work of the party, however, goes on at the *national convention* held every four years during the summer before the presidential election.

The national convention is attended by delegates chosen by the states in various ways. In 1976 the Republican convention had 2,257 delegate seats, and the Democratic convention had 3,008 delegate seats. The delegates to the convention adopt a party platform and elect the party's presidential nominee.

The *party platform* is actually written by a Platform Committee and then approved by the convention. It is generally a long document that states the party's position on many issues, and can be used as a basis for the party's electioneering. If the party is in power, the platform will boast of the party's achievements. If the party is out of power, the platform will criticize the policies of the other party. The platform will emphasize the party's differences with the other major party, and minimize the divisions within the party.

Frequently groups of convention delegates will organize into factions or *caucuses* in order to press for statements representing their minority political views to be included in the platform. In 1972, minority caucuses at the Democratic national convention pressed unsuccessfully for planks (parts of the platform) on abortion law reform, gay liberation, tax reform, and welfare rights.

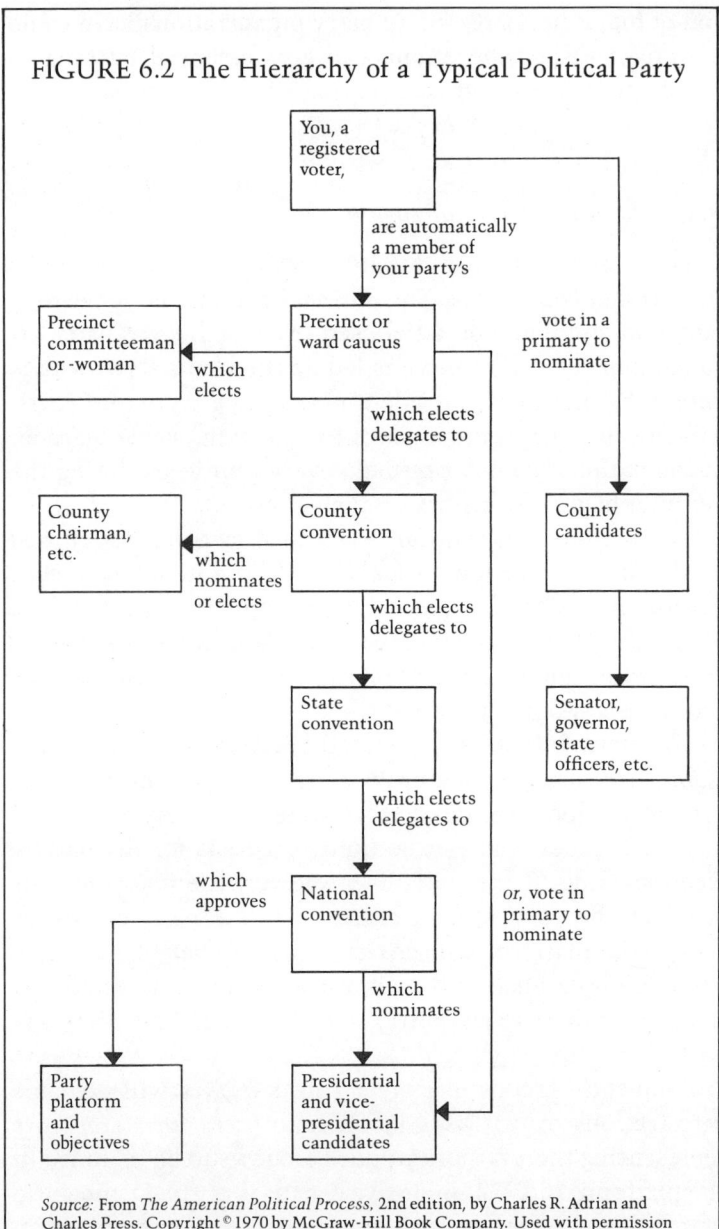

FIGURE 6.2 The Hierarchy of a Typical Political Party

Source: From *The American Political Process*, 2nd edition, by Charles R. Adrian and Charles Press. Copyright © 1970 by McGraw-Hill Book Company. Used with permission of McGraw-Hill Book Company. (Based on data from the Committee on Political Education, Labor and Politics, AFL-CIO, Washington, D.C., 1960.)

The high point of the convention comes when the delegates vote for the party's presidential nominee. Usually the candidates have been campaigning throughout the country to show their popularity with the voters and to influence convention delegates from each of the states to vote in their favor. Most states hold *presidential primaries* in which candidates from the same party run against each other, competing for popular support and for the right to send delegates pledged to their candidacy to the national convention. For the first few days of the convention, candidates and their campaign workers try to line up delegates who will support them.

Toward the end of the convention, the names of the candidates are placed in nomination, with nominating speeches by famous party figures. A roll-call vote of the delegates is then taken. Each state, in alphabetical order, announces the tally of its delegate votes. The final party nominee for the office of president is elected by a simple majority vote. In 1924, the Democratic convention took 103 ballots before it was able to reach a majority decision. Generally, however, the presidential nominee is chosen on the first ballot.

The presidential nominee chooses a vice presidential running mate who is then formally approved by the convention. Usually the main goal is to "balance the ticket." Jimmy Carter, a moderate WASP (white Anglo-Saxon Protestant) from the South, chose Walter Mondale, a more liberal senator from the Midwest, to be his running mate in 1976. Or the vice presidential nominee may be a well-known competitor of the presidential nominee, as was Lyndon Johnson when John F. Kennedy chose him in 1960. Sometimes he is a political unknown and therefore not going to offend anyone immediately as was Spiro Agnew when Nixon chose him in 1968.

The national convention is the starting point of the fall presidential campaign. Party workers and party supporters, their enthusiasm sparked by the convention proceedings, set out to make their party's nominee the winner of the presidential election in November.

VIEW FROM THE OUTSIDE: THE TWO-PARTY SYSTEM

In the United States we have a *two-party system* on the national level, meaning that two major parties dominate national politics. In a *one-party system*, a single party monopolizes the organization of power and the positions of authority. In a *multiparty system*, more than two political parties compete for power and authority.

From the Civil War until the election of Dwight David Eisenhower to the presidency in 1952, the eleven southern states of the Civil War Confederacy had virtually one-party systems. These states were so heavily Democratic that the Republicans were a permanent minority. The important electoral contests took place in the primaries, where blacks were systematically excluded. Multiparty systems have also existed in the United States. New York state, for example, has a four-party system today in which Democrats, Republicans, Liberals, and Conservatives compete in state and local elections. Nationally, however, the United States has a two-party system.

Causes of the Two-Party System

There are four main reasons for the continued dominance of two parties in America. The first is the *historic dualism* of American political conflict. The first major political division among Americans was dual, or two-sided, between Federalists and Anti-Federalists. It is said that this original two-sided political battle established the dual nature of political conflict in this country.

The second reason is the *moderate views of the American voter*. Americans may be moderate because their political party system forces them to choose between two moderate parties; or, American parties may be moderate because Americans do not want to make more extreme political choices. As with the chicken and the egg, it's tough to know which came first.

Third, the *structure of our electoral system* encourages two-party dominance. We elect one representative at a time from each district to Congress, which is called election by *single-member districts*. The winning candidate is the one who gets the most votes, or a *plurality*. (A majority of votes means more than fifty percent of the votes cast; a plurality simply means more votes than anyone else.) This system makes it difficult for minor party candidates to win elections, and without election victories minor parties tend to fade fast.

Many countries with multiparty systems elect representatives by *proportional representation*. That is, each district has more than one representative, and each party that receives a certain number of votes gets to send a proportionate number of representatives to the legislature. For example, in a single-member district, a minor party that received ten percent of the vote would not be able to send its candidate to Congress. In a multimember district the size of ten congressional districts, however, that ten percent of the vote would mean that one out of the ten representatives sent from the district would be a minor party member.

Finally, the Democratic and Republican parties continue to dominate national politics because they are flexible enough to *adopt some of the programs proposed by third parties*, and thus win over third-party supporters. The Socialist party in America, even during its strongest period, always had difficulty achieving national support partly because the Democratic party was able to *co-opt*, or win over, the support of most of organized labor with prolabor economic programs. The Republicans lured voters away from George Wallace's American Independent Party (AIP) by emphasizing law and order and deemphasizing civil rights in its 1968 presidential campaign.

Consequences of the Two-Party System

The moderate "umbrella" nature of our parties can be considered a plus or a minus. Our party system prevents the country from being *polarized,* or severely divided, by keeping factions with radical views from winning much power. But this also means that extreme dissenting opinions get little consideration by the voters. When a candidate does take a strong stand on issues, especially in a national election, he or she usually loses. The two most lopsided presidential elections in our history reflect this fact. Barry Goldwater, the conservative Republican candidate for president in 1964, and George McGovern, the liberal Democratic candidate for president in 1972, were both overwhelmingly defeated in their election campaigns.

As we discussed earlier, the two parties competing for national office must appeal to a majority of voters to win, and thus both parties tend to shy away from taking extreme positions. Parties and their candidates avoid being specific about programs they might enact when in office, for discussing specific programs will win the support of some voters, but lose the support of many others. When they need majority support, politicians try not to commit themselves to positions on controversial issues. Politicians whose party is out of power also realize that they have more to gain by simply attacking the party in power than by proposing alternative programs. All these factors mean that when it comes to taking a public stand, politicians often must talk a lot, but say as little as possible.

WRAP-UP

Voters are the broadest, most representative player in the political game. Directly or indirectly they legitimate how the government is run and choose who is to run it. There are many factors, like political socialization, party membership, religion, race, and class, which influence how people vote or even *if* they vote. The political game tends to discourage voting by the working class by deemphasizing class issues. The growth of nonvoting poses serious questions to the representative nature of government and the responsiveness of people to their government.

The political parties provide a major link between voters and their elected officials. Historically the parties have evolved into a two-party system with the Democrats and Republicans dominating elections for more than a century. The parties are weakly organized on a national level and generally have only slightly stronger local organizations. Through a process of primaries, nominating conventions, and election campaigns, they put their label on candidates for positions of national leadership. Both the party structure and the historical tone of American politics lead to moderate positions by the competing parties and, some contend, little difference between the two.

Predictions of the decline and fall of the two-party system of Democrats and Republicans are undoubtedly overstated. Despite the increase in nonvoting and the decrease in party loyalty among those who do vote, both parties still have a few cards left to play. They have shown great flexibility in the past in adapting to the demands of new political groups, whether blacks, women, or blue-collar supporters of Governor Wallace. A similar flexibility in dealing with issues such as full employment, tax reform, consumer protection, and street crime, will allow them to continue as vital links between the people and their government. Directly confronting these issues of economic and political justice will allow the parties to bring the nonvoter back into electoral politics. To not do so will lead to the questioning of their own role as political players, and the search by turned-off voters for other ways of influencing the political game.

THOUGHT QUESTIONS

1. If you voted in the last election, what influenced the way you voted? Can you relate your political views to your family, religion or class background?
2. If you didn't vote, what led you not to vote? Was it a conscious decision? What would lead you to vote in the future?

3. How would the development of a multiparty system on the national level change the role and nature of our political parties? What would be the advantages and disadvantages of such a system?
4. Should our political parties be strengthened? If not, why not? If so, how?

SUGGESTED READINGS

Flanigan, William H., and Nancy Zingale. *Political Behavior of the American Electorate,* 3rd ed. Boston: Allyn & Bacon, 1975. Pb.
A short, comprehensive survey of voting behavior.

Reeves, Richard. *Convention.* New York: Harcourt, Brace, Jovanovich, 1977.
The fast-paced story of the 1976 Democratic presidential convention focusing on the spicy human-interest side of a political happening.

Riordan, William L. *Plunkitt of Tammany Hall.* New York: Dutton, 1963. Pb.
The witty, straightforward confessions of a New York City political boss covering the politics of his party machine around the turn of the century.

Sale, Kirkpatrick. *Power Shift.* New York: Vintage Books, 1975. Pb.
A readable argument that political power in the country is now shifting to the South and Southwest, challenging the dominance of the eastern establishment.

Sorauf, Frank J. *Party Politics in America,* 2nd ed. Boston: Little, Brown, 1972.
A thorough analysis of the role and organizaton of American political parties.

Thompson, Dr. Hunter S. *Fear and Loathing on the Campaign Trail '72.* New York: Popular Library, 1973. Pb.
Rolling Stone's Outlaw Journalist writes a hip, slightly crazed journal of what it's like to be in the middle of a presidential campaign.

Verba, Sidney, and Norman H. Nie. *Participation in America: Political Democracy and Social Equality.* New York: Harper and Row, 1972.
An in-depth study of the connections between people's social and economic positions and their political opinions and participation.

Interest Groups and the Media 7

The Constitution does not take into account interest groups and the media. Except for the First Amendment's guarantee of freedom of the press, neither is mentioned in the document. The framers of the Constitution recognized various interests in society but not their role in government. And although they made wide use of the press in their efforts to get the Constitution adopted, they could not foresee the influence of modern media on politics. Indeed, what could the framers have said about these two political players? Their development has filled gaps left by the Constitution in the political process.

Both interest groups and media provide ways for people to participate in the political process. Interest groups provide the means for people with common concerns to make their interests known to government officials. The media are a communications link (and an actor in their own right) through which people keep informed of political events. In providing instruments of power, the two can influence the political game they play and the people they serve as shown in the case study of an election to the Senate. Who they are, what they do, and how interest groups and media shape and are shaped by politics in America, are the questions at the heart of what follows.

INTEREST GROUPS

Alexis de Tocqueville, in his famous book *Democracy in America*, wrote in 1835 that Americans have a tendency to form "associations," and have perfected "the art of pursuing in common the object of their common desires."[1] One type of association is the *interest group* or *pressure group*, a group of people who organize to pursue a common interest by applying pressure on the political process. As we have seen, American parties do not provide for expressing specific interests or positions. Interest groups partly fill this gap.

How Do Interest Groups Differ from Parties?

Party organization and the electoral system are based on geographic divisions. Our senators and representatives represent us on the basis of the state or the district in which we live. But within one district there might be very important group interests that are not represented. People of different religions, races, ethnic backgrounds, income levels, or occupations may have different political concerns. Interest groups have developed to give Americans with common causes a way to express their concerns to political decision-makers.

Interest groups may try to influence the outcome of elections, but, unlike parties, they do not compete for public office. Although a candidate for office may be sympathetic to a certain group, or may in fact be a member of that group, he or she does not run as a candidate of the group.

Interest groups may be more tightly organized than political parties. They are often financed through contributions or dues-paying memberships. Organizers communicate with members through newsletters, mailings, and conferences. Union members, for example, usually receive regular correspondence from the union leadership informing them about union activities, benefits, and positions they are expected to support.

---

[1] Alexis de Tocqueville, *Democracy in America,* Vol. 2 (New York: Vintage Books, 1945), p. 115.

Types of Interest Groups

The largest and probably the most important type of interest group is the economic interest group, including business, professional, labor, and farming groups. James Madison, in *The Federalist Papers*, expressed the fear that if people united on the basis of economic interests, all the have-nots in society would take control of the government. This has obviously not happened. The most influential groups in the political process are those with the most money.

Business groups have a common interest in making profits. This also involves supporting the economic system that makes profits possible. The Chamber of Commerce, the National Association of Manufacturers, and the National Small Business Association are well-known business groups. Large powerful companies, like American Telephone and Telegraph (AT&T), United States Steel, and General Motors often act as interest groups by themselves.

Professional groups include the American Medical Association, the National Association of Realtors, and the Amer-

TABLE 7.1. Interest Group Contributions to 1976 Congressional Campaigns (by category)

Category of interest group	Amount reported
Agriculture	$ 1,534,447
Business	7,091,375
Health	2,694,910
Lawyers	241,280
Labor	8,206,578
Ideological	1,503,394
Miscellaneous	1,299,928
TOTAL	$22,571,912

Source: *Congressional Quarterly* (April 16, 1977), p. 710.

TABLE 7.2. Major Interest Group Contributors in 1976

	Total Contributions
American Medical Associations	$1,790,879
Dairy committees	1,362,159
AFL-CIO, COPE	996,910
Maritime-related unions	979,691
United Auto Workers	845,939
Coal, oil, and natural gas interests	809,508
National Education Associations	752,272
National Association of Realtors	605,973
Financial institutions	529,193
Intl. Assn. of Machinists	519,157
United Steelworkers of America	463,033
American Dental Associations	409,835

Source: *Congressional Quarterly* (April 16, 1977), p. 710.

ican Bar Association, all of which have powerful lobbies in Washington.

Labor unions, like the American Federation of Labor and the Congress of Industrial Organizations (the AFL-CIO), and the International Brotherhood of Teamsters, are among the most influential interest groups in the country. Their leaders, who tend to stay in power longer than most politicians, are powerful political figures in their own right. Newer and smaller unions, like the United Farm Workers, an organization of mainly Chicano farm laborers, are less effective than older, wealthier unions.

Agricultural business interests have a long history of influential lobbying activity. The American Farm Bureau Federation, the National Farmers Union, and the National Grange are among the most powerful groups in Washington. Specialized groups, like the Associated Milk Producers, Inc. (AMPI), also have a large influence on farm legislation.

Some interest groups are organized around religious, social, or political concerns. Groups like the NAACP, the Urban League, and the Southern Christian Leadership Conference (SCLC) focus on economic interests as only one aspect of their efforts on behalf of blacks in America. Groups like the Sierra Club are concerned with legislation to protect the environment. Some interest groups, such as the liberal Americans for Democratic Action (ADA) and the conservative Americans for Constitutional Action (ACA) represent groups of people who share similar political ideas.

Lobbying

When interest groups put pressure on the government to act in their favor we call this *lobbying*. Interest groups today maintain professional staffs of lobbyists in Washington to protect their interests. These staffs often include former members of Congress or former employees of executive bureaucracies who are experienced in the techniques of political influence. According to the 1946 Federal Lobbying Act, interest groups must register with the clerk of the House and the secretary of the Senate if they want to influence legislative action, but this act is easy to get around and is frequently not enforced.

Direct lobbying usually takes place in congressional committees and executive bureaucracies. Although lobbying the legislature gets most of the publicity, usually lobbyists devote more attention to executive agencies in attempting to influence their regulations. It is sometimes said that the real decisions of government are made among lobbyists, bureaucrats and congressional committees — the so-called "Golden Triangle." Lobbyists provide information about their particular industry or population group to committees and bureaucracies. In turn, lobbyists are given an opportunity to present their case for or against legislative proposals or executive programs.

Indirect lobbying may involve massive letter-writing campaigns run by lobbyists in Washington. The National Rifle Association successfully used this tactic to fight gun-control legislation. More subtle lobbying efforts involve "nonpolitical" public relations. For example, oil companies responded to criticism about increased prices with advertising showing their concern for the public welfare. Another form of indirect lobbying is for interest groups to convince other interest groups to support their goals. If the Automobile Association of America (AAA) favors new highway construction, it will try to raise support from other groups with similar interests, such as trucking companies, camping clubs, automobile manufacturers, and construction unions.

Interest groups also use the courts to influence the political process. They may bring lawsuits and file *amicus curiae* (friend of the court) briefs in suits initiated by others. Class-action suits are brought by interest groups in order to get a favorable court ruling on issues that affect a whole class or group of people in a similar situation.

Interest groups often use demonstration techniques to influence politicians. Strikes and boycotts, for example, are important techniques, particularly for labor unions. Some interest groups are adept at using media to spread propaganda about their interests. Mobil Oil Company, for example, publishes columns in advertising space purchased in major newspapers across the country.

Campaign Contributions and Electioneering

The most controversial aspects of lobbying relate to elections. By contributing money to a political campaign, interest groups can reward a politician who has supported them in the past and encourage candidates to give support in the future. Often groups "hedge their political bets" by helping to finance the campaigns of two opposing candidates.

During the Watergate investigations, many lobbying scandals involving campaign contributions came to light. In the Spring of 1971, ITT (International Telephone and Telegraph), a powerful multinational corporation, made a commitment of $400,000 to help finance the 1972 Republican convention in San Diego, California. Around the same time,

President Nixon ordered the Justice Department to drop the antitrust suit pending against ITT. Although the president later revoked his order (he was advised that he was playing with "political dynamite"), the ITT suit was settled out of court shortly afterward. When the press began to expose ITT's contribution and the scandal surrounding it, the Republican party decided to move the convention site to Miami.

Another scandal involved the Associated Milk Producers, Inc. (AMPI). After AMPI pledged over $2 million to the 1972 Nixon campaign, the president recommended that milk price supports be raised to help the dairy industry. In both these cases, and many others like them, it is impossible to prove that the politician actually has been bribed by interest group money. Politicians themselves claim that money gives the interest groups *access* to political decision makers but not *influence* over them. The line between bribery of public officials and "politics as usual" is often blurred.

Many campaign contributions bend the law even if they don't quite break it. Corporations and labor unions are not allowed to give political gifts, but they have found ways of getting around this. They may donate services, such as the use of a private plane or a credit card. They may form a special political group to give the contribution, so that it does not come directly from the corporation or union. COPE (the Committee on Political Education), for example, is the political "education" arm of the AFL-CIO. Or, they may have individual executives or officers give contributions that the company or union will refund secretly. Contributions given by secret means are said to have been "laundered," meaning that they were made to look "clean" or legal.

In 1974, the efforts of reform groups, such as Common Cause, combined with the effects of the Watergate scandals, led to stricter campaign financing regulations (see pages 121–125). These laws are still very controversial, and their effectiveness is open to debate.

Critics of the present interest group structure claim that

the loudest voices in Washington belong to the groups with the most money. Many voices in America are barely heard, and these tend to be the voices of people who have the greatest needs. Despite recent efforts by Ralph Nader's organization and other public interest groups, the interest group system on the whole still has a strong bias in favor of the people who have enough money to make their lobbying effective.

Political Movements

Clearly there are gaps left in the political process by the bias toward wealthy and powerful established interest groups. Political movements have sprung up to fill those gaps. Movements allow underrepresented groups to express their demands for change. They have historically provided a means for Americans to use mass support in place of massive money to influence the political process.

What Is a Political Movement? Political movements have three main characteristics that set them apart from most interest groups. First, the *structure* of political movements is *flexible and unstable.* Movements rarely have a permanent form; they are always in the process of becoming. This often makes them hard to identify. Sometimes parts of a movement are permanent organizations, or become permanent, taking the form of interest groups or parties. Parts of the civil rights movement of the 1950s and 1960s, like the Southern Christian Leadership Conference (SCLC), became stable interest groups and are still active. Other parts, like the NAACP (founded in 1910), had been active as interest groups long before the civil rights movement. Other groups went south to register voters or participate in freedom rides but never became formal organizations.

Second, the interests expressed by movements relate to *proposals for major changes in society.* Political movements generally demand change in who gets what, when, and how, and in who gets to participate in political decision making. The civil rights movement aimed at winning for black Americans (who) the basic rights and liberties enjoyed by white Americans (what) as quickly as possible (when) through nonviolent protest (how).

Third, movements depend for their success on their *ability to mobilize as many people as possible.* The success of the anti-Vietnam War movement rested on the number of supporters directly involved in the movement's activities. Widespread support shows political decision makers that the goals of change are popular, and puts pressure on them to give in to some or all of the movement's demands.

Why Do Political Movements Arise? Movements develop out of a combination of four essential ingredients. The first is *discontent caused by relative deprivation.* Political movements always relate to a feeling of discontent: movement supporters feel deprived of something relative to someone else. That the poor in America are richer than the poor in many other countries does not lessen their discontent. That American women are more equal to men than are women in other societies does not lessen their feeling of deprivation. Both groups feel deprived relative to others in their own environment.

A second ingredient needed for a political movement to get started is what is sometimes called the *historical moment* or the *precipitating factor.* The historical moment is usually an event or situation that focuses people's general feelings of discontent and moves them to take action. It might be a severe depression which makes economic hardship impossible to bear any longer, or a particular event, like the invasion of Cambodia in 1970 which caused large numbers of people to mobilize in support of the antiwar movement. This historical moment helps *raise the consciousness,* or simply activate, many people. They see that their discontent is caused by some outside identifiable force, and that by organizing together they can create a change in their common conditions.

The third and fourth ingredients are *leaders* and *targets*. If leaders are present at the historical moment, they help people make the connection between their discontent and a political target. Often the target is a particular member of the elite who is accused of being responsible for people's deprivation. Once the target is identified, leaders and followers develop tactics and strategies to achieve the change they desire. Movements are well-known for the nonviolent and violent demonstration tactics they use to focus attention on their cause. But movements use many other tactics, and other political actors (labor unions, for example) use demonstration tactics, so it is misleading to try to identify movements by tactics alone.

Movements lose their force if the authorities (1) do something to cure the discontent, (2) alter policies to reduce the "historical moments," (3) eliminate the movement leadership, or (4) eliminate the target of movement activity. Even with no response from authorities, movements often lose momentum. It is difficult to keep large numbers of people involved in any sustained political activity. And the rewards of movement activity are often few and far between.

MEDIA

After Watergate and Vietnam, few people would argue that the media is not a powerful political player. The way we see politics and what we think is important are largely given to us by the press. Certainly politicians are affected by and recognize those facts. For example, the physical capabilities of politicians are very important to the public's impression of their suitability for office. After he was shot, Alabama Governor George Wallace was frequently pictured as an invalid in a wheelchair. Yet 40 years earlier the press had agreed as a matter of courtesy never to publish photos of Franklin Roosevelt in his wheelchair (to which he was confined by polio). An example of media influence over policy occurred when Walter Cronkite, anchorman of CBS news, turned against the war in Vietnam. Reportedly President Johnson then concluded that all hope of uniting the people behind his war policy was lost. CBS's view of political reality was, apparently, a match for any president.

The media have often been labeled "the fourth branch of government," rivaling the three official branches in political power. Although overstated (the press can't actually *do* what the other three branches can), the way the media shape political attitudes makes it important to understand. This part of the chapter will attempt to come to grips with the following questions: What are the media? What do media do? Who controls media? How do media influence politics, and how are they influenced by the other political players?

What Are the Media?

Media are those means of communication that permit messages to be made public. Media such as TV, radio, magazines, and newspapers provide important links connecting people to one another. But these are links (unlike the telephone and the mail) with an important quality: they have the ability to communicate messages from a single source to a great many people at roughly the same time.

The major forms of media we will concentrate on are television and newspapers. With almost 125 million TV sets in America, television not surprisingly dominates the mass media. Its political impact is illustrated not only by an exceptional event, such as the 1976 presidential debates watched by seventy million Americans, but also by the networks' evening news programs which reach more than forty-five million people each night. Television is in turn dominated by the three major networks, CBS, NBC, and ABC. These corporations each own five TV stations (the legal limit). But the *networks* mainly function as agencies which produce and sell programs with advertising to local broadcast stations called *affiliates*. (In 1978, NBC had 212 affiliates, CBS 198, and ABC 195.) The networks have contracts with their affiliates which enable them to buy or produce programs and to sell time to advertisers for the programs on a national basis. They then offer these programs, with ads, to the affiliates, who can sell time locally to advertisers — "and now a word from our local stations." The affiliates get the shows, and the networks get the national coverage which allows them to sell time at some $1 million for six minutes of advertising during prime evening viewing hours.

Newspapers are much more varied. They range in quality from the utterly respectable *The New York Times*, which carries national and international news collected by its own reporters, to small-town dailies which relay crop reports and local fires but provide only a sketchy coverage of national

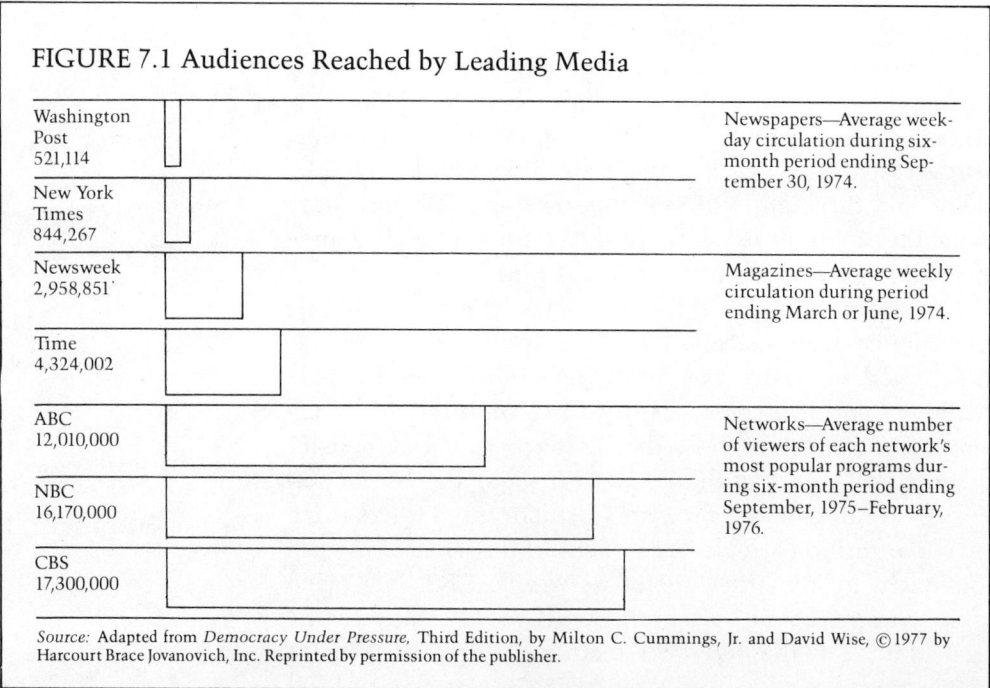

FIGURE 7.1 Audiences Reached by Leading Media

Washington Post 521,114	Newspapers—Average weekday circulation during six-month period ending September 30, 1974.
New York Times 844,267	
Newsweek 2,958,851	Magazines—Average weekly circulation during period ending March or June, 1974.
Time 4,324,002	
ABC 12,010,000	Networks—Average number of viewers of each network's most popular programs during six-month period ending September, 1975–February, 1976.
NBC 16,170,000	
CBS 17,300,000	

Source: Adapted from *Democracy Under Pressure*, Third Edition, by Milton C. Cummings, Jr. and David Wise, © 1977 by Harcourt Brace Jovanovich, Inc. Reprinted by permission of the publisher.

events, reprinted from the wire services. (*Wire services* are specialized agencies like Associated Press (AP) and United Press International (UPI) that gather, write, and sell news to the media that subscribe to them.)

Newspapers are also getting less numerous and less competitive. At the turn of the century there were 2,600 daily papers. By 1975, despite the enormous growth in population, there were under 1,750. The same period has seen the decline of competing newspapers in the same city. In 1910 over half of the cities and towns in America had dailies owned by two or more companies. Today only four percent of United States communities have competing newspaper ownerships. The rest have only one newspaper or else all the papers are controlled by the same owner. Of our major cities only New York, Boston, and Philadelphia have three separately owned daily papers. We'll get to the reasons for this trend shortly.

What Do the Media Do?

The media provide three major types of messages in linking people together. Through *news reports, entertainment programs,* and *advertising,* the media help shape attitudes on many things — including politics.

In news reports the media supply up-dated factual accounts of what journalists believe to be the most important events, issues, and developments occurring in the world. By reporting certain things (President Ford bumping his head) and ignoring others (President Kennedy's back trouble), the media tell us what is important. Media coverage gives status to people and events — a national TV interview or a picture on the cover of *Time* magazine creates a "national figure." By doing this the media also put together an agenda of national priorities — what should be taken seriously, what lightly, and what ignored entirely. The media attention given to the arms race, environmental pollution, or corruption in government will largely determine how important most people think these issues are. How the issue is presented will influence whether certain explanations of these problems are acceptable or not. If urban crime, for example, is associated with the need for larger police forces or the failure of federal programs, rather than with the distribution of wealth in the country or urban poverty, then this will direct the acceptable range of debate and the likely solutions.

Entertainment programs give people images of "normal" behavior. Certain standards are upheld by heroes who are rewarded, and violated by outlaws who are punished. In general, social and political conflict is changed into personal drama on these shows. The issue of black poverty is presented as whether a handsome young black actor can "go straight" and stay in college and turn his back on his violent street friends. People are rarely shown organizing to solve common problems. Instead they meet difficulties in their own homes, or within their own consciences, even when these problems are shared by their friends and neighbors. Whether media are reflecting reality here is of course a debatable point.

Finally, the programs and news that media present are built around a constant flow of advertisements. TV programs are constructed to reach emotional high points just before the commercials so that the audience will stay put during the advertisement. Newspapers devote much more space to ads than news, leading one English author to define

---

FRED FLINTSTONE FOR PRESIDENT IN 1996?

An international study has shown that while only half the adults around the world could identify a picture of their national leader, 90 percent of American 3-year-olds could identify a photograph of cartoon character Fred Flintstone.

Another survey asked 4- to 6-year-olds which they preferred, "television or daddy?" Forty-four percent replied "television."

a journalist as "someone who writes on the back of advertisements." The ads themselves encourage audiences to buy many things by showing them the real or imaginary pleasures of owning them. They show generally well-off Americans enjoying the material rewards that come from conforming to the norms of society. Whether this is true is again a very debatable and very political question.

Media and the Marketplace of Ideas

The framers of the Constitution believed that a free flow of information from a great many sources was basic to maintaining the system of government they set up. Ideas would compete with one another without restraint in the "marketplace of ideas." Fearing that the greatest enemy of free speech was the government, the framers added the First Amendment forbidding government officials from "abridging the freedom of speech, or of the press." The phrase has since been extended to include radio and TV. The principle, however, remains the same, as Judge Learned Hand wrote:

> Right conclusions are more likely to be gathered out of a multitude of tongues than through any kind of authoritative selection. To many this is, and always will be folly; but we have staked upon it our all.

The ability of media to fulfill this goal of presenting a variety of opinions, representing the widest range of political ideas, has not surprisingly been limited in practice. It is limited both by what the media are and what the government does.

Media, such as TV stations and newspapers, are basically privately owned economic assets bought and sold to make a profit. Sound business judgment rather than the needs of a community determine what media there will be in any local area. Profitability, rather than public service has led to the increasing concentration of media ownership. For example, the decrease in competing newspapers mentioned before has been a reflection of the increase in *chains*, which are companies that combine different media in different cities under a single owner. Over half of the nation's newspapers today are owned by chains, as are many TV and radio stations. Newhouse Publications, one of the largest chains, owns twenty-two daily papers, seven TV stations, seven radio stations, its own wire service, and twenty national magazines including *Vogue* and *Mademoiselle*.

The media industry is also very profitable. A 100 percent return on investment each year for a TV station in a major city is not uncommon. Pre-tax profits for the TV industry as a whole reached a high of 200 percent in 1974 and never fell below fifty-three percent in the previous fifteen years. Newspapers, although their rate of profit isn't as high, earn even more in total income than TV. These profits are made possible by the advertising carried by the media.

Advertisers approach the media with certain expectations: They want their ads to be seen by as many people as possible; they want the people seeing the ads to be potential customers; and they don't want the surrounding programs or articles to detract from the ads. As a result, advertising helps make the programs — both news and entertainment — as inoffensive and conventional as possible in order to keep the customer satisfied. For example, drug companies would prefer not to sponsor programs where poor people are shown not meeting their medical bills. David Susskind, a TV interviewer, once had a list of possible guests cut by one-third by his sponsors because of their political views. And one of TV's biggest sponsors, Procter and Gamble, has a censorship code which reads in part: "Members of the armed forces must not be cast as villains." Even newscasts, by attempting to be "objective," avoid antagonizing the audience and advertisers but often deprive the public of the interpretation and debate needed to understand what's going on. In presenting two sides of an issue, the important questions the public should ask are, *which* two sides are presented, and what position is shown as the point of balance, or "happy medium"?

Media and Government

Government officials have a number of formal and informal means for regulating and influencing the media. Their formal powers include the requirement that radio and TV stations renew their broadcast licenses with a regulatory commission, the Federal Communications Commission, every three years. Although this is usually a formality, the threat of losing a license can be an effective means of pressuring broadcasters hostile to a particular administration or policy. The FCC also tries to enforce certain standards in the industry. Its *fairness doctrine* requires that contrasting views on controversial issues be presented. If the stations do not give a balanced presentation they may have to provide

> **THE PRESS ON THE PRESS**
>
> "The duty of the press is to print the truth and raise hell."
> — Mark Twain
>
> "Newspapers start when their owners are poor, and take the part of the people and so they build a large circulation, and, as a result, advertising. That makes them rich and the publishers naturally begin to associate with other rich men . . . then they forget all about the people." — Joseph Patterson, Publisher, *New York Daily News*
>
> "If, over the last generation, the politicians and the bureaucrats in Washington have made such a mess of things with the press keeping some kind of watch over them, what would they have done with nobody watching?" — David Brinkley, TV Newsman
>
> "Personally I would rather leave my money for a newspaper than for a cathedral, a gymnasium, or even a home for street-walkers with fallen arches, but I have seldom been able to assemble more than $4.17 at one time." — A. J. Liebling, press critic
>
> "The freedom to inform is now the counterpart of what was once the freedom to build castles." — Jean Sauvy, Economist

air time to correct the balance. In theory this ensures that broadcasters do not use the valued public airwaves for propaganda purposes. In practice it has sometimes been used against certain political views, illustrated by President Johnson's use of it in 1964 to intimidate pro-Goldwater radio stations. More importantly, the "fairness doctrine" has been criticized for encouraging media to steer clear of controversy.

The examples of government leaders informally pressuring media are numerous. As seen in the box below ("Dealing with the Media"), the Nixon administration took a very

> **DEALING WITH THE MEDIA**
> *Jeb Magruder's ideas for fighting media "bias" against the Nixon administration*
> "Plant a column with a syndicated columnist which raises the question of objectivity and ethics in the news media. . . .
>
> "Arrange for an article on the subject in a major consumer magazine authorized by Stewart Alsop, [William F.] Buckley or [James J.] Kilpatrick. . . .
>
> "Ask the Vice-President to speak out on this issue. . . .
>
> "Have Rogers Morton [Chairman of the Republican National Committee] go on the attack in a news conference. . . . Have him charge that the great majority of the working press are Democrats and this colors their presentation of the news. Have him charge that there is a political conspiracy in the media to attack this Administration. . . .
>
> "Arrange for an 'expose' to be written by an author such as Earl Mazo or Victor Lasky. Publish in hardcover and paperback. . . .
>
> "Have outside groups petition the FCC and issue public statements of concern over press objectivity.
>
> "Generate a massive outpouring of letters-to-the-editor.
>
> "Have a Senator or Congressman write a public letter to the FCC suggesting the 'licensing' of individual newsmen . . ."
> — 1970 memo from Magruder to other White House staff members, in "Annals of Television: Shaking the Tree," by Thomas Whiteside, *New Yorker*, March 17, 1975, p. 46.

hard line toward the media — with poor results. President Kennedy tried to get *The New York Times* to transfer its reporter in Vietnam because the president was unhappy with his news reports. Most of the time presidents try to get on the good side of the media by giving favored reporters exclusive "leaks" of information and by controlling information going to the public through TV, radio, and newspapers. This is called *news management* and was probably done most successfully by the Kennedy administration.

Press conferences have been used by presidents since Theodore Roosevelt to get their views directly across to the public. Radio allowed even more direct access to the public without the interference of reporters. Franklin Roosevelt's radio "fireside chats" during the Depression were a skillful use of direct communication. TV allows similar direct contact but, as seen in Richard Nixon's career, this can be dangerous as well. In 1952 Nixon's televised "Checkers speech" in which he pleaded not guilty to charges of graft saved him from being dropped as Eisenhower's vice presidential candidate. But in 1960, as a presidential candidate in a televised debate, Nixon's streaky makeup and heavy beard showed up badly next to his attractive opponent, John Kennedy. In his successful 1968 campaign he used TV to sell a "New Nixon" — the old one being tarnished by previous political defeats. Finally, as a disgraced former president, Nixon admitted wrongdoing (though nothing illegal) in a series of TV interviews with David Frost in May, 1977. Presidents and TV can be a very difficult political marriage.

To make things easier a president has a large staff of media experts, speech writers, and public relations people to perfect his media image. Gerald Rafshoon, an Atlanta advertising expert, heads up the present effort to bolster Jimmy Carter's image before the American public. Call-in shows, town hall meetings, and overnight stays in average American homes are designed to preserve and promote the president's "folksy" image. Some of these activities have been called *pseudoevents* — not real events at all, but staged in order to be reported. A congressional hearing designed not so much to gather information for legislation but to gain publicity for the committee members is another example of a pseudoevent.

Media and the Public

Political scientist E. E. Schattschneider once pointed out that the "definition of alternatives is the supreme instrument of power." By "definition of alternatives" he meant the ability to set limits on political debates, to define what is politically important and what is not, and to make certain solutions reasonable and acceptable and others not. Media to a great extent have this power. Who influences the exercise of this power is another question.

Certainly the media managers (editors, newscasters, producers, reporters) have an important role in shaping political views. It was these managers whom Vice President Agnew saw as too powerful and attacked as "the nittering nabobs of negativism." The owners of media, whether of TV networks or newspaper chains, play a part in selecting who will handle the day-to-day running of the press and what the general "slant" of the media they own will be. Advertisers, by buying space in some programs or papers and not in others, affect the messages the public gets. Government and politicians have a whole catalogue of laws and tactics to pressure media to conform to their political priorities for themselves and the country. And the public, by watching or not watching certain programs, by buying or not buying certain papers, by demanding or not demanding access to the *means* of free speech, can help shape the output of mass communications.

No matter who we think controls the media, the messages that the media provide clearly reflect the power of those in the political game. The official players, through press conferences, speeches, and news releases, can be fairly sure of reaching the public through the media. Through paid advertising those with wealth can claim media time to persuade the public to act in certain ways — such as buying the goods they produce. The ability of nonelite groups to address each other, as well as their political representatives, is much more limited. The practice of giving air time to community groups has not gone very far in this country (certainly not as far as in the Netherlands, where any group with enough members is entitled to a certain amount of time on TV each week to present its programs). Free speech without a more widespread access to the *means* of free speech must remain a limited right for most people.

Case Study:
Electing a Senator[2]

Elections provide an opportunity for the media and interest groups to influence who will be the players and what will be the policies of the political game. In Maryland Senator Joseph Tydings' 1970 campaign for re-election against J. Glenn Beall the activities of these groups was of vital importance. Not only did the voters and the two parties play a role, but interest groups and the media were major factors in the outcome of the election.

The Setting

The politics of Maryland are not that different from the rest of the country. Most of the voters in the state are found in the suburbs of Washington and in the urban areas of Baltimore. They are mainly Democrats and, when put together with conservative rural Democrats, one finds seventy percent of the voters declared Democrats and only twenty-seven percent Republicans. This has meant a strong grass-roots Democratic organization able to dominate most local and state legislative offices. However, in statewide and national elections where publicity and media campaigning are more important, the Maryland Republicans have done much better. In the eight elections for the United States Senate between 1945 and 1970, the Republicans won five times.

One the Republicans didn't win was Joseph Tydings' easy 1964 victory against J. Glenn Beall, Sr., the incumbent Republican senator and father of Tydings' 1970 opponent. Tydings, whose father had also been a senator from Maryland, had run against the Democratic party organization's candidate in the 1964 primary and throughout his political career was not on close terms with the state party. As a young

---

[2] Adapted from John F. Bibby and Roger H. Davidson, "I Guess I Was Just Too Liberal: Joseph Tydings of Maryland," in *On Capitol Hill* (Hinsdale, Illinois: The Dryden Press, Inc., 1972), pp. 25–51.

political reformer he continued his independent ways in the Senate. A strong supporter of civil rights legislation and urban programs, Tydings broke with the Johnson Administration over the Vietnam War in 1967 and later endorsed his friend Robert Kennedy for the presidency. His opposition to the war and defense spending had labeled Tydings as a liberal.

Perhaps his most controversial action as a senator was in sponsoring gun-control legislation which provided for federal registration of guns and licensing of gun owners. Although the bill did not pass, Tydings had aroused the opposition of many gun owners, and in 1970 he was the "number-one target" of the national gun lobby. Trying to make this and other controversial stands a virtue, Tydings campaigned on the theme, "He never ducks the tough ones." Even though he lost forty percent of the vote in winning the Democratic primary, the senator was considered a strong favorite for re-election in 1970.

So strong, in fact, that the Republicans had difficulty finding a candidate to run against him. Finally, following reports that the Nixon White House had urged him to run, Republican Congressman J. Glenn Beall, Jr., announced his candidacy. Beall had the advantage of his father's well-known name in the state, and, having been in Congress only one term, was not strongly identified with any particular issue. As a pleasant, uncontroversial candidate, Beall could make Tydings and his record the main issue in the campaign.

The Campaign

Senator Tydings' first decision in seeking re-election was whether to rely on the local Democratic party organization or build his own campaign structure. Given the party regulars' dislike of Tydings, he chose to create a volunteer organization. Along with some professional staff, the organization was made up of people who had worked in his first campaign, those whom Tydings had helped during his years in office, and others who stopped by to volunteer. At the same time, the Tydings campaign tried to stay on good terms with the party organization. The party was backing a popular governor running for re-election and although most organization Democrats supported Tydings after he won the primary, few did much for him.

Campaigning followed the traditional route. Concentrating on the heavily populated areas, there was early morning handshaking at plant gates (workers are less eager to go to work than to go home in the afternoon), shopping-center tours accompanied by sports stars, candidates' wives giving coffees for women's groups, stops at local headquarters to meet volunteers and have pictures taken, and appearances at big events in the evening. As a campaigner Tydings was generally considered cold and aloof before large groups while Beall was described by his ads as "a man you can walk up to and talk to."

Interest Groups. Interest groups played a prominent role in the campaign. Labor unions supported and gave money to Tydings, while more conservative business groups backed Beall. The most visible interest group, however, was the gun-control lobby whom Tydings had earlier antagonized.

Gun owners throughout the country poured money into a local group called Citizens Against Tydings (CAT). Some $60,000 was used for tens of thousands of bumper stickers and pamphlets, thirty full-page newspaper ads, and dozens of radio announcements. The National Rifle Association was not allowed to campaign directly because of tax laws, but clearly the effort had their blessing. Surveys had shown that the majority of Maryland voters supported gun control, but for the sizable minority who intensely opposed it, the issue was of prime importance.

Tydings took on the issue directly. Citing crime rates from firearms and statements by law enforcement officials, he accused out-of-state gun interests of "bullying" tactics and of lying about his bill. In one TV ad the names and ages of Marylanders killed by guns were rolled slowly across the screen as Tydings appealed for his position on gun control. While Beall benefitted from the issue and opposed gun registration as useless ("criminals won't register their guns anyway"), he described himself as a middle of the roader. Beall was trying to avoid becoming a one-issue candidate, captured by an interest group.

Media. Media was used by both candidates to reach voters and also acted independently as an important player in the campaign.

Most of the half-million dollars spent by each campaign went into media advertising. Tydings' ads stressed his experience, his independence, and his personal concern about people (to counter his image of being cold). Sixty-second TV spots showed his contributions to the state and featured Tydings with cops and kids. Media ads were also pinpointed to certain audiences: appeals to working people were broadcast on country-and-western radio stations; the senator's wife made an ad aimed at housewives that was shown on daytime television; black politicians' endorsements ran on stations playing soul music. Press releases, endorsements, and challenges to opponents by both sides kept a constant stream of "news" going to the press.

Both candidates appeared for a series of TV debates broadcast statewide. Since Tydings was better known, the debates probably aided Beall by giving the lesser known candidate free exposure. Beall also benefitted from the wide publicity given Vice President Agnew's hard-hitting attack on Tydings as a "radical liberal" and from President Nixon's campaigning in Baltimore. Beall saved most of his media money for the last week before the election. Concentrating on Tydings' record, he called him a "lackey" for "ultraliberal" groups.

But the press didn't act only as a sounding board for the candidates. Most of the major newspapers of the region, like the Washington *Star* and the Baltimore *Sun*, endorsed Tydings. At least as important, however, was an article in *Life,* a photo-feature magazine, charging that the senator had helped a company he partly owned get a loan from the government. Tydings repeatedly denied the accusation and charged the White House with pushing *Life* into running the story. The government agency involved cleared Tydings of any involvement in the loan decision but the declaration of his innocence was not publicly released until after the election. Although it's unclear how many votes were changed, the Tydings staff devoted a tremendous amount of time to answering the charges and once again Tydings was put on the defensive.

The Election

In spite of these setbacks, most of the polls throughout the campaign showed Tydings with a large lead. At the same time, he was widely disliked for his stands on particular issues and considered to be "not a personal senator." Just as important, while only twenty-seven percent of the voters considered themselves liberals, over half considered Tydings one. Nonetheless, with two and one-half times more Democrats in the state than Republicans, a popular Democratic governor running for re-election, and a spirited volunteer staff and adequate funding, Tydings still looked like a winner.

He wasn't. Tydings lost by some 25,000 votes out of almost one million cast (forty-eight percent to Beall's fifty-one percent, with a minor candidate getting one percent). Perhaps the key factor in his loss was the very light turnout in heavily Democratic Baltimore, especially in the black and working-class districts. Forty-six percent of the registered voters showed up, compared with sixty percent in previous nonpresidential elections. A heavy rain and lack of enthusiasm for Tydings combined to make nonvoters significant in Tydings' defeat.

When the head of Tydings' campaign was asked why the senator had lost, he replied, "Well, the left-handed Lithuanian vote didn't go for him." In a sense, he meant that the margin was so thin and the deciding factors so numerous, it would be impossible to point to any one cause. Tydings blamed the gun lobby which was quite willing to take the credit. The senator's image of remoteness didn't help, nor did the *Life* article or the party organization's indifference to his candidacy. Tydings himself became the major issue in the campaign. Pleasant J. Glenn Beall offered an uncontroversial alternative or, in Baltimore, an excuse to stay home.

The fragile nature of Beall's victory was shown six years later when the Democrats ran Congressman Paul Sarbanes and easily retook the seat. Tydings, running again, was defeated in the Democratic primary.

WRAP-UP

Both interest groups and media reflect the views of organizations that have not been established primarily to influence politics. Interest groups provide the means for business, labor, professional, or citizens' organizations to make their views known to government officials. They unify people with common concerns to bring pressure through campaign contributions, lobbying, or publicity, on decision makers. Not surprisingly those interest groups with the most resources or wealth tend to be the most effective. Some people, feeling both a lack of influence through established interest groups and a high level of discontent, will form political movements to exert influence for their cause. These rest on wide popular support and seek broad political changes. They also tend to rise and fall in certain fairly brief periods of history.

Media, on the other hand, seem to be everywhere. While being both a communications link and a profitable economic asset, media also influence politics. Through news reports, entertainment, and advertisements, media directly and indirectly shape political attitudes. What is and is not broadcast and printed establishes political figures, sets priorities, focuses attention on issues, and largely makes politics understandable to most people. The media are in turn affected by the corporations that own them, the advertisers that pay for their messages, the managers who run them, and the public that consumes what they offer. Government officials grant them licenses (if they're TV or radio), stage pseudoevents for their own benefit, and distribute or withhold information as it serves those officials' interests. As both a political player and a communications link, the media are among the most powerful, complex, and controversial influences in American politics.

By providing access to the political game, interest groups and media have the potential of allowing wide public influence over how the game is played. The rise of public-oriented interest groups (consumers, environmentalists, etc.) and of media outlets for community groups (public TV stations) shows the possibilities of these instruments of power being used by a broader cross-section of the public. But in the main the wide public use of interest groups and media is more a potential trend than an actual practice. These instruments of power remain in the hands of the powerful.

THOUGHT QUESTIONS

1. Which interests are represented best by American interest groups? How would you remedy the abuses of interest groups so that groups that are now poorly represented would be guaranteed an equal voice?
2. How would you analyze political movements such as the women's and black movements according to the characteristics outlined in the chapter?
3. Does the First Amendment right to free speech and a free press conflict with the commercial nature of media in the United States? Should the media be run to make a profit?
4. What are the arguments for and against changing the media to make it more available for differing political viewpoints? Must this mean more government control and regulation?

5. Based on your study of voters and parties, and of Maryland's election of a senator, how would you run a political campaign like Tydings'? What issues would you stress? What voters would you focus the campaign on reaching? And what would you use (i.e., media, mail, personal contact) to get your message across?

SUGGESTED READINGS

Interest Groups

Flexner, Eleanor. *Century of Struggle: The Women's Rights Movement in the United States.* New York: Atheneum, 1968. Pb.
 A history of the struggle of women to obtain equality in America.
Goulden, Joseph. *The Superlawyers.* New York: Dell, 1972. Pb.
 A gossipy account of the powerful world of the leading Washington law firms and the wealthy interests for whom they lobby.
Lewis, Anthony. *Portrait of a Decade: The Second American Revolution.* New York: Vintage, 1967. Pb.
 An account of the civil rights movement.
Mintz, Morton, and Jerry S. Cohen. *America, Inc.* New York: Dell, 1971. Pb.
 A solid muckraking description of "who owns and operates the United States" focusing on the power of big business in politics.
Truman, David B. *The Governmental Process*, 2nd ed. New York: Knopf, 1971.
 The classic examination and defense of interest group politics in America.

Media

Crouse, Timothy. *The Boys on the Bus.* New York: Ballantine, 1974. Pb.
 The amusing inside story of press coverage in the 1972 presidential campaign with character studies of the major reporters.
McGinnis, Joe. *The Selling of the President, 1968.* New York: Pocket Books, 1968. Pb.
 An entertaining account of how Richard Nixon used the media to create and sell a "New Nixon" image to the American voter.
McLuhan, Marshall, and Quentin Fiore. *The Medium is the Massage.* New York: Bantam Books, 1967. Pb.

> This is the only predominantly picture book in the lists of suggested readings. It is also the easiest place to start in understanding McLuhan, a guru of the 60s, who has important things to say about the media today.

Phillips, Kevin P. *Mediacracy: American Parties and Politics in the Communications Age.* New York: Doubleday, 1975.
> The rise of a liberal elite controlling various communications empires is argued and criticized from a conservative viewpoint.

Schiller, Herbert I. *The Mind Managers.* Boston: Beacon Press, 1973. Pb.
> An insightful radical argument by a leading scholar in the field of how and why media managers manipulate minds.

Shanks, Bob. *The Cool Fire: How to Make it in Television.* New York: Vintage Books, 1976. Pb.
> A breezy behind-the-cameras look at how this "electronic wallpaper" works and doesn't work, and why.

Who Wins, Who Loses: Pluralism versus Elitism 8

Is it clear now what American politics is about? Or, in describing the players and rules, the terms and institutions, have we lost sight of the game? This chapter will give us a chance to step back a bit and ask a few basic questions: Who's running the game? Who (if anyone) has control? Who wins, who loses? Who plays and who doesn't play?

It should not be too surprising that there is no accepted answer to these basic questions. Rather, there are two major competing approaches to an answer. The dominant one is *pluralism.* Its competitor, the *power elite* school of thought, has attracted a growing number of supporters seeking explanations for the turmoil and frustration of the 1960s.

PLURALISM

Pluralism is a *group theory of democracy.* Pluralism states that society contains many conflicting groups with access to government officials, and that these groups compete with one another to influence policy decisions. Although people as individuals can't have much influence over politics, they can through their membership in various groups. These groups bargain both among themselves and with government institutions. The compromises which result become public policy.

Several key concepts make up the pluralist argument: fragmentation of power, bargaining, compromise, and consensus.

Fragmentation of power is the pluralists' way of saying that no one group dominates the political game. Power is divided, though not equally, among a large number of groups

— labor unions, corporations, citizen groups, and many others. To gain their goals, the groups must *bargain* with each other. Within this bargaining process the government, though it may have its own interests, acts essentially as a referee. The government will make sure the rules of the game are followed and may intervene to help groups who consistently have less power than their opponents. It is also to the advantage of all the groups to follow the "rules of the game," since the bargaining-compromise method is the most effective way to win changes.

The result of this many-sided bargaining process is inevitably a series of *compromises.* Since no group has dominant power, each must take a little less than it wants in order to gain the support of the others. This accommodation is made easier because both the interests and membership of the groups overlap. An individual may even be a member of two groups with different views on an issue. His or her membership in both will tend to reduce the conflict between them. For example, a black doctor may be a member of the American Medical Association (AMA), which opposes an expanded program of government-directed medical care, and also a member of the National Association for the Advancement of Colored People (NAACP), which supports such a program. As a member of both, he or she may influence the groups to reach a compromise with each other.

Underlying this bargaining-compromise process is a *consensus,* an agreement on basic political questions that most of the groups are reasonably satisfied with. This agreement on the rules of the game, and also on most of its results, is the basic cooperative cement that holds society together. Aspects of this consensus in American society are things like the general agreement on the importance of basic liberties, on the goal of equality of opportunity for all citizens, on the necessity for compromise, and on the duty of citizens to participate in politics. The pluralists maintain not only that there is widespread participation in political decisions but also that the decisions themselves have the general agreement (or consensus) of society behind them.

What we have then in the pluralist view is a process of bargaining among organized groups, and also between these groups and various agencies of the government. The bargaining results in a series of compromises which become public policy and determine who gets what, when, and how. A widespread consensus on the rules and results of this process keeps the political game from degenerating into unmanageable conflict.

Examples of Pluralism

Examples of the whole bargaining-compromise process, pluralists claim, are easy to find in American politics. When Ralph Nader, the consumer advocate, proposes that automobile makers be required to install more safety devices in their cars, numerous interests get involved in the process of

turning that proposal into law. The car manufacturers worry about the increased costs resulting in less sales and less profits, and they may try to limit the safety proposals. Labor unions may want to make sure that the higher costs do not result in lower wages. Insurance companies may be interested in how greater safety will affect the claims they have to pay out. Oil companies may worry about the effect on gasoline consumption. Citizens' groups, like Common Cause, may try to influence the legislation so that it provides the greatest protection for the consumer. The appropriate committees of the House and Senate, and the relevant parts of the bureaucracy, will weigh the competing arguments and pressures as they consider bills covering automobile safety. The resulting legislation will reflect the relative power of the competing groups as well as the compromises they have reached.

THE PLURALIST VIEW

"The fact is that the Economic Notables operate within that vague political consensus, the prevailing system of beliefs, to which all the major groups in the community subscribe.... Within limits, they can influence the content of that belief system; but they cannot determine it wholly...." (p. 84)

"In the United States the political stratum does not constitute a homogeneous class with well-defined class interests." (p. 91)

"Thus the distribution of resources and the ways in which they are or are not used in a pluralistic political system like New Haven's constitute an important source of both political change and political stability. If the distribution and use of resources gives aspiring leaders great opportunities for gaining influence, these very features also provide a built-in throttle that makes it difficult for any leader, no matter how skillful, to run away with the system." (p. 310) — Robert A. Dahl, *Who Governs?* (New Haven: Yale University Press, 1961).

One of the best known studies attempting to support the pluralist model is Robert Dahl's book on politics in New Haven, Connecticut, *Who Governs?* Dahl tried to find out who actually has influence over political decisions in an American city. He examined several important issues, such as urban development and public education, to see who made the key decisions in these areas. He concluded that different groups influenced decisions in the different areas. The people who had the most influence over education policy were not the same as those influencing urban development or political nominations. There was, Dahl concluded, no single economic and social elite wielding political power in New Haven.

Criticisms of Pluralism

Who Governs? and other studies supporting pluralist ideas have run into numerous criticisms. One major argument faults pluralism for emphasizing *how* the political game is played rather than *why* people play it. Critics say that pluralism does not give enough importance to how benefits really are distributed. A consensus that equal opportunity is good is not the same as actually having equality. A system of democratic procedures may simply be a cover for the most powerful interests getting their way. The argument often goes on to say that there can be no political democracy without social and economic conditions also being equal for all. Critics of pluralism often ask: What good are the rules of the game to the majority of people who never get a chance to play?

Critics of studies like Dahl's have pointed out that those with power cannot always be identified from an examination of key decisions. Powerful elites may *prevent* certain issues from ever reaching the public arena for a decision. Whether housing in New York City should be taken over by the local government or whether public transportation should be free are not the type of issues on which people get a chance to vote. The pluralistic appearance of politics may merely mask domination by a small number of powerful elites.

POWER ELITE

Many of pluralism's critics believe the power elite approach more realistically describes the American political game. Power elite supporters see society as dominated by a unified and nonrepresentative elite. This elite secures the important decision-making positions for its members while encouraging powerlessness below. Those in power do not represent the varied interests in society. Instead they look after their own interests and prevent differing views from surfacing. American politics is not a collection of pluralist groups maintaining a balance of power among themselves, but an elite of economic, political, and military leaders in unchallenged and unresponsive control of the political game.

How the Power Elite Rules

This single elite rules the country through the positions its members occupy, according to this view. Power does not come from individuals but from *institutions*. Thus, to have power you need a role of leadership in a key institution of the society — you have to be a full admiral in the navy, or the chairman of the board of directors of General Motors. These leadership roles are not open to everyone. They are open only to the rich and the powerful, the *ruling class* of the country, whose names can be found on the social register and whose children go to the "right" schools. This influential class controls the country's economy and is in basic agreement that political power should be used to preserve the economic status quo.

The results of this elite control, needless to say, are dif-

ferent from the pluralist outcome. Political decisions, rather than representing a consensus in the society, merely represent the *conflict* within it. Society is not held together by widespread agreement but by force and control: the control the elite has over the majority. The only consensus that exists is everyone's agreement that some have power and others do not. Politics is a constant conflict between those with power, who seek to keep it, and those without power, who seek to gain it. The policies that result from the political game reflect the conflict between elite and majority and the domination of the latter by the former.

The best-known study of elite control in America, *The Power Elite,* was written in 1959 by a sociologist, C. Wright

Mills. Mills maintained that American politics is dominated by a unified group of leaders from the corporations, the military, and the political arena. They make most of the important policy decisions, and they cooperate among themselves because they need each other. Mills noted the frequent movement among the three areas, with business leaders taking jobs in high levels of government, military leaders getting positions in corporations, and so forth. Supporters of Mills' ideas often point to President Eisenhower's farewell address in which he warned of a vast "military-industrial complex" whose influence "is felt in every city, every state house, every office of the federal government."

Criticisms of the Power Elite Theory

Critics have been quick to do battle with the power elite theory. Although they may agree that only a small number of people participate in politics, they argue that this minority of activists is much less unified than Mills maintains. They point to Watergate as an example of how some elites checked others. These elites compete, and democracy consists of people choosing among them through the vote. Besides, the elite critics argue, the political ideals of democracy are probably carried out better by these elites than they would be by the uninformed majority. Public surveys, these critics contend, have repeatedly shown a lack of democratic ideals among the working class. Hence greater participation of the people might curiously enough mean less liberty and justice, not more.

Another criticism aimed at some of the less careful elitists is that they are supporting a conspiracy theory. Their argument becomes circular: American politics is a secret conspiracy which can't be proved because it is a secret conspiracy. The existence of such an elite, critics charge, is thus an unprovable assumption which serves only to remove politics from analysis and thereby allow the lazy to hold on to their biases.

> **THE POWER ELITE VIEW**
>
> "The power elite is composed of men whose positions enable them to transcend the ordinary environments of ordinary men and women; they are in positions to make decisions having major consequences. . . . They rule the big corporations. They run the machinery of the state and claim its prerogatives. They direct the military establishment. They occupy the strategic command posts of the social structure, in which are now centered the effective means of the power and the wealth and the celebrity which they enjoy." (pp. 3–4)
>
> "Within American society, major national power now resides in the economic, the political, and the military domains." (p. 6)
>
> "The men of the higher circles are not representative men; their high position is not a result of moral virtue; their fabulous success is not firmly connected with meritorious ability. . . . They are not men held in responsible check by a plurality of voluntary associations which connect debating publics with the pinnacles of decision. Commanders of power unequaled in human history, they have succeeded within the American system of organized irresponsibility." (p. 361) — C. Wright Mills, *The Power Elite* (New York: Oxford University Press, 1959).

THE DEBATE

The debate between the pluralists and the elitists does not usually come down to *whether* a small number of people dominate the political game. Even in the pluralist model, the bargaining among the groups is carried on by relatively few leaders representing their groups. Clearly only a minority of people directly participate in politics, and this small group has more influence than the majority of people. The central questions are how *competitive* and *representative* these elites are.

To what degree do elites compete rather than cooperate with one another over who gets what, when, and how? How much conflict is there between, say, heads of government agencies and corporations over regulation and taxes? Or, how much do they share views on major questions of policy, and cooperate among themselves regardless of the "public good"? That brings us to the question of how *representative* these elites are of the broader public. Do powerful minorities reflect, however imperfectly, the wishes of the majority? And if so, do they represent what the public really thinks or what they have manipulated us into thinking?

For example, it is frequently charged that, in general, TV programs are a "cultural wasteland." But do we know why? Some say it's because an elite seeking its own profits controls what we see. Others argue that the abundant violence and silly commercials reflect what the majority wants, as shown by numerous opinion polls. But do these polls reflect what people actually want or what they are conditioned to want? Is there a real public opinion, or just one produced by an elite to further its own interests? The argument can continue endlessly.

There may well be no "right" answer to the argument between pluralists and the power elite school. It may depend on which political conflict we are talking about. Sometimes, as in the town meetings held in many New England towns, we can see a number of different views being expressed on an issue and a fairly democratic decision being reached. In other areas, such as the making of foreign policy, a small number of high officials meeting secretly decide policies that will affect the lives of millions. We can conclude that the issue being decided is likely to affect how decisions will be made. Pluralism may be most appropriate in describing a small community's politics, but the power elite idea may help us understand how foreign policy is made.

The concepts we adopt as most accurately reflecting political reality are bound also to reflect our own ideals. The pluralists and elitists are asking and answering not only what *is* but what *should be.* The pluralists state that politics in America is democratic, with widespread participation in decisions that most people agree with. The elitists say that politics is dominated by an elite that controls and manipulates the rest of us in its own interest. The elitists contend that basic changes in the American system are needed to create a pluralist democracy, whereas the pluralists argue that we have one and that the means for change are available within it.

What do you think? The position you take is based not only on your understanding and study of politics, but also on your ideals and experience in politics. Further, the position you take will guide your political choices.

WRAP-UP

Throughout the book we have spoken about politics as a game. We have discussed the nature of the political game and what the competition is about. We talked about the rules of the conflict, many of them set forth in the Constitution, and how they have changed. Most of the book has been devoted to the governmental and nongovernmental players, their history, structures, and powers. And in this last chapter we have looked at two schools of thought which try to sum up and analyze who wins and loses and how the game is really played. But we're not quite finished.

We said in the beginning that most of us are spectators of the game — nonparticipants. But just as politics is a very special kind of game, so are we a very special kind of audience. We *can* participate in the game, and by participating, change the way the game is played as well as its outcome. As a respected scholar of politics has written:

> Political conflict is not like a football game, played on a measured field by a fixed number of players in the presence of an audience scrupulously excluded from the playing field. Politics is much more like the original primitive game of football in which everybody was free to join, a game in which the whole population of one town might play the entire population of another town moving freely back and forth across the countryside.
>
> Many conflicts are narrowly confined by a variety of de-

vices, but the distinctive quality of political conflicts is that the relations between the players and the audience have not been well defined and there is usually nothing to keep the audience from getting into the game.[1]

We should not expect the powers that be to encourage us to participate. Our participation will change their power, and they cannot be expected to welcome that. But their resistance should only strengthen our determination. "Power to the People" need not only be a slogan and a goal. It can be a fact as well.

THOUGHT QUESTIONS

1. Which of the case studies in the other chapters tend to support the pluralist approach? Which support the power elite approach?
2. Pluralism has been described as essentially "liberal," whereas elitism can be either "radical" or "conservative." Do you agree?
3. Which approach, pluralism or elitism, do you feel best describes the political game in your community? Give examples.

SUGGESTED READINGS

Dahl, Robert A. *Who Governs?* New Haven: Yale University Press, 1961. Pb.
A case study showing pluralism operating in New Haven's city government.

Evans, M. Stanton. *Clear and Present Dangers.* New York: Harcourt Brace Jovanovich, 1975. Pb.
As the subtitle says, "A conservative view of America's government."

Hodgson, Godfrey. *America in Our Time.* New York: Vantage Books, 1976. Pb.
Written by a British journalist, this is a clear intelligent history of what happened to America and why in the 1960s and 70s.

Mills, C. Wright. *The Power Elite.* Oxford: Oxford University Press, 1959. Pb.
The well-known attempt to show that an elite governs America.

Parenti, Michael. *Democracy for the Few.* 2nd ed. New York: St. Martins Press, 1977. Pb.
A short radical text asserting the hypocrisy of American democracy.

[1] E. E. Schattschneider, *The Semisovereign People* (New York: Holt, Rinehart & Winston, 1960), p. 18.

APPENDIXES

The Declaration of Independence

THE UNANIMOUS DECLARATION OF THE THIRTEEN UNITED STATES OF AMERICA

When in the Course of human events, it becomes necessary for one people to dissolve the political bands, which have connected them with another, and to assume among the powers of the earth, the separate and equal station to which the Laws of Nature and of Nature's God entitle them, a decent respect to the opinions of mankind requires that they should declare the causes which impel them to the separation. — We hold these truths to be self-evident, that all men are created equal, that they are endowed by their Creator with certain unalienable Rights, that among these are Life, Liberty and the pursuit of Happiness. — That to secure these rights, Governments are instituted among Men, deriving their just powers from the consent of the governed, — That whenever any Form of Government becomes destructive of these ends, it is the Right of the People to alter or to abolish it, and to institute new Government, laying its foundation on such principles and organizing its powers in such form, as to them shall seem most likely to effect their Safety and Happiness. Prudence, indeed, will dictate that Governments long established should not be changed for light and transient causes; and accordingly all experience hath shown, that mankind are more disposed to suffer, while evils are sufferable, than to right themselves by abolishing the forms to which they are accustomed. But when a long train of abuses and usurpations, pursuing invariably the same Object evinces a design to reduce them under absolute Despotism, it is their right, it is their duty, to throw off such Government, and to provide new Guards for their future security. — Such has been the patient sufferance of these Colonies; and such is now the necessity which constrains them to alter their former Systems of Government. The history of the present King of Great Britain is a history of repeated injuries and usurpations, all having in direct object the establishment of an absolute Tyranny over these States. To prove this, let Facts be submitted to a candid world. — He has refused his Assent to Laws, the most wholesome and necessary for the public good. — He has forbidden his Governors to pass Laws of immediate and pressing importance, unless suspended in their operation till his Assent should be obtained; and when so suspended, he has utterly neglected to attend to them. — He has refused to pass other Laws for the accommodation of large districts of people, unless those people would relinquish the right of Representation in the Legislature, a right inestimable to them and formidable to tyrants only. — He has called together legislative bodies at places unusual, uncomfortable, and distant from the depository of their public Records, for the sole purpose of fatiguing them into compliance with his measures. — He has dissolved Representative Houses repeatedly, for opposing with manly firmness his invasions on the rights of the people. — He has refused for a long time, after such dissolutions, to cause others to be elected; whereby the Legislative powers, incapable of Annihilation, have returned to the People at large for their exercise; the State remaining in the meantime exposed to all the dangers of invasion from without, and convulsions within. — He has endeavored to prevent the population of these States; for that purpose obstructing the Laws for Naturalization of Foreigners; refusing to pass others to encourage their migrations hither, and raising the conditions of new Appropriations of Lands. — He has obstructed the Administration of Justice, by refusing his Assent to Laws for establishing Judiciary powers. — He has made Judges dependent on his Will alone, for the tenure of their offices, and the amount and payment of their salaries. — He has erected a multitude of New Offices, and sent hither swarms of Officers to harass our people, and eat out their substance. — He has kept among us, in times of peace, Standing Armies without the Consent of our legislatures. — He has affected to render the Military independent of and superior to the Civil power. — He has combined with others to subject us to a jurisdiction foreign to our constitution, and unacknowledged by our laws; giving his Assent to their Acts of pretended Legislation. — For quartering large bodies of armed troops among us: — For protecting them, by a mock Trial, from punishment for any Murders which they should commit on the Inhabitants of these States: — For cutting off our Trade with all parts of the world: — For imposing Taxes on us without our Consent: — For depriving us in many cases, of the benefits of Trial by Jury: — For transporting us beyond Seas to be tried for pretended offenses: — For abolishing the free System of English Laws in a neighboring Province, establishing therein an Arbitrary government, and enlarging its Boundaries so as to render it at once an example and fit instrument for introducing the same absolute rule into these Colonies: — For taking away our Charters, abolishing our most valuable Laws, and altering fundamentally the Forms of our Governments: — For suspending our own Legislatures, and declaring themselves invested with power to legislate for us in all cases whatsoever. — He has abdicated Government here, by declaring us out of his Protection and waging War against us. — He has plundered our seas, ravaged our Coasts, burnt our towns, and destroyed the lives of our people. — He is at this time transporting large armies of foreign Mercenaries to complete the works of death, desolation and tyranny, already begun with circumstances of Cruelty & perfidy, scarcely paralleled in the most barbarous ages, and totally unworthy the Head of a civilized nation. — He has constrained our fellow Citizens taken Captive on the High Seas to bear Arms against their Country, to become the executioners of their friends and Brethren, or to fall themselves by their hands. — He has excited domestic insurrections amongst us, and has endeavored to bring on the inhabitants of our frontiers, the merciless Indian Savages, whose known rule of warfare, is an undistinguished destruction of all ages, sexes and conditions. In every stage of these Oppressions We have Petitioned for Redress in the most humble terms: Our repeated Petitions have been answered only by repeated injury. A Prince whose character is thus marked by every act which may define a Tyrant, is unfit to be the ruler of a free people. Nor have We been wanting in attentions to our British brethren. We have warned them from time to time of attempts by their legislature to extend an unwarrantable jurisdiction over us. We have reminded them of the circumstances of our emigration and settlement here. We have appealed to their native justice and magnanimity, and we have conjured them by the ties of our common kindred to disavow these usurpations, which would inevitably interrupt our connections and correspondence. They too have been deaf to the voice of justice and of consanguinity. We must, therefore, acquiesce in the necessity, which denounces our Separation, and hold them, as we hold the rest of mankind, Enemies in War, in Peace Friends. —

We, therefore, the Representatives of the United States of America, in General Congress, Assembled, appealing to the Supreme Judge of the world for the rectitude of our intentions do, in the Name, and by the Authority of the good People of these Colonies, solemnly publish and declare, That these United Colonies are, and of Right ought to be Free and Independent States; that they are Absolved from all Allegiance to the British Crown, and that all political connection between them and the State of Great Britain, is and ought to be totally dissolved; and that as Free and Independent States, they have full Power to levy War, conclude Peace, contract Alliances, establish Commerce, and to do all other Acts and Things which Independent States may of right do. — And for the support of this Declaration, with a firm reliance on the protection of divine Providence, we mutually pledge to each other our Lives, our Fortunes and our sacred Honor.

The Constitution of the United States

We the People of the United States, in Order to form a more perfect Union, establish Justice, insure domestic Tranquility, provide for the common defence, promote the general Welfare, and secure the Blessings of Liberty to ourselves and our Posterity do ordain and establish this CONSTITUTION for the United States of America.

ARTICLE I

Section 1. All legislative Powers herein granted shall be vested in a Congress of the United States, which shall consist of a Senate and House of Representatives.

Section 2. (1) The House of Representatives shall be composed of Members chosen every second Year by the People of the several States, and the Electors in each State shall have the Qualifications requisite for Electors of the most numerous Branch of the State Legislature.

(2) No Person shall be a Representative who shall not have attained to the Age of twenty-five Years, and been seven Years a Citizen of the United States, and who shall not, when elected, be an Inhabitant of that State in which he shall be chosen.

(3) [Representatives and direct Taxes[1] shall be apportioned among the several States which may be included within this Union, according to their respective Numbers, which shall be determined by adding to the whole Number of free Persons, including those bound to Service for a Term of Years, and excluding Indians not taxed, three fifths of all other Persons.][2] The actual Enumeration shall be made within three Years after the first Meeting of the Congress of the United States, and within every subsequent Term of ten Years, in such Manner as they shall by Law direct. The Number of Representatives shall not exceed one for every thirty Thousand, but each State shall have at Least one Representative; and until such enumeration shall be made, the State of New Hampshire shall be entitled to choose three,

---

[1] The Sixteenth Amendment replaced this with respect to income taxes.
[2] Repealed by the Fourteenth Amendment.

Massachusetts eight, Rhode-Island and Providence Plantations one, Connecticut five, New York six, New Jersey four, Pennsylvania eight, Delaware one, Maryland six, Virginia ten, North Carolina five, South Carolina five, and Georgia three.

(4) When vacancies happen in the Representation from any State, the Executive Authority thereof shall issue Writs of Election to fill such Vacancies.

(5) The House of Representatives shall choose their Speaker and other Officers; and shall have the sole Power of Impeachment.

Section 3. (1) The Senate of the United States shall be composed of two Senators from each State, [chosen by the Legislature][3] thereof, for six Years; and each Senator shall have one Vote.

(2) Immediately after they shall be assembled in Consequence of the first Election, they shall be divided as equally as may be into three Classes. The Seats of the Senators of the first Class shall be vacated at the Expiration of the second Year, of the second Class at the Expiration of the fourth Year, and of the third Class at the Expiration of the sixth Year, so that one-third may be chosen every second year; [and if Vacancies happen by Resignation, or otherwise, during the Recess of the Legislature of any State, the Executive thereof may make temporary Appointments until the next Meeting of the Legislature, which shall then fill such Vacancies].[4]

(3) No person shall be a Senator who shall not have attained to the Age of thirty Years, and been nine Years a Citizen of the United States, and who shall not, when elected, be an Inhabitant of that State for which he shall be chosen.

(4) The Vice President of the United States shall be President of the Senate, but shall have no Vote, unless they be equally divided.

(5) The Senate shall choose their other Officers, and also a President pro tempore, in the Absence of the Vice President, or when he shall exercise the Office of President of the United States.

(6) The Senate shall have the sole Power to try all Impeachments. When sitting for that Purpose, they shall be on Oath or Affirmation. When the President of the United States is tried, the Chief Justice shall preside: And no Person shall be convicted without the Concurrence of two thirds of the Members present.

(7) Judgment in Cases of Impeachment shall not extend further than to removal from Office, and disqualification to hold and enjoy any Office of honor, Trust or Profit under the United States: but the Party convicted shall nevertheless be liable and

---

[3] Repealed by the Seventeenth Amendment, Section 1.
[4] Changed by the Seventeenth Amendment.

subject to Indictment, Trial, Judgment and Punishment according to Law.

Section 4. (1) The Times, Places and Manner of holding Elections for Senators and Representatives, shall be prescribed in each State by the Legislature thereof; but the Congress may at any time by Law make or alter such Regulations, except as to the Places of choosing Senators.

(2) The Congress shall assemble at least once in every Year, and such Meeting shall [be on the first Monday in December,]⁵ unless they shall by Law appoint a different Day.

Section 5. (1) Each House shall be the Judge of the Elections, Returns and Qualifications of its own Members, and a Majority of each shall constitute a Quorum to do Business; but a smaller Number may adjourn from day to day, and may be authorized to compel the Attendance of absent Members, in such Manner, and under such Penalties as each House may provide.

(2) Each House may determine the Rules of its Proceedings, punish its Members for disorderly Behavior, and, with the Concurrence of two thirds, expel a Member.

(3) Each House shall keep a Journal of its Proceedings, and from time to time publish the same, excepting such Parts as may in their Judgment require Secrecy; and the Yeas and Nays of the Members of either House on any question shall, at the Desire of one fifth of those Present, be entered on the Journal.

(4) Neither House, during the Session of Congress, shall, without the Consent of the other, adjourn for more than three days, nor to any other Place than that in which the two Houses shall be sitting.

Section 6. (1) The Senators and Representatives shall receive a Compensation for their Services, to be ascertained by Law, and paid out of the Treasury of the United States. They shall in all Cases, except Treason, Felony and Breach of the Peace, be privileged from Arrest during their Attendance at the Session of their respective Houses, and in going to and returning from the same; and for any Speech or Debate in either House, they shall not be questioned in any other Place.

(2) No Senator or Representative shall, during the Time for which he was elected, be appointed to any civil Office under the Authority of the United States, which shall have been created, or the Emoluments whereof have been increased during such time; and no Person holding any Office under the United States, shall be a Member of either House during his Continuance in Office.

Section 7. (1) All Bills for raising Revenue shall originate in the

⁵ Changed by the Twentieth Amendment, Section 2.

House of Representatives; but the Senate may propose or concur with Amendments as on other Bills.

(2) Every Bill which shall have passed the House of Representatives and the Senate, shall, before it become a Law, be presented to the President of the United States; If he approve he shall sign it, but if not he shall return it, with his Objections to that House in which it shall have originated, who shall enter the Objections at large on their Journal, and procced to reconsider it. If after such Reconsideration two thirds of that House shall agree to pass the Bill, it shall be sent, together with the Objections, to the other House, by which it shall likewise be reconsidered, and if approved by two thirds of that House, it shall become a Law. But in all such Cases the Votes of both Houses shall be determined by Yeas and Nays, and the Names of the Persons voting for and against the Bill shall be entered on the Journal of each House respectively. If any Bill shall not be returned by the President within ten Days (Sundays excepted) after it shall have been presented to him, the Same shall be a Law, in like Manner as if he had signed it, unless the Congress by their Adjournment prevent its Return, in which Case it shall not be a Law.

(3) Every Order, Resolution, or Vote to which the Concurrence of the Senate and House of Representatives may be necessary (except on a question of Adjournment) shall be presented to the President of the United States; and before the Same shall take Effect, shall be approved by him, or being disapproved by him, shall be repassed by two thirds of the Senate and House of Representatives, according to the Rules and Limitations prescribed in the Case of a Bill.

Section 8. (1) The Congress shall have Power To lay and collect Taxes, Duties, Imposts and Excises, to pay the Debts and provide for the common Defense and general Welfare of the United States; but all Duties, Imposts and Excises shall be uniform throughout the United States;

(2) To borrow money on the credit of the United States;

(3) To regulate Commerce with foreign Nations, and among the several States, and with the Indian Tribes;

(4) To establish an uniform Rule of Naturalization, and uniform Laws on the subject of Bankruptcies throughout the United States;

(5) To coin Money, regulate the Value thereof, and of foreign Coin, and fix the Standard of Weights and Measures;

(6) To provide for the Punishment of counterfeiting the Securities and current Coin of the United States;

(7) To establish Post Offices and post Roads;

(8) To promote the Progress of Science and useful Arts, by securing for limited Times to Authors and Investors the exclusive Right to their respective Writings and Discoveries;
(9) To constitute Tribunals inferior to the supreme Court;
(10) To define and punish Piracies and Felonies committed on the high Seas, and Offenses against the Law of Nations;
(11) To declare War, grant Letters of Marque and Reprisal, and make Rules concerning Captures on Land and Water;
(12) To raise and support Armies, but no Appropriation of Money to that Use shall be for a longer Term than two Years;
(13) To provide and maintain a Navy;
(14) To make Rules for the Government and Regulation of the land and naval Forces;
(15) To provide for calling forth the Militia to execute the Laws of the Union suppress Insurrections and repel Invasions;
(16) To provide for organizing, arming, and disciplining the Militia, and for governing such Part of them as may be employed in the Service of the United States, reserving to the States respectively, the Appointment of the Officers, and the Authority of training the Militia according to the discipline prescribed by Congress;
(17) To exercise exclusive Legislation in all Cases whatsoever, over such District (not exceeding ten Miles square) as may, by Cession of particular States, and the Acceptance of Congress, become the Seat of the Government of the United States, and to exercise like Authority over all Places purchased by the Consent of the Legislature of the State in which the Same shall be, for the Erection of Forts, Magazines, Arsenals, dock-Yards, and other needful Buildings; — And
(18) To make all Laws which shall be necessary and proper for carrying into Execution the foregoing Powers, and all other Powers vested by this Constitution in the Government of the United States, or in any Department or Officer thereof.

Section 9. (1) The Migration or Importation of such Persons as any of the States now existing shall think proper to admit, shall not be prohibited by the Congress prior to the Year one thousand eight hundred and eight, but a tax or duty may be imposed on such Importation, not exceeding ten dollars for each Person.
(2) The Privilege of the Writ of Habeas Corpus shall not be suspended, unless when in Cases of Rebellion or Invasion the public Safety may require it.
(3) No Bill of Attainder or ex post facto Law shall be passed.
(4) No Capitation, or other direct, Tax shall be laid, unless in Pro-

portion to the Census or Enumeration herein before directed to be taken.[6]

(5) No Tax or Duty shall be laid on Articles exported from any State.

(6) No Preference shall be given by any Regulation of Commerce or Revenue to the Ports of one State over those of another: nor shall Vessels bound to, or from, one State, be obliged to enter, clear, or pay Duties in another.

(7) No Money shall be drawn from the Treasury, but in Consequence of Appropriations made by Law; and a regular Statement and Account of the Receipts and Expenditures of all public Money shall be published from time to time.

(8) No Title of Nobility shall be granted by the United States: And no Person holding any Office of Profit or Trust under them, shall, without the Consent of the Congress, accept of any present, Emolument, Office, or Title, of any kind whatever, from any King, Prince, or foreign State.

Section 10. (1) No State shall enter into any Treaty, Alliance, or Confederation; grant Letters of Marque and Reprisal; coin Money; emit Bills of Credit; make any Thing but gold and silver Coin a Tender in Payment of Debts; pass any Bill of Attainder, ex post facto Law, or Law impairing the Obligation of Contracts, or grant any Title of Nobility.

(2) No State shall, without the Consent of the Congress, lay any Imposts or Duties on Imports or Exports, except what may be absolutely necessary for executing its inspection Laws: and the net Produce of all Duties and Imposts, laid by any State on Imports or Exports, shall be for the Use of the Treasury of the United States; and all such laws shall be subject to the Revision and Control of the Congress.

(3) No State shall, without the Consent of Congress, lay any duty of Tonnage, keep Troops, or Ships of War in time of Peace, enter into any Agreement or Compact with another State, or with a foreign Power, or engage in War, unless actually invaded, or in such imminent Danger as will not admit of delay.

ARTICLE II

Section 1. (1) The executive Power shall be vested in a President of the United States of America. He shall hold his Office during the Term of four Years, and, together with the Vice-President, chosen for the same Term, be elected, as follows:

---

[6] Changed by the Sixteenth Amendment.

(2) Each State shall appoint, in such Manner as the Legislature thereof may direct, a Number of Electors, equal to the whole Number of Senators and Representatives to which the State may be entitled in the Congress; but no Senator or Representative, or Person holding an Office of Trust or Profit under the United States, shall be appointed an Elector.

[The Electors shall meet in their respective States, and vote by Ballot for two persons, of whom one at least shall not be an Inhabitant of the same State with themselves. And they shall make a List of all the Persons voted for, and of the Number of Votes for each; which List they shall sign and certify, and transmit sealed to the Seat of the Government of the United States, directed to the President of the Senate. The President of the Senate shall, in the Presence of the Senate and House of Representatives, open all the Certificates, and the Votes shall then be counted. The Person having the greatest Number of Votes shall be the President, if such Number be a Majority of the whole Number of Electors appointed; and if there be more than one who have such Majority, and have an equal Number of Votes, then the House of Representatives shall immediately choose by Ballot one of them for President; and if no Person have a Majority, then from the five highest on the List the said House shall in like Manner choose the President. But in choosing the President, the Votes shall be taken by States, the Representation from each State having one Vote; A quorum for this purpose shall consist of a Member or Members from two-thirds of the States, and a Majority of all the States shall be necessary to a Choice. In every Case, after the Choice of the President, the Person having the greatest Number of Votes of the Electors shall be the Vice-President. But if there should remain two or more who have equal Votes, the Senate shall choose from them by Ballot the Vice-President.][7]

(3) The Congress may determine the Time of choosing the Electors, and the Day on which they shall give their Votes; which Day shall be the same throughout the United States.

(4) No person except a natural born Citizen, or a Citizen of the United States, at the time of the Adoption of this Constitution, shall be eligible to the Office of President; neither shall any Person be eligible to that Office who shall not have attained to the Age of thirty-five Years, and been fourteen Years a Resident within the United States.

(5) In case of the Removal of the President from Office, or of his Death, Resignation, or Inability to discharge the Powers and

---

[7] This paragraph was superseded in 1804 by the Twelfth Amendment.

Duties of the said Office, the same shall devolve on the Vice-President, and the Congress may by Law provide for the Case of Removal, Death, Resignation or Inability, both of the President and Vice-President, declaring what Officer shall then act as President, and such Officer shall act accordingly, until the Disability be removed, or a President shall be elected.[8]

(6) The President shall, at stated Times, receive for his Services, a Compensation, which shall neither be increased nor diminished during the Period for which he shall have been elected, and he shall not receive within that Period any other Emolument from the United States, or any of them.

(7) Before he enter on the Execution of his Office, he shall take the following Oath or Affirmation: — "I do solemnly swear (or affirm) that I will faithfully execute the Office of President of the United States, and will to the best of my Ability, preserve, protect and defend the Constitution of the United States."

Section 2. (1) The President shall be Commander in Chief of the Army and Navy of the United States, and of the Militia of the several States, when called into the actual Service of the United States; he may require the Opinion in writing, of the principal Officer in each of the executive Departments, upon any subject relating to the Duties of their respective Offices, and he shall have Power to Grant Reprieves and Pardons for Offenses against the United States, except in Cases of Impeachment.

(2) He shall have Power, by and with the Advice and Consent of the Senate, to make Treaties, provided two-thirds of the Senators present concur; and he shall nominate, and by and with the Advice and Consent of the Senate, shall appoint Ambassadors, other public Ministers and Consuls, Judges of the supreme Court, and all other Officers of the United States, whose Appointments are not herein otherwise provided for, and which shall be established by Law: but the Congress may by Law vest the Appointment of such inferior Officers, as they think proper, in the President alone, in the Court of Law, or in the Heads of Departments.

(3) The President shall have Power to fill up all Vacancies that may happen during the Recess of the Senate, by granting Commissions which shall expire at the End of their next Session.

Section 3. He shall from time to time give to the Congress Information of the State of the Union, and recommend to their Consideration such Measures as he shall judge necessary and expedient; he may, on extraordinary Occasions, convene both Houses, or either of them, and in Case of Disagreement between

---

[8] Changed by the Twenty-fifth Amendment.

them, with Respect to the Time of Adjournment, he may adjourn them to such Time as he shall think proper; he shall receive Ambassadors and other public Ministers; he shall take Care that the Laws be faithfully executed, and shall Commission all the Officers of the United States.

Section 4. The President, Vice President and all civil Officers of the United States, shall be removed from Office on Impeachment for, and Conviction of, Treason, Bribery, or other high Crimes and Misdemeanors.

ARTICLE III

Section 1. The judicial Power of the United States, shall be vested in one supreme Court, and in such inferior Courts as the Congress may from time to time ordain and establish. The Judges, both of the supreme and inferior Courts, shall hold their Offices during good Behavior, and shall, at stated Times, receive for their Services a Compensation which shall not be diminished during their Continuance in Office.

Section 2. (1) The judicial Power shall extend to all Cases, in Law and Equity, arising under this Constitution, the Laws of the United States, and Treaties made, or which shall be made, under their Authority; — to all Cases affecting Ambassadors, other public Ministers and Consuls; — to all Cases of admiralty and maritime Jurisdiction; — to Controversies to which the United States shall be a Party; — to Controversies between two or more states; — [between a State and Citizens of another State];[9] — between Citizens of different States; — between Citizens of the same State claiming Lands under Grants of different States, and [between a State, or the Citizens thereof, and foreign States, Citizens or Subjects].[10]

(2) In all Cases affecting Ambassadors, other public Ministers and Consuls, and those in which a State shall be Party, the supreme Court shall have original Jurisdiction. In all the other Cases before mentioned, the supreme Court shall have appellate Jurisdiction, both as to Law and Fact, with such Exceptions, and under such Regulations as the Congress shall make.

(3) The trial of all Crimes, except in Cases of Impeachment, shall be by Jury; and such Trial shall be held in the State where the said Crimes shall have been committed: but when not commit-

---

[9] Restricted by the Eleventh Amendment.
[10] Restricted by the Eleventh Amendment.

ted within any State, the Trial shall be at such Place or Places as the Congress may by Law have directed.

Section 3. (1) Treason against the United States, shall consist only in levying War against them, or in adhering to their Enemies, giving them Aid and Comfort. No Person shall be convicted of Treason unless on the Testimony of two Witnesses to the same overt Act, or on Confession in open Court.

(2) The Congress shall have Power to declare the Punishment of Treason, but no Attainder of Treason shall work Corruption of Blood, or Forfeiture except during the Life of the Person attainted.

ARTICLE IV

Section 1. Full Faith and Credit shall be given in each State to the public Acts, Records, and judicial Proceedings of every other State. And the Congress may by general Laws prescribe the Manner in which such Acts, Records and Proceedings shall be proved, and the Effect thereof.

Section 2. (1) The Citizens of each State shall be entitled to all Privileges and Immunities of Citizens in the several States.

(2) A Person charged in any State with Treason, Felony, or other Crime, who shall flee from Justice, and be found in another State, shall on demand of the executive Authority of the State from which he fled, be delivered up, to be removed to the State having Jurisdiction of the Crime.

(3) [No Person held to Service or Labor in one State, under the Laws thereof, escaping into another, shall, in Consequence of any Law or Regulation therein, be discharged from such Service or Labor, but shall be delivered up on Claim of the Party to whom such Service or Labor may be due.][11]

Section 3. (1) New States may be admitted by the Congress into this Union; but no new State shall be formed or erected within the Jurisdiction of any other State; nor any State be formed by the Junction of two or more States, or Parts of States, without the Consent of the Legislatures of the States concerned as well as of the Congress.

(2) The Congress shall have Power to dispose of and make all needful Rules and Regulations respecting the Territory or other Property belonging to the United States; and nothing in this Constitution shall be so construed as to Prejudice any Claims of the United States, or of any particular State.

[11] This paragraph has been superseded by the Thirteenth Amendment.

Section 4. The United States shall guarantee to every State in this Union a Republican Form of Government, and shall protect each of them against Invasion; and on Application of the Legislature, or of the Executive (when the Legislature cannot be convened) against domestic Violence.

ARTICLE V

The Congress, whenever two-thirds of both Houses shall deem it necessary, shall propose Amendments to this Constitution, or, on the Application of the Legislatures of two-thirds of the several States, shall call a Convention for proposing Amendments, which, in either Case, shall be valid to all Intents and Purposes, as part of this Constitution, when ratified by the Legislature of three-fourths of the several States, or by Conventions in three-fourths thereof, as the one or the other Mode of Ratification may be proposed by the Congress; Provided that no Amendment which may be made prior to the Year One thousand eight hundred and eight shall in any Manner affect the first and fourth Clauses in the Ninth Section of the first Article; and that no State, without its Consent, shall be deprived of its equal Suffrage in the Senate.

ARTICLE VI

(1) All Debts contracted and Engagements entered into, before the Adoption of this Constitution, shall be as valid against the United States under this Constitution, as under the Confederation.
(2) This Constitution, and the Laws of the United States which shall be made in Pursuance thereof; and all Treaties made, or which shall be made, under the Authority of the United States, shall be the supreme Law of the Land; and the Judges in every State shall be bound thereby, any Thing in the Constitution or Laws of any State to the Contrary notwithstanding.
(3) The Senators and Representatives before mentioned, and the Members of the several State Legislatures, and all executive and judicial Officers, both of the United States and of the several States, shall be bound by Oath or Affirmation, to support this Constitution; but no religious Test shall ever be required as a Qualification to any Office or public Trust under the United States.

ARTICLE VII

The Ratification of the Conventions of nine States, shall be sufficient for the Establishment of this Constitution between the States so ratifying the Same.

DONE in Convention by the Unanimous Consent of the States present the Seventeenth Day of September in the Year of our Lord one thousand seven hundred and Eighty seven and the Independence of the United States of America the Twelfth. In Witness whereof We have hereunto subscribed our Names.

Go. WASHINGTON
President and deputy from Virginia

ARTICLES IN ADDITION TO, AND AMENDMENT OF, THE CONSTITUTION OF THE UNITED STATES OF AMERICA, PROPOSED BY CONGRESS, AND RATIFIED BY THE LEGISLATURES OF THE SEVERAL STATES, PURSUANT TO THE FIFTH ARTICLE OF THE ORIGINAL CONSTITUTION.

AMENDMENT I[12]

Congress shall make no law respecting an establishment of religion, or prohibiting the free exercise thereof; or abridging the freedom of speech, or of the press; or the right of the people peaceably to assemble, and to petition the Government for a redress of grievances.

AMENDMENT II

A well regulated Militia, being necessary to the security of a free State, the right of the people to keep and bear Arms, shall not be infringed.

AMENDMENT III

No Soldier shall, in time of peace be quartered in any house, without the consent of the Owner, nor in time of war, but in a manner to be prescribed by law.

---

[12] The first ten amendments were adopted in 1791.

AMENDMENT IV

The right of the people to be secure in their persons, houses, papers, and effects, against unreasonable searches and seizures, shall not be violated, and no Warrants shall issue, but upon probable cause, supported by Oath or affirmation, and particularly describing the place to be searched, and the persons or things to be seized.

AMENDMENT V

No person shall be held to answer for a capital, or otherwise infamous crime, unless on a presentment or indictment of a Grand Jury, except in cases arising in the land or naval forces, or in the Militia, when in actual service in time of War or public danger; nor shall any person be subject for the same offense to be twice put in jeopardy of life or limb; nor shall be compelled in any criminal case to be witness against himself, nor be deprived of life, liberty, or property, without due process of law; nor shall private property be taken for public use without just compensation.

AMENDMENT VI

In all criminal prosecutions, the accused shall enjoy the right to a speedy and public trial, by an impartial jury of the State and district wherein the crime shall have been committed, which district shall have been previously ascertained by law, and to be informed of the nature and cause of the accusation; to be confronted with the witnesses against him; to have compulsory process for obtaining witnesses in his favor, and to have the Assistance of Counsel for his defense.

AMENDMENT VII

In Suits at common law, where the value in controversy shall exceed twenty dollars, the right of trial by jury shall be preserved, and no fact tried by a jury, shall be otherwise reexamined in any Court of the United States, than according to the rules of the common law.

AMENDMENT VIII

Excessive bail shall not be required, nor excessive fines imposed, nor cruel and unusual punishments inflicted.

AMENDMENT IX

The enumeration in the Constitution, of certain rights, shall not be construed to deny or disparage others retained by the people.

AMENDMENT X

The powers not delegated to the United States by the Constitution, nor prohibited by it to the States, are reserved to the States respectively, or to the people.

AMENDMENT XI[13]

The Judicial power of the United States shall not be construed to extend to any suit in law or equity, commenced or prosecuted against one of the United States by Citizens of another State, or by Citizens or Subjects of any Foreign State.

AMENDMENT XII[14]

The Electors shall meet in their respective states and vote by ballot for President and Vice-President, one of whom, at least, shall not be an inhabitant of the same state with themselves; they shall name in their ballots the person voted for as President, and in distinct ballots the person voted for as Vice-President, and they shall make distinct lists of all persons voted for as President, and of all persons voted for as Vice-President, and of the number of votes for each, which lists they shall sign and certify, and transmit sealed to the seat of the government of the United States, directed to the President of the Senate; — The President of the Senate shall, in presence of the Senate and House of Representatives, open all the certificates and the votes shall then be counted; — The person

---

[13] Adopted in 1798.
[14] Adopted in 1804.

having the greatest number of votes for President, shall be the President, if such number be a majority of the whole number of Electors appointed; and if no person have such majority, then from the persons having the highest numbers not exceeding three on the list of those voted for as President, the House of Representatives shall choose immediately, by ballot, the President. But in choosing the President, the votes shall be taken by states, the representation from each state having one vote; a quorum for this purpose shall consist of a member or members from two-thirds of the states, and a majority of all the states shall be necessary to a choice. [And if the House of Representatives shall not choose a President whenever the right of choice shall devolve upon them, before the fourth day of March next following, then the Vice-President shall act as President, as in the case of the death or other constitutional disability of the President.][15] — The person having the greatest number of votes as Vice-President, shall be the Vice-President, if such number be a majority of the whole number of Electors appointed, and if no person have a majority, then from the two highest numbers on the list, the Senate shall choose the Vice-President; a quorum for the purpose shall consist of two-thirds of the whole number of Senators, and a majority of the whole number shall be necessary to a choice. But no person constitutionally ineligible to the office of President shall be eligible to that of Vice-President of the United States.

AMENDMENT XIII[16]

Section 1. Neither slavery nor involuntary servitude, except as a punishment for crime whereof the party shall have been duly convicted, shall exist within the United States, or any place subject to their jurisdiction.

Section 2. Congress shall have power to enforce this article by appropriate legislation.

AMENDMENT XIV[17]

Section 1. All persons born or naturalized in the United States, and subject to the jurisdiction thereof, are citizens of the United States and of the State wherein they reside. No state shall make or enforce any law which shall abridge the privileges or immunities of citizens of the United States; nor shall any State deprive any person of life, liberty, or property, without due process of

---

[15] Superseded by the Twentieth Amendment, Section 3.
[16] Adopted in 1865.
[17] Adopted in 1868.

law; nor deny to any person within its jurisdiction the equal protection of the laws.

Section 2. Representatives shall be apportioned among the several States according to their respective numbers, counting the whole number of persons in each State, excluding Indians not taxed. But when the right to vote at any election for the choice of electors for President and Vice-President of the United States, Representatives in Congress, the Executive and Judicial officers of a State, or the members of the Legislature thereof, is denied to any of the male inhabitants of such State, being twenty-one years of age, and citizens of the United States, or in any way abridged, except for participation in rebellion, or other crime, the basis of representation therein shall be reduced in the proportion which the number of such male citizens shall bear to the whole number of male citizens twenty-one years of age in such State.

Section 3. No person shall be a Senator or Representative in Congress, or elector of President and Vice-President, or hold any office, civil or military, under the United States, or under any State, who, having previously taken an oath, as a member of Congress, or as an officer of the United States, or as a member of any State legislature, or as an executive or judicial officer of any State, to support the Constitution of the United States, shall have engaged in insurrection or rebellion against the same, or given aid or comfort to the enemies thereof. But Congress may by a vote of two-thirds of each House, remove such disability.

Section 4. The validity of the public debt of the United States, authorized by law, including debts incurred for payment of pensions and bounties for services in suppressing insurrection or rebellion, shall not be questioned. But neither the United States nor any State shall assume or pay any debt or obligation incurred in aid of insurrection or rebellion against the United States, or any claim for the loss or emancipation of any slave; but all such debts, obligations and claims shall be held illegal and void.

Section 5. The Congress shall have power to enforce, by appropriate legislation, the provisions of this article.

AMENDMENT XV[18]

Section 1. The right of citizens of the United States to vote shall not be denied or abridged by the United States or by any State

---

[18] Adopted in 1870.

on account of race, color, or previous condition of servitude.

Section 2. The Congress shall have power to enforce this article by appropriate legislation.

AMENDMENT XVI[19]

The Congress shall have power to lay and collect taxes on incomes, from whatever source derived, without apportionment among the several States, and without regard to any census or enumeration.

AMENDMENT XVII[20]

The Senate of the United States shall be composed of two Senators from each State, elected by the people thereof, for six years; and each Senator shall have one vote. The electors in each State shall have the qualifications requisite for electors of the most numerous branch of the State legislatures.

When vacancies happen in the representation of any State in the Senate, the executive authority of such State shall issue writs of election to fill such vacancies: *Provided,* That the legislature of any State may empower the executive thereof to make temporary appointments until the people fill the vacancies by election as the legislature may direct.

This amendment shall not be so construed as to affect the election or term of any Senator chosen before it becomes valid as part of the Constitution.

AMENDMENT XVIII[21]

Section 1. After one year from the ratification of this article the manufacture, sale, or transportation of intoxicating liquors within, the importation thereof into, or the exportation thereof from the United States and all territory subject to the jurisdiction thereof for beverage purposes is hereby prohibited.

---

[19] Adopted in 1913.
[20] Adopted in 1913.
[21] Adopted in 1919. Repealed by Section 1 of the Twenty-first Amendment.

Section 2. The Congress and the several States shall have concurrent power to enforce this article by appropriate legislation.

Section 3. This article shall be inoperative unless it shall have been ratified as an amendment to the Constitution by the legislatures of the several States, as provided in the Constitution, within seven years from the date of the submission hereof to the States by the Congress.

AMENDMENT XIX[22]

The right of citizens of the United States to vote shall not be denied or abridged by the United States or by any State on account of sex.

Congress shall have power to enforce this article by appropriate legislation.

AMENDMENT XX[23]

Section 1. The terms of the President and Vice-President shall end at noon on the 20th day of January, and the terms of Senators and Representatives at noon on the 3rd day of January, of the years in which such terms would have ended if this article had not been ratified; and the terms of their successors shall then begin.

Section 2. The Congress shall assemble at least once in every year, and such meeting shall begin at noon on the 3rd day of January, unless they shall by law appoint a different day.

Section 3. If, at the time fixed for the beginning of the term of the President, the President elect shall have died, the Vice-President elect shall become President. If a President shall not have been chosen before the time fixed for the beginning of his term, or if the President elect shall have failed to qualify, then the Vice-President elect shall act as President until a President shall have qualified; and the Congress may by law provide for the case wherein neither a President elect nor a Vice-President elect shall have qualified, declaring who shall then act as President,

---

[22] Adopted in 1920.
[23] Adopted in 1933.

or the manner in which one who is to act shall be selected, and such person shall act accordingly until a President or Vice-President shall have qualified.

Section 4. The Congress may by law provide for the case of the death of any of the persons from whom the House of Representatives may choose a President whenever the right of choice shall have devolved upon them, and for the case of the death of any of the persons from whom the Senate may choose a Vice-President whenever the right of choice shall have devolved upon them.

Section 5. Sections 1 and 2 shall take effect on the 15th day of October following the ratification of this article.

Section 6. This article shall be inoperative unless it shall have been ratified as an amendment to the Constitution by the legislatures of three-fourths of the several States within seven years from the date of its submission.

AMENDMENT XXI[24]

Section 1. The eighteenth article of amendment to the Constitution of the United States is hereby repealed.

Section 2. The transportation or importation into any State, Territory, or possession of the United States for delivery or use therein of intoxicating liquors, in violation of the laws thereof, is hereby prohibited.

Section 3. This article shall be inoperative unless it shall have been ratified as an amendment to the Constitution by conventions in the several States, as provided in the Constitution, within seven years from the date of the submission hereof to the States by the Congress.

AMENDMENT XXII[25]

Section 1. No person shall be elected to the office of the President more than twice, and no person who has held the office of President, or acted as President, for more than two years of a term to which some other person was elected President shall be elected to the office of the President more than once. But this

---

[24] Adopted in 1933.
[25] Adopted in 1951.

Article shall not apply to any person holding the office of President when this Article was proposed by the Congress, and shall not prevent any person who may be holding the office of President, or acting as President, during the term within which this Article becomes operative from holding the office of President or acting as President during the remainder of such term.

Section 2. This article shall be inoperative unless it shall have been ratified as an amendment to the Constitution by the legislatures of three-fourths of the several States within seven years from the date of its submission to the States by the Congress.

AMENDMENT XXIII[26]

Section 1. The District constituting the seat of Government of the United States shall appoint in such manner as the Congress may direct:

A number of electors of President and Vice-President equal to the whole number of Senators and Representatives in Congress to which the District would be entitled if it were a State, but in no event more than the least populous State; they shall be in addition to those appointed by the States, but they shall be considered, for the purposes of the election of President and Vice-President, to be electors appointed by a State; and they shall meet in the District and perform such duties as provided by the twelfth article of amendment.

Section 2. The Congress shall have power to enforce this article by appropriate legislation.

AMENDMENT XXIV[27]

Section 1. The right of citizens of the United States to vote in any primary or other election for President or Vice-President, for electors for President or Vice-President, or for Senator or Representative in Congress, shall not be denied or abridged by the United States or any state by reasons of failure to pay any poll tax or other tax.

Section 2. The Congress shall have power to enforce this article by appropriate legislation.

[26] Adopted in 1961.
[27] Adopted in 1964.

AMENDMENT XXV[28]

Section 1. In case of the removal of the President from office or of his death or resignation, the Vice-President shall become President.

Section 2. Whenever there is a vacancy in the office of the Vice-President, the President shall nominate a Vice-President who shall take office upon confirmation by a majority vote of both Houses of Congress.

Section 3. Whenever the President transmits to the President pro tempore of the Senate and the Speaker of the House of Representatives his written declaration that he is unable to discharge the powers and duties of his office, and until he transmits to them a written declaration to the contrary, such powers and duties shall be discharged by the Vice-President as Acting President.

Section 4. Whenever the Vice-President and a majority of either the principal officers of the Executive departments or of such other body as Congress may by law provide, transmit to the President pro tempore of the Senate and the Speaker of the House of Representatives their written declaration that the President is unable to discharge the powers and duties of his office, the Vice-President shall immediately assume the powers and duties of the office as Acting President.

Thereafter, when the President transmits to the President pro tempore of the Senate and the Speaker of the House of Representatives his written declaration that no inability exists, he shall resume the powers and duties of his office unless the Vice-President and a majority of either the principal officers of the executive departments or of such other body as Congress may by law provide, transmit within four days to the President pro tempore of the Senate and the Speaker of the House of Representatives their written declaration that the President is unable to discharge the powers and duties of his office. Thereupon Congress shall decide the issue, assembling within forty-eight hours for that purpose if not in session. If the Congress, within twenty-one days after receipt of the latter written declaration, or, if Congress is not in session, within twenty-one days after Congress is required to assemble, determines by two-thirds vote of both houses that the President is unable to discharge the powers and duties of his office, the Vice-President shall continue to discharge the same as Acting President; otherwise, the President shall resume the powers and duties of his office.

[28] Adopted in 1967.

AMENDMENT XXVI[29]

Section 1. The right of citizens of the United States, who are 18 years of age or older, to vote shall not be denied or abridged by the United States or any state on account of age.

Section 2. The Congress shall have power to enforce this article by appropriate legislation.

PROPOSED AMENDMENTS:
(EQUAL RIGHTS AMENDMENT)[30]

Section 1. Equality of rights under the law shall not be denied or abridged by the United States or by any State on account of sex.

Section 2. The Congress shall have the power to enforce, by appropriate legislation, the provisions of this article.

Section 3. This amendment shall take effect two years after the date of ratification.

(D.C. VOTING RIGHTS)[31]

Section 1. For purposes of representation in the Congress, election of the President and Vice President, and article V of this Constitution, the District constituting the seat of government of the United States shall be treated as though it were a State.

Section 2. The exercise of the rights and powers conferred under this article shall be by the people of the District constituting the seat of government, and as shall be provided by the Congress.

Section 3. The twenty-third article of amendment to the Constitution of the United States is hereby repealed.

Section 4. This article shall be inoperative, unless it shall have been ratified as an amendment to the Constitution by the legislatures of three-fourths of the several States within seven years from the date of its submission.

---

[29] Adopted in 1971.

[30] Approved by Congress in 1972 and sent to the states for ratification. On October 6, 1978, Congress voted to extend the deadline for ratification from March 29, 1979 to June 30, 1982; marking the first time the ratification period was ever extended. As of November 1978, 35 states, out of a needed 38, had voted for ratification.

[31] Proposed Amendment passed by Congress and sent to the states for ratification on August 28, 1978.

Index

Adams, John, 138
Advisory committees, reduction of, 78
Affirmative action, 152
  and reverse discrimination, 151
Agnew, Spiro, 103, 207
Agricultural interest groups, 190
Alien and Sedition Acts of 1798, 43–44
American Bar Association (ABA), 157
Anarchy, defined, 7
Appropriations bills, 109
Appropriations committees, 118
Arthur, Chester, and civil service reform, 76
Articles of Confederation (1781–89), 23–24
Associated Milk Producers (AMPI), 190
  campaign contributions by, 193
Authority
  defined, 6
  final, of Supreme Court, 136–137, 158
  obedience to, 6–7

Badillo, Herman, 115–116
Baker v. *Carr* (1962), 142
Bakke case, 151
Barber, James David, 61–62
Beall, J. Glenn, Jr., election campaign of, 209–213
Beard, Charles, 26–27
Biden, Joseph, 94
Bill. *See* Legislation
Bill of Rights
  on free speech, 43
  ratification struggle for, 29–30
Black, Hugo, on free speech, 46
Blacks, in Congress, 94, 96t, 97t
Brooke, Edward, 94
Brown v. *Board of Education*, 150
Buchanan, James, presidential style of, 59
Buckley, James, 125
Bureaucracy, federal
  and president, 66–67, 78–79
  problems of, 75–78
  role of, 69–70
  structure of, 70–75
Bureaucrat, defined, 69
Burger, Warren, 142–143
Business groups, 189

Cabinet departments, 71, 73
  rivalries between, 79
Calhoun, John C., 92
Cambodian invasion, and antiwar movement, 195
Campaign contributions
  by interest groups, 189t, 190t, 192–194, 210
  regulation of, 122–125, 193
Campaign Finance Reform Bill
  opposition to, 125
  passage of, 122–124
  and Watergate scandal, 121–122

Carter, Jimmy
  and bureaucratic reform, 77–78
  and cabinet, 73
  and Gettysburg address in style of, 63
  and media, 69, 206
  on Mondale, 55
  personality type of, 62
  presidential style of, 61
  and steel industry, 82–83, 84–85
  White House staff of, 70
Caucus
  defined, 102
  in national conventions, 177
Central Intelligence Agency (CIA), 65, 70, 73
Certiorari, writ of, 136
Checks and balances, 31–32
Chief of state, president as, 63–64
Circuit courts of appeals, 132
Civilian supremacy principle, over military, 66
Civil rights
  Congress and, 150–151
  presidents and, 149
  Supreme Court and, 36–37, 142, 147, 150, 151–152
Civil Rights Act of 1875, 147
Civil rights movement, and free speech, 46
Civil Service
  Carter's reform of, 77–78
  rise of, 76, 77
  (*See also* Bureaucracy, federal)
Civil Service Reform Act of 1883, 76
Civil Service Reform Act of 1978, 77
Civil War, Lincoln's leadership in, 58

Class differences, in voter participation, 164–165, 167–168
Clay, Henry, 92
Cloture, defined, 108
Colonial government, and U.S. Constitution, 22
Commander in Chief, president as, 65–66
Committees on Committees, of Republican party, 103
Committees (Congress), 109–110
  assignments to, 103, 104
  chairmen of, 113–114
  in House of Representatives, 116–118
  in Senate, 118–119
  Speaker and, 102
  specialization and reciprocity in, 114–116
  types of, 110–113
Common Cause, and campaign finance reform, 122, 124
Compromise
  and pluralism, 220
  in U.S. Constitution, 24–25
Confederation, Articles of, 23–24
Conference committee, 111
Conflict
  and elite control, 225
  government regulation of, 7–8, 10–11
  political, 229–230
Congress, U.S.
  accomplishments of, 127–128
  calendar of, 105–106
  careerism in, 98–99
  civil rights in, 147, 150–151
  committee system in, 109–119

and constitutional amendments, 38, 39–40
Ninetieth, 97t
Ninety-fifth, 94, 96t
operation of, 104–109, 126–127
  in Campaign Finance Reform Bill, 121–125
powers of, 32, 66, 91–92
  nonlegislative, 119-121
  and presidential veto, 109
and president, 67–68
representation in, 92–93
size of, 93
suppression of free speech by, 43–44, 45
and Supreme Court, 155–156
unicameral, 23
(*See also* Government; House of Representatives; Senate)
Congressional Budget Office, 119–120
Congressional districts
  malapportionment and gerrymandering in, 99
  reapportionment of, 99–100, 142, 153–154
Congressional investigations, 120
Congress members
  age of, 94
  characteristics of, 96–97t, 98
  election of incumbents, 101
  mavericks, 115–116
  qualifications for, 95
  role of, 94–95
  (*See also* Senators)
Consensus, in society, 220
Conspiracy theory, of politics, 226
Constitution, U.S.
  compromise in, 24–25, 28
  congressional powers in, 91

framers of, 25–27
  Federalists *vs.* Anti-Federalists, 27–28
freedom of speech in, 43–47, 201
historical background of, 21–24
on judicial power, 131
limitations of power in, 8
methods of change in, 37–40, 136–137
motivation behind, 26–27
presidential power in, 32, 53–54, 66
principles of, 30–37
ratification of, 28–30
Supreme Court and, 154–155
survival of, 40–41, 48–49
as symbol, 48–49
Constitutional amendments
First, 43
numbers of, 37–38
process for, 38–39
Seventeenth, 95
Tenth, 34
Thirteenth, 25
Twenty-second, 40, 54
Constitutional Convention (1787), 24–25
delegates to, 25–26
Continental Congresses, 22–23
Conventions. *See* National convention; State convention
Coolidge, Calvin, 59
Council of Economic Advisors, 71
Court of Claims, U.S., 132
Court of Military Appeals, U.S., 132–133
Courts of appeals, 132
Court system, federal, 131–135
  (*See also* Supreme Court)
Cracking, defined, 99

Criminal defendents, rights of, 142, 143
Cuban missile crisis (1962), 8
Custodial view, of presidential power, 59
Custom, in constitutional change, 40

Dahl, Robert, on pluralist model, 222, 223
Daley, Richard, 176
Debate, congressional, 105–106
  filibuster of, 106–108
Declaration of Independence, 21, 23
  signers of, 26
Democracy
  defined, 8
  framers of constitution on, 26–27
  group theory of. *See* Pluralism
Democracy in America (de Tocqueville), 187–188
Democratic party
  in Congress, 102–103, 104
  origins of, 170
  in presidential elections, 171–172
  supporters of, 172–173
  (*See also* Political parties)
de Tocqueville, Alexis, 187–188
Diplomacy. *See* Foreign policy
Discharge calendar, 105–106
Douglas, William O.
  on free speech, 42
  on obscenity, 154
Dred Scott decision, 137, 140, 153
Dumping, of steel, 83

Economic Interpretation of the Constitution of the United States, An (Beard), 26–27

Economics, scope of, 12
Eisenhower, Dwight D.
  on military-industrial complex, 226
  personality type of, 62
  presidential style of, 60
  on Warren court, 143
Elections
  campaign contributions in, 124–125, 189t, 190t, 192–194
  constitutional provisions for, 32, 95
    presidential, 54–57
  of incumbents, 101
  interest groups in, 210–211
  media influence on, 208–213
  presidential, 54–55
    party alignment in, 171–172
    and party conventions, 177, 179
    voter participation in, 161–162, 163t
  (*See also* Political parties)
Electoral college, 54–55
Elite
  at Constitutional Convention, 26–27
  defined, 5
  political control by, 224–227
Equal Rights Amendment (ERA), 38
Espionage Act of 1917, 44
Executive agencies, 73–74
Executive agreements, 65
Executive branch, 53–87
Executive office of president, 70–71, 72t, 78
Executive privilege, 67–68

Fairness doctrine, of FCC, 203–204

Federal Aviation Administration (FAA), 15
Federal Communications Commission (FCC), 74, 203–204
Federal Elections Campaign Act. *See* Campaign Finance Reform Act
Federalism
  and colonial government, 22
  principle of, 34–35
  in U.S. Constitution, 30
Federalist Papers, The, 27, 29, 31
Federalists *vs.* Anti-Federalists, 27–28, 169–170
  at Constitutional Convention, 28–30
Federal regulations, reform of, 78
Federal Trade Commission, and interest groups, 75
Filibuster, 106, 108
Finance Committee, Senate, 118
Force
  in government, 10–11
  and power, 4, 7
Ford, Gerald, 102
  and campaign finance bill, 124, 125
  use of veto by, 60–61
Foreign policy
  presidential role in, 64–65, 92
  Senate and, 118–119
Foreign Relations Committee, Senate, 118–119
Frankfurter, Felix, 145, 146
Franklin, Benjamin, 25
Freedom of speech, 42
  constitutional guarantees of, 43
  controversies over, 46–47
  and media, 201–203, 207
  suppression of, 43–44
  Supreme Court defense of, 44–46

Gag Rule, 44
Garfield, James, 76
General Accounting Office (GAO), 119–120
General Services Administration (GSA), 74
Gerry, Elbridge, 99
Gerrymandering, 99
  in twelfth congressional district of New York, 100
GI Supreme Court. *See* Court of Military Appeals, U.S.
Gladstone, William, on U.S. Constitution, 41
Glenn, John, 94
Government
  constitutional restraints on, 30, 31–32, 35–37
  defined, 8–9
  democratic, 8
  function of, 9–11, 31
  and media, 203–206
  national *vs.* state, 34–35
  need for, 7–8
  structure of, 30, 33*t*
  (*See also* Congress, U.S.; Constitution, U.S.; Politics)
Government corporations, 73–74
Gun-control lobby, in election campaign, 210–211

Hamilton, Alexander
  attitude to people, 27
  at Constitutional Convention, 25
  and Federalists, 29, 170
Hand, Learned, 201

Harding, Warren, 59
Harlan, John, on *Plessy* v. *Ferguson*, 148
Hays, Wayne
  and campaign finance reform bill, 124
  resignation of, 113
Heinz, H. John, 125
Henry, Patrick, 26
History, scope of, 12
Hofstadter, Richard, 32
Holmes, Oliver Wendell, Jr.
  on free speech, 42, 44
  and judicial restraint, 145, 146
  on Supreme Court powers, 37
Hoover, Herbert, 59
House of Representatives
  committees of, 116–118
  districts of, 99–100
  election to, 32
  makeup of, 92–99
  organization of, 100–103
  (*See also* Congress, U.S.; Senate, U.S.)
Humphrey, Muriel, 94

Impeachment, 92, 121
Income, national distribution of, 6
Incumbency, advantages of, 101
Interest groups
  campaign contributions of, 189–190t, 192–194, 210
  lobbying by, 112, 191–192
  nature of, 188
  and regulatory commissions, 75
  types of, 189–191
  (*See also* Political movements)

International Telephone and Telegraph (ITT), campaign contributions of, 192–193
Interstate Commerce Commission (ICC), 74
Item veto, 67

Jackson, Andrew, 60
  and Democratic party, 170
  and slavery issue, 44
  and spoils system, 76
  and Supreme Court, 156
Jefferson, Thomas, 26
  on judicial review, 139
  presidential power under, 58
Jim Crow laws, 147
Johnson, Andrew, 121
Johnson, Lyndon
  and media, 69
  as party leader, 68
  personality type of, 62
  presidential style of, 60
Joint committees, 112–113
Judges, federal
  appointment of, 133–134
  Supreme Court, 136t
Judicial activism *vs.* judicial restraint, 144–146
Judicial branch, 131–158
Judicial interpretation, and constitutional change, 39
Judicial review, 36–37
  defined, 138
  in *Marbury* v. *Madison*, 138–139
  use of, 144–146
Jurisdiction of courts, 134–135

Kennedy, John F., 60, 117
  and media, 205, 206
  personality type of, 62

and steel industry, 81–82, 84, 85
use of federal troops by, 66
Kissinger, Henry, 70

Labor unions, political influence of, 190
Lame duck presidents, 54
Lasswell, Harold, definition of politics, 4, 12–13
Legal profession, and Supreme Court, 157
Legislation
  in committee, 110–111, 116–119
  and constitutional change, 39–40
  passage of, 104–109
  presidential influence on, 67
Legislative branch, 91–128
Legislators. *See* Congress members; Senators
Lincoln, Abraham
  and cabinet, 73
  election of, 170–171
  presidential style of, 58, 59–60
Lobbyists
  defined, 112
  for gun control, 210–211
  methods of, 191–192
Locke, John, 22

McCarthy, Eugene, 125
McCarthy, Joseph, R., 45, 120
Machines, party, 175
McCulloch v. *Maryland* (1819), 140
McDonnell Douglas, FAA and, 15
Madison, James, 25, 29

on government, 31
and *Marbury* v. *Madison*, 139
on property owners, 27
Magna Charta (1215), 22
Magruder, Jeb, on media, 205
Majority leaders, 102, 104
Majority party, 100–101
Malapportionment, 99
Marbury v. *Madison* (1803), 138–139
Marshall, John, 138
  court of, 145–146
  Jackson on, 156
  in *Marbury* v. *Madison*, 138–139
  in *McCulloch* v. *Maryland*, 140
Marshall, Thurgood, 145
Maverick congressmen, 115–116
Mayflower Compact (1620), 22
Media
  audience of, 198t
  freedom of, 201–203, 207
  and government, 203–206
  influence of, 196–197, 199–200, 206–207
    in elections, 208–213
    and presidential popularity, 69
  newspaper, 198–199
  television, 197–198
Media managers, 207
Meredith, James, 66
Military-industrial complex, 226
Mill, John Stuart, on free speech, 42
Mills, C. Wright, 225–226, 227
Mills, Wilbur, resignation of, 113
Minority leaders, 102, 104
Minority party, 101
Miranda decision, 142–143

Missouri Compromise (1820), 140, 153
Missouri ex. rel. Gaines v. *Canada* (1938), 149
Mondale, Walter, 55, 103

Nader, Ralph, 75, 77
National Association for the Advancement of Colored People (NAACP), 194
National committees, 177
National conventions, 177–179
National Rifle Association, 210
National Security Council (NSC), 70–71
National security *vs.* free speech, 45–46
National supremacy principle
 establishment of, 140
 vs. states' rights, 34–35
Near v. *Minnesota* (1931), 45
Neustadt, Richard, 79
Newspapers
 ownership of, 199, 201–202
 role of, 204
 types of, 198–199
 (*See also* Media)
Nixon, Richard
 on campaign finance bill, 125
 Checkers, speech, 206
 and media, 69, 204–205, 206
 personality type of, 62
 presidential style of, 60
 resignation of, 121, 122
 and Supreme Court, 134, 143
 use of executive privilege by, 68
Northwest Ordinance, 23

Obscenity, Supreme Court on, 143, 154

Office-holding terms, 23
 and checks and balances, 32
 of congressmen and senators, 95, 125–126
 presidential, 54
Office of Management and Budget (OMB), 71
O'Neill, Thomas "Tip," 102
One man, one vote principle, 142

Packing, defined, 99
Patronage. *See* Spoils system
Pendleton Act. *See* Civil Service Reform Act
Personality, and presidential style, 61–62
Platform party, 77
Plessy v. *Ferguson* (1896), 147–148
 Harlan on, 148
 reversal of, 150
Pluralism
 concept of, 219–221
 criticism of, 223–224
 examples of, 221–223
 vs. power elite, 227–229
Poage, W. R., 94
Pocket veto, 109
Policy committee, Democratic, in Senate, 104
Political machines, 175
Political movements, 194–196
Political parties
 caucus of, 102
 defined, 169
 function of, 174–175
 history of, 169–171
 and independent voter, 173–174
 organization of, 175–179
 and presidential leadership, 68

in two-party system, 180–182
(*See also* Democratic party;
Republican party)
Political power. *See* Power;
Presidential power
Political questions
defined, 153
and Supreme Court, 153–154
Political science, focus of, 11–13
Politics
defined, 3–4
as game, 16–17
involvement in, 13–16
pluralistic *vs.* power elite
view of, 219–229
study of, 11–13
(*See also* Government)
Pornography
and free speech, 47
Supreme Court on, 143
Poverty, 6
Power
and authority, 6–7
decentralization of, 169
defined, 4
definition of alternatives in, 206–207
fragmentation of, 219–220
governmental, 8, 30
checks and balances in, 31–32
federalism and, 34–35
limited, 35–36
separation of, 30–31
legitimate, 6
as means to end, 5
(*See also* Power elite theory;
Presidential power)
Power Elite, The (Mills), 225–226, 227
Power elite theory
criticism of, 226
vs. pluralism, 227–229
political control in, 224–226, 227
Precedent, in Supreme Court
decisions, 155
Presidential Character, The
(Barber), 61–62
Presidential power
activist view of, 59–60
congressional limitations on, 91
constitutional provisions for, 32, 53
custodial view of, 59
examples of, 79–85
expansion of, 55, 58
persuasion in, 79
residual, 58
(*See also* Power; Veto power)
President *pro tem*, of Senate, 103–104
Presidents, U.S.
appointments of, 76
and Senate confirmation, 120–121
and bureaucracy, 78–79
ceremonial role of, 63–64
chronology of, 56–57t
election methods for, 54–55
executive office of, 70–71
history of, 55–58
and media, 69, 204–206
personality categories for, 61–62
requirements for office, 54
role of, 62–68
and Supreme Court, 143
term of, 40
types of, 59–61
(*See also* Vice president)
Press. *See* Media
Press conferences, 205–206
Pressure groups. *See* Interest groups
Primary elections, 179

Professional groups, 189–190
Pseudoevents, 206
Psychology, scope of, 12
Public opinion
  and media, 206–207
  political parties and, 174–175
  president and, 69

Racial discrimination. *See* Civil rights
Rafshoon, Gerald, 206
Randall, Nick Joe, 94
Rayburn, Sam, 115, 117
Reciprocity rule, in congressional committees, 114–116
Regulatory commissions, 74–75
  and economic interests, 14–15
Reorganization authority bill (1977), 78
Representatives, congressional. *See* Congress members
Republican party
  in Congress, 102–103, 104
  origins of, 170
  in presidential elections, 171–172
  supporters of, 172–173
  (*See also* Democratic party; Political parties)
Residual power, of presidency, 58
Reverse discrimination, and Bakke case, 151
Rider, to legislation, 109
Roosevelt, Franklin D., 149
  and Democratic party, 171
  fireside chats of, 206
  presidential style of, 58, 60
  and Supreme Court, 141, 146

Roosevelt, Theodore, presidential style of, 60
Rule of law, 36
Rules Committees, 116–117, 119
Ruling class. *See* Elite; Power elite theory

Schattschneider, E. E., 206
Schenck, Charles T., 44
Schenck v. *U.S.* (1919), 44
Schmitt, Harrison H., 94
Secession issue, at Constitutional Convention, 25
Segregation, role of judiciary in, 146–152
Select committees, 112
Senate, U.S.
  committees of, 118–119
  and federal judges, 134
  filibuster in, 106, 108
  makeup of, 92–99
  organization of, 103–104
  and presidential appointments, 120–121
  treaty-making power of, 65, 120
  (*See also* Congress, U.S.; House of Representatives)
Senate Rule, 22,108
Senatorial courtesy, 134
Senators
  age of, 94
  characteristics of, 96–97t
  election of, 32, 95
    case study, 208–213
  incumbents in, 101
  (*See also* Congress members)
Seniority system, in congressional committees, 113–114

Separate but equal doctrine, 146–152, 158
Separation of powers, 30–31
  and executive privilege, 68
Shays' Rebellion (1786), 24, 26
Skokie (Illinois), free speech issue in, 47
Slavery issue
  at Constitutional Convention, 25
  and suppression of free speech, 44
  Supreme Court on, 140
Smith Act of 1940, 42, 45, 46
Speaker of the House, 101–102
Specialization rule, in congressional committees, 114–116
Spoils system, 76
Standing committees, 110–111
Stare decisis policy, 149, 155
State convention, constitutional amendment by, 38–39
State courts, and concurrent jurisdiction, 135
States
  and Articles of Confederation, 23
  Congressional representation of, 24–25
States' rights, and national supremacy, 34–35
Steel industry, presidential confrontations with, 79–85
Steering committees, Democratic in Congress, 103, 104
Stewardship, presidency as, 60
Subcommittees, 111
Supreme Court, U.S.
  and Bakke decision, 151
  and campaign finance bill, 125
  cases before, 135–136
  and constitutional change, 39, 136–137
  and judicial review, 36–37
  jurisdiction of, 135
  justices of, 135, 136t
  free speech defense in, 44–46
  history of, 137–141
  and malapportionment, 99
  and obscenity, 154
  political role of, 144
    in separate but equal doctrine, 146–152
  power of, 144–146
    limitations on, 152–156
  strengths of, 156–157, 158
  in Truman's seizure of steel mills, 81
  trends in, 141–144
  and U.S. president, 143
Sweatt v. *Painter* (1950), 149
Symbolic speech, defined, 46

Taft, William Howard, personality type of, 62
Television
  network system of, 197–198
  political impact of, 197
  profits of, 202
  sponsors on, 203
  (*See also* Media)
Tennessee Valley Authority (TVA), 73
Terms of office. *See* Officeholding terms
Thurmond, Strom, filibuster record of, 108
Treaty-making powers, Senate and, 65, 120
Truman, Harry, 60, 149
  personality type of, 62
  on political parties, 173

Truman [cont.]
    and steel industry, 80–81, 84, 85
    on vice presidency, 55
Tydings, Joseph, re-election campaign of, 208–213

U.S. district courts, 131–132
U.S. Postal Service, 73–74

Veto power, 32, 67
    congressional limitation on, 91, 108–109
    Ford's use of, 60–61
Vice presidents
    chronology of, 56–57t
    function of, 55
    as Senate president, 103–104
Vietnam War
    opposition to, 195
    settlement of, 65
Vinson, Fred M., on free speech, 42, 45
Voter apathy, reasons for, 165–169
Voter participation
    class and, 164–165
    by independents, 173–174
    and political socialization, 162, 163
    in presidential elections, 161–162, 163t
Voting Rights Amendment, Washington, D.C., 38

Wage Stabilization Board (WSB), 80
War making power
    congressional, 66
    Constitution on, 40
    of president, 58, 66, 137
War Powers Act of 1973, 66
Warren, Earl, 46, 142, 145
    Eisenhower on, 143
Washington, George
    on political parties, 173
    and presidential power, 58
Watergate scandal, campaign contributions in, 121–122, 192–193
Ways and Means Committee, 117–118
Wealth, distribution of, 5–6, 9–10
Webster, Daniel, 92
Whips, majority and minority, 102, 104
Whiskey Rebellion, 58
White House, mice in, 74
White House staff, 70
Who Governs? (Dahl), 222, 223
Wilson, Charles, 80, 84
Wilson, Woodrow, on congressional power, 92
World War I, suppression of free speech rights in, 44

Young, Milton, 94

Zero-based budgeting, 77–78